The Practice of Technology

The Practice of Technology

Exploring Technology, Ecophilosophy, and
Spiritual Disciplines for Vital Links

Alan Drengson

STATE UNIVERSITY OF NEW YORK PRESS

Published by
State University of New York Press, Albany

For information address State University of New York Press,
State University Plaza, Albany,
NY 12246

Production by Laura Starrett
Marketing by Fran Keneston

Library of Congress Cataloging in Publication Data

Drengson, Alan R.
    The practice of technology : exploring technology, ecophilosophy,
and spiritual disciplines for vital links / Alan R. Drengson.
        p.   cm.
    Includes bibliographical references and index.
    ISBN 0-7914-2669-6 : $59.50. — ISBN 0-7914-2670-X (pbk.) : $19.95
    1. Technology—Philosophy.   I. Title.
    T14.D74—1995
    601—dc20   95-1305
                                                CIP

10 9 8 7 6 5 4 3 2 1

Contents

Acknowledgments

So many people, books, authors and institutions have helped me to write this book. Thanks to Doug Tompkins and the Foundation for Deep Ecology for their generous support without which this book would not now be complete. Thanks to Jerry Mander, Bill Devall, Arne Naess, Yuichi Inoue, and Kirke Wolfe for their valuable ideas and insights. Thanks to the Ecoforestry Institute for their information on ecoforestry. Thanks to my editor and agent Eileen King, Genie Computing, and the University of Victoria. Thanks to my wife, Victoria Stevens, and our children Alice, Jane and Anna for teaching me more about the feminine side of the practice of technology, and also about beginner's mind. Finally, there are many authors who have helped me to organize and present the core ideas and insights of this book. Those who have most influenced me are: E. F. Schumacher, K. Ueshiba and M. Ueshiba, Frederick Streng, Friedrick Rapp, Arne Naess, Gary Snyder, and Wendell Berry.

Portions of this book have appeared in different form in the following periodicals under the titles noted. Permission to reprint this material is much appreciated.

The following previously published articles formed the basis for Chapters of this book as noted below.

"Four Philosophies of Technology," *Philosophy Today*, vol. 26. no. 2/4 (Summer 1982), pages 103–117. This article was also published in an anthology edited by Larry Hickman, *Philosophy, Technology and Human Affairs*, Ibis Press 1985, College Station, Texas A & M University. This anthology was later revised and published under the title of *Technology as a Human Affair*, by McGraw-Hill in 1990. Chapter 6.

"The Sacred and the Limits of the Technological Fix," *Zygon*, vol. 19, no. 3 (September 1984), pages 259–275. Chapter 8.

"Art and Imagination in Technological Society," *Research in Philosophy and Technology*, vol. 6 (Fall 1983), pages 77–91. Chapter 9.

"Toward a Redefinition of Progress in Agricultural Technology and

Practice: From Industrial Paradigms to Natural Patterns," *Quarterly Journal of Ideology*, vol II, no. 2 (September 1987), pages 59–66. Chapter 10.

"Toward a Philosophy of Appropriate Technology," *Humboldt Journal of Social Relations*, vol. 9, no. 2 (Spring/Summer 1982), pages 161–176. Chapter 11.

"Mastery and Masters," *Philosophy Today*, vol. 27, no. 3/4 (Fall 1983), pages 230–246. Chapter 12.

To my brother, Mike Drengson, and my father, Alvin Drengson, for their affection, friendship and all they taught me about technology practices. And also to the peoples of the First Nations from whose wise practices we must learn.

Preface
Backgrounds of This Book

In 1974, at the University of Victoria, where I teach philosophy, I was asked to serve on a committee to create and administer an experimental program in environmental studies. This experimental program, which is now a regular one, is interdisciplinary. The reason for this is that the environment is one whole—it is not cut up into specialties, disciplines and departments—and part of our difficulty in dealing with environmental problems is that we do not approach them as a unified whole. We did not have at the university, nor could we find, any existing program that brought all of our specialized knowledge together so that we could clearly see the overall nature of the problems. There was and remains an urgent need for such interdisciplinary programs.

In order to contribute a philosophical dimension to this program I developed a course in Environmental Philosophy. While teaching this course the need to address the role technology plays in environmental problem creation and solution became evident; hence, I designed and introduced Philosophy of Technology, a course that provides a comprehensive look at human technology on all levels of development, assessing its philosophical and valuational dimensions, its role in causing environmental problems, and possible ways in which its practice might be reformed and redesigned so as to prevent problems from arising. This book grew out of work done in connection with the Philosophy of Technology course and out of published research arising from my work in this area.

The articles I wrote while researching the philosophy of technology cover a wide range of topics, from the function of imagination in technological societies to the spiritual dimensions of the practice of technology. Unifying themes, sometimes explicitly stated, sometimes not, run through these essays. Two major themes deserve mention here: the philosophy of appropriate design and the view of technology as a whole practice. These essays always incorporated the environmental dimension. It became obvious to me and my students, as we pondered the issues surrounding the practice of technology, that environmental problems in industrial society cannot be solved by simply changing legal requirements for assessing possible damages of contemplated actions or through the enforcement of minimal standards. Major practices that have vast impacts on the land, soil, air, and water are never subjected to such impact assessments or standards. Agriculture, as it is conventionally practiced; forestry, as it is carried on in the West; automobile commuting; the use of rivers and lakes to dump waste materials: these are destructive practices that continue to grow unabated, despite decades of environmental legislation. There has been some regulation of auto exhaust and a switch to lead-free gas; there has been some attempt to clean up municipal sewage. But overall the problems have grown in magnitude and intensity, due partly to increasing numbers of people adopting the industrial way of life, partly to increasing population pressures, partly to existing economic structures. But at the heart of all these causes lie the technology practices of the West, with their associated technocratic worldview based on modern philosophy.

Whatever our numbers, the use of inappropriate, nonecosophic technology practices (that is, practices lacking ecological harmony and wisdom) will have negative impacts on ourselves, our communities, and nature. In this book, we assume the importance of responsible control of human population growth; it is possible and should be a priority. However, even if we do control our numbers and over time reduce total human population, we still have to discipline our lifestyles: change our consumptive practices, the way we garden and landscape, our habits of saving and recycling, how we heat and cool our homes, how we travel and recreate, and how we work. Without these changes, all policies, laws and population control will be for naught. This is so, not only because we will continue to increase the impact of each human being on the environment through the power of technology, but also because new technologies, and some older ones too, are potentially (or are already) so destructive that their widespread use will destroy wild creatures and the wilderness and alter the flora and fauna of the Earth in ways that will be nonrestorable. However, we still have enough of the natural systems left to embark on a priority program of restoration, along with a redesign and retooling of technology practices to prevent this disaster escalating.

An earlier book, *Beyond Environmental Crisis* (New York: Peter Lang Publishers, 1989), addressed the philosophical dimensions of the environmental crisis. It set forth a way of appropriate philosophizing that lays bare the philosophical dimensions of the environmental crisis and is creative enough to lead us to design a more comprehensive, appropriate philosophy for human life on Earth. This philosophical approach I call comparative, creative ecophilosophy; its ultimate aim is ecosophy, or ecological wisdom, manifested as ecological harmony. In that book, I examined the environmental crisis as one of culture, consciousness, and character. I showed that to address the problems we have to see and think comprehensively, grasp the interrelationships in our search for self-confirmation, completion, and self-realization, and see our failure to achieve completion as a lack of both community with others and communion with nature.

In industrial society, life becomes abstract, cut off from firsthand experience with nature, lacking in genuine human relationships; community is destroyed by the organizational processes; meaningful work is lost to the mechanization of production; and life and nature are desacralized and treated as nothing more than raw material. These losses and divisions give rise to a deep longing and a frustrating quest for self-completion, which often results in a pursuit of thrills and other compensatory activities and addictions. The whole system is characterized by violence resulting from exerting "power-over" control. To understand the deep needs of the human person is to see how we find our completion through a process of maturation that enables us to extend our sense of compassionate identification to a wider and wider sphere of relationships, not only with other humans but with other beings as well, and eventually with all of nature. This is the practice of ecosophy.

But, in addition, we must recognize that the philosophy of industrial culture is rooted in an approach to the world that necessarily divides the human person into parts and the world into fragments. The organization of industrial society for productive activity and profits reorders the whole range of values of earlier societies. It intensifies the urbanization of human life, destroys rural culture, and turns the whole planet into a giant manufacturing and marketing system, in which the major media become primarily marketing tools and time-filling entertainment. The depopulated wilderness and farmland become only raw materials. Forests are just logs for timber and fiber. The models and paradigms under which industrial philosophy operates must be replaced by new ones. Drawing from ancient wisdom and contemporary understanding of both ecological processes and transpersonal human development, we can provide a new vision of human possibilities and of nature, based on ecocentric values. *Beyond Environmental Crisis* illustrates how such a redesign in philosophical approach and philosophy of life can be undertaken and continued as an ongoing activity in the realization of ecosophy.

Here we bring this approach to bear on the question of technology. What is the role of technology practice in human life, and why do our current practices impact upon us and the Earth in negative ways? How do we gain a holistic understanding of technology practices, so that we can change these practices to conform with ecosophic values? How do we create new practices with ecosophy built into their conception, inception, and application? What are the ecosophic criteria we must use, and how must we apply them to the practice of technology? What we seek is technosophia, that is, the wisdom to create nonviolent technology practices in harmony with nature. These are the overriding concerns of this book.

Prologue
The Interconnected Nature
of the Problems

Every major problem reported in popular media has both an environmental and a technological dimension, regardless of what the problem is: violence in urban streets, drug abuse, smog, the greenhouse effect, chemical contamination of food, the threat of nuclear war, political tyranny, the erosion of soil, the undermining of civil liberties, the AIDS epidemic. Why should our modern technological society, which was supposedly built on democratic values and freedom, using rational science and technology, blessed by the free market system, produce such a host of problems? Are these problems caused by just a few malcontents and criminals among us? Or are they the result of all of us living irresponsibly? These seem to be the two most ready answers circulated by the media.

Consider the problem of drug abuse, for example. In the United States this is treated as a most serious threat to human life and national security. It is difficult to understand how it could be a national security issue, unless we look at the economic dimensions of the problem. The economic impacts of the illegal drug market are quite astounding. It is estimated that (in the United States alone) the illegal drug trade represents a total of from $45 to $110 billion annually, money which escapes all regulation and taxation. Much of this money leaves the country, but much of it is laundered and put back into circulation to buy property and legitimate businesses. The marketing and consumption of illegal drugs has become very big business, threatening to rival and displace the trade in other established legal drugs. Clearly, the problem for national security is not that the United States is under threat from a foreign power, but that its citizens are ignoring government attempts to control their lifestyles and habits, and that their demands are helping to finance a vast underground market that is taking money out of the rest of the economy.

In terms of public health problems, disease, and deaths, the adverse effects of illegal drugs are dwarfed by those of such legal drugs as coffee, alcohol and tobacco. The total number of deaths from illegal drugs in the United States in 1988 was less than 4,000. The total number of deaths from alcohol and tobacco was over a million. About 50 percent of all traffic deaths are alcohol related. Alcohol is involved in child abuse, domestic violence, and other crime. Why then is there no war on alcohol? Why is there no war on tobacco, similar to the war on illegal drugs?

If we look at the statistics for prescription and over the counter drugs we find a similar situation. The problems, deaths, and illnesses associated with legal drugs far outweigh those associated with illegal drugs. A few illegal drugs, moreover, account for a major share of the problems attributed to illegal drugs in general. Crack cocaine is one of the major sources of profits and also one of the most addictive and destructive drugs. Marijuana, in contrast, is nonaddictive, is far less profitable and is rarely implicated in crimes of violence. Yet all illegal drugs are treated as if they were the same. Moreover, what started as a war against drug *abuse* was slowly transformed into a war against illegal drug *use* and now there is even a newer, broader category called *substance* abuse. The latter, by the light of reason, should include using too many consumer goods, but there is no war on over-consumption—damaging as it is to the environment.

The question of illegal drugs and the war on them does not seem to have anything to do with the environment and technology, and it is certainly not the subject of this book. However, it is an excellent example that illustrates the ways in which current intractable problems have both technological and environmental dimensions. Let us see why.

In the first place, the illegal market relies heavily on such things as modern transportation, communications, weapons, and chemical processing equipment to carry out its activities. The raw materials for many illegal drugs are produced in countries far from the major lucrative markets. The large amounts of materials involved require a sophisticated system of processing, transport, storage, wholesaling, and marketing. In fact, the international drug trade follows the pattern of multinational corporations in the way it conducts business, except that it has to do so underground, in the shadows, because it is illegal. In addition, because of the large sums of money involved, the international drug business must depend on the international financial system, which is in place to facilitate the conduct of legitimate business. To wage a war on drugs the U.S. government resorts to the use of sophisticated equipment, and in order to intercept information and shipments it utilizes complex and costly military hardware operated by highly trained personnel. The war on drugs would not be possible without the vast infrastructure of government, military and other forms of corporate organization. The use of surveillance equipment, urine and blood analysis equipment, recorders, video devices, computers, radar-equipped planes, and technically trained experts: these are all part of the war on drugs. And this describes only part of the effort.

The illegal drug trade has many impacts on the environment. First, large amounts of cannabis are cultivated to produce hash and marijuana. Cannabis is a plant that requires much water and sunlight, and well-drained soil; these are also requirements for agricultural crops. Raising cannabis competes with raising food crops, and farmers who raise cannabis to sell on the international market must get their food from somewhere else. What this means (and this applies to cocaine as well) is that more total land and resources must be brought under cultivation both to feed hungry people and to feed the demand for illegal drugs, which are used mostly as intoxicants for recreational purposes. In addition, the fields of marijuana and coca plants are often sprayed with herbicides in government eradication programs, and these sprays have adverse environmental impacts. Another environmental impact of the war on illegal drugs is that it diverts resources and attention away from more urgent, serious problems that our other practices are causing to the Earth's atmosphere, water, and habitats. And there are other environmental effects as well.

Although these negative consequences of the war on illegal drugs illustrate our point, we should also mention in passing another serious consequence of the illegal drug trade and the war on it. The attempt to control the problem as it is usually perceived has led to political grandstanding and demagoguery, promoted covert racism, and the introduction of laws and law enforcement practices that violate basic rights and freedoms, and are an affront to the dignity of every free human being.

What is true of the war on drugs and the illegal drug trade is true of every other major problem in industrial society. The problems are intractable, and seem to call for extreme measures that are usually seen as requiring further legislation, centralization, and enforcement, and additional applications of technological power. It is a mistake to blame these problems on a few "bad guys" or on everyone. The reason we do not make progress in solving the problems caused by acid rain, or in preserving the ancient forests, or in halting soil erosion, or in controlling urban violence, for example, is that our analyses of these problems are not complete and comprehensive. We do not focus on the role that our technology practices and organizational structures play in the whole range of problems besetting industrial culture. We do not as a society critique the worldview of industrial culture and its philosophy of nature and humanity.

This book takes a comprehensive and integrated look at technology and its role in producing our many problems, and at ways in which we can reconceptualize our understanding of technology so as to imagine and then create new and alternative forms of practice that will not be problem creating. In order to pursue these aims we begin by introducing the concept of technology *practice*. The title of this book, *The Practice of Technology*, was chosen because I believe we need to look at the whole context of technological process and activity. The word "practice" helps us see this context. It also helps us to make a connection with daily life and spiritual practices or disciplines. Our work and technology practice must be reintegrated with a larger vision of life that includes fully conscious efforts toward self-realization, resulting not from gadgets and things, but from self-discipline learned through a practice in a context of ecocentric values.

The concept of "technology practice" comes from Arnold Pacey's book, *The Culture of Technology*. Pacey (1983) shows how technology is part of culture, and how, as an expression of culture, it interacts with nature and human life to produce new cultural forms. Pacey's thesis is supported by anthropological, historical, and philosophical studies of technology. Here we will enlarge on his concept of technology practice in order to pursue our ultimate objective: not only to critique existing practices, but to envisage alternatives that are appropriate and ecosophic. Our aim is to re-vision technology practices so that they become part of a solution to our many problems rather than a major source of further problems. As it is, we often respond to problems caused by our production and distribution processes in ways that cause other problems to which we respond in the same way. In so doing we create more and more complex problems, illustrated by our attempt control the use of illegal drugs mainly through the power of law enforcement.

To give another example, consider farming. Conventional industrial farming methods use capital-intensive heavy machinery, chemical fertilizers, petrochemical insecticides, fungicides, and herbicides. Some of the results of these practices, coupled with the monoculture cropping of highly specialized plant annuals, are soil erosion; destruction of soil communities and soil fertility; pollution of streams, lakes, and ground water; and contamination of the food supply. When we try to solve these problems by further uses of the same methods we produce yet other problems. Insecticide-resistant bugs and antibiotic resistant strains of bacteria are just two examples of this third level of problems produced, and there are others as well.

There are alternatives to our current bad technology practices. It is possible to redesign these practices so that they do not generate problems in the first place. It is possible to redesign farming so that its practices contribute to soil health and to the flourishing of plant and animal communities. In forestry, too, we can remove forest materials while preserving full functioning forest ecosystems. Our aim is to explore such possibilities for appropriate design of ecosophic practices, especially at the conceptual or philosophical level. Once we envisage alternatives and have a clear idea of how to proceed, we can easily bring together the information and knowledge we need to realize ecosophic aims—we can practice techno-sophia.

We now face a crisis that requires us to place ecosophic criteria and ecocentric values at the basis of everything we do. When we do this in all of our activities: education, research, production, recreation, and govern-ment, we will create communities, selves, and societies appropriate to the Age of Ecology. As we continue to rectify our relationships on all levels: within the self, between self and others, within our communities, be-tween human communities and nations, and between humans and na-ture, we will be moving to the Age of Ecosophy. However, the Age of Ecosophy is also a Kingdom (space) we can each enter on our own here and now; a community can enter it before other communities have taken the necessary steps. It is a condition most humans must enter, if we are to save the Earth from destruction. How quickly and vitally we act will depend on how seriously we take our current predicament. But we must have the vision and creative imagination to act. This book aims to free the imagination.

I have written this book with the platform principles of the Deep Ecology movement in mind: that we cannot go on with business as usual, that we must make fundamental changes in our values and practices if we are to avoid destroying the ecological communities of this planet. Sup-porters of the movement believe, even if human life were not threatened, that we should all work to make changes to enter ecosophy, for they believe that all beings have a right to flourish and that humans as self-conscious beings have no moral or spiritual right to interfere with other beings, except to meet *vital* needs. Humans pride themselves on being *Homo sapiens*, wise humans. If we are one of the most highly evolved forms of consciousness on this planet, certainly our claim to wisdom should be measured by the breadth and depth of our compassion. Com-passion for other humans and for other beings is a fundamental guide to this philosophical undertaking, and is a central feature of ecosophy.

If we embrace the above platform principles of the Deep Ecology movement, we are committed to making necessary cultural and personal changes. It is our conception of self as an isolated entity, and of our human species as exempt from ecological limitations and separate from the rest of creation, that are part of the engendering conditions of the modern Western crisis with nature. This concept of self and human exclu-siveness are part of a complex worldview which is communicated trans-generationally. This worldview is interconnected with our culture's orga-nizational structures, technical and other knowledge, and our practices.

This book stresses the critical importance of technology practices and their design in relation to the environmental crisis. It advocates a holistic approach to understanding and designing technology, but it focuses most on the *cultural dimensions* of technology practices. If we are to redesign our practices and reduce our population, we need to make major changes in our culture, that is, in our values, commitments, and ultimate meanings; these must be scrutinized for redesign. These cultural elements are conveyed through our mythologies and sacred ideals, which need to be deeply examined.

Our Western conceptions of self and society shape our technology practices and give direction to our economic and political life. All aspects of our current crisis are part of a larger world which has its own ecology. A key to understanding this ecology is found by examining our most general, common, narrative (Western) tradition. We take "narrative tradition" to refer to those shared beliefs and ultimate values which tell about our lives and destiny. These stories are our ultimate accounts of meaning, without which human society cannot flourish. They rest upon the secularization of earlier, Christian teachings, which in turn are bound up with an even earlier oral tradition predating but incorporated in Genesis. Our mythology includes not only the early stories such as Adam and Eve but a great diversity of other tales up through such events as the Moon landing. What do these stories mean to us?

As self-reflective beings, conscious of our own cultural context, we ought to design new ecologically and socially responsible technology practices, as well as create the skills of restoring and caring for the land. Our technology has a cultural mythology behind and within it which says things about our values and ideas with respect to self, power, control, values, and destiny. We will explore different ways of seeing the technology manifest in our culture, and our culture manifest in the technology we offer to the world. Technology reflects the culture which is its context. Anyone who doubts this has only to study it cross-culturally.

Democracy arose in the modern West as a result of deep cultural changes from Medieval Feudalism. A money economy and private ownership emerged in conjunction with market capitalism, shifting the emphasis away from the communal values of Feudalism. This shift was facilitated by turning Christian religion into a secular doctrine of commercial humanism. Redemption comes through our own individual efforts by participating in the creation of a human world of perfect technological control and progress. Personal merit depends on our own work and accomplishment. Our destiny is in our own hands, for God created us in His image and gave the Earth to us as a gift.

The rise of modern Western industrial society was facilitated then, by transmutation of a theocentric tradition into a secular, human centered one. Technological change became the source of the miraculous. Divine power is unnecessary. The West's destiny is to take this modern progress to the rest of the world for its benefit, just as we had earlier taken Christianity to the world for its salvation.

Part of this mythology is based on an ancient story about the human (Adam and Eve) fall from grace. Our ancestors sinned against God by disobeying His order not to eat the fruit of the tree of knowledge of good and evil. This injunction warned that to eat this fruit is to become as gods, that is, creators. This is because the fruits of self-knowledge include not only a loss of innocence, an increased sense of mortality, and the burden of being responsible, but *the capacity to choose with knowledge*. The Garden of Eden (also the womb, our home place, our original life in nature, our innocence) was the paradise we had to leave. But Christianity promised a Kingdom of Heaven as a non-Earthly paradise to which we individually go, if we seek salvation and put our faith in Christ, that is, sacrifice self-seeking. Throughout the Middle Ages, Christian communal and religious organizations tempered both self-seeking and technological innovation by branding them as prideful and arrogant. There were stringent laws against usury. Personal salvation requires humility and self-sacrifice. Thus, entry into the Kingdom of Heaven depends on our own personal effort.

Technological change, in the modern period, becomes the primary means to change human destiny so as to create a perfect world on Earth. A perfect world, like Eden and Heaven, is free of trial and woe (weeds and drought); through science and technology we will control everything around us. In modern Western mythology technological change *is* progress. We will create a new and better world in which we will control even the weather. We will design our moods, our appearance, our environment, our animals, our plants, our genes, everything. We get personal meaning by participating in this grand story of human progress as increasing control and increasing levels of material wealth and consumption for the greatest number.

Social justification for progress follows from its ties to a democratic, participatory ethos (a reaction against authoritarian structures). Science belongs to no one. It is democratic. Each of us is capable of observing the world with our own senses. Technology is just an extension of physical capacities and is in itself value neutral. Like the hand, it is good or bad depending on the user. These are taken for granted. All values are at the lowest common denominator (money), and so no one is excluded (for everyone can get money in some way or other). In the market everyone and anyone can play.

Western democratic traditions exalt the rights of the person over collectives. Ownership through purchase bestows almost complete freedom to do what you like with the land. Everything is done for the self in the West, except to give it an authentic place, community, and access to wisdom. The Western ideal of progress by human design is an expression of the aspirations of the individualist self. But what or who is this *designing* self?

In individualist market driven society, products are sold by being covertly linked with symbols and myths of personal worth and ultimate meaning. The drive for individual paradise (as a result of a loss of access to joy and ecstasy) leads to insatiable cravings which suit a market system based on ever-rising levels of demand, production, and consumption. The rise of modernism created new social and economic institutions in part because of the character structure reared on freedom and conditioned love. Such character gives rise to cravings for which compensatory gratifications are sought. Individual wealth is a powerful means for realizing such compensations.

In modern Western mythology it is assumed that the natural world is primarily raw material to be manipulated in the ways science discovers. This, too, is rooted in Christian beliefs. Only humans have souls, according to its dominant institutional teachings. Thus, modern science and Christianity agree that the world has only instrumental value. For both, it is devoid of consciousness. We have not only a right but an obligation to use its raw material to alleviate human ignorance and suffering. In such charity on behalf of all humans we take up the salvational cross of Christianity in secular guise.

As noted, this book does not examine the economic and political dimensions of the environmental crisis, although it briefly comments on them. Instead, it focuses on the myths and stories that we tell ourselves trans-generationally so as to give meaning to our lives and actions. These trans-generational tales ground our history and are a key to understanding who and what we are. They not only perpetuate our situation and the way we are in the world, they also confirm and give our lives meaning. Even Modernism's insistence on science is part of trans-generational mythology, especially when applied to technology. These tales are a crucial link between technology, ecophilosophy, and the spiritual dimensions of human life.

The spiritual dimensions of human life cannot be understood independent of the mythological and visionary, for they give our actions a meaningful context. Our myths live us, for we enact these stories, often without even being aware of it. We perpetuate the child rearing practices of our ancestors by treating our children exactly as adults treated us when we were children. In much the same way, we pass on the forms and patterns of behavior tied in with larger cultural stories. Although, to be sure, the public schools and media have done much to limit parent to child education and to dispose of tradition.

Humans are not just meaning seeking beings, we are meaning creating beings. We *need* meaning. It is *vital* for individuals and cultures. It is vital that we understand our own participation in larger personal and cultural stories and myths. Meaning and values are the foundation of any cultural order, tradition, and life. Where practices are based only on instrumental values and change, no solid, *place-specific* wisdom can develop. Human meaning must be realized in a cultural context and place in which we dwell, and this requires communities. Individualism and the corporate economy have destroyed most resource based communities, and modern urban centers are not conducive to community. In many respects, modern Western culture has been placeless and has lost its sense of direction. Its mythology has been hidden in abstractions which are contextless, much in the way the Kingdom of Heaven is a utopia in the literal sense, a non-place. The future has become our aspiration, not the present.

The impulse to control everything is not just a manifestation of an explicit intent to dominate, it is the result of the insecurities and unmet needs that are part of the Western psyche and character structure. If we stay in a place and daily practice an awareness increasing discipline (such as meditation), and a spiritual discipline (for example, Aikido), we begin to see more and more deeply into our *total* context, including our history and culture. To get to the roots of the environmental crisis in our own personal lives, we must go deeply into ourselves. If we are to understand it *culturally*, we must probe our most sacred beliefs.

If we are to restore our lives to social and ecological responsibility and balance, we must go deeply into our places and learn to rebuild community from the ecological wisdom to be found in those places. We must return to our historical roots and re-envision our noble ideals and stories in an ecologically conscious way, if we are to define and develop nonviolent technology practices whose design and use expresses ecocentrically creative mythologies and stories. We must find the new roots of our trans-generational enactments in the soil of the Earth, in its forests, waters, mountains, and grasslands. Aboriginal dwellers can help North Americans to gain deeper insight into the places they inhabit.

But how can recreating our mythologies make any difference to our situation? Are we not controlled by the economic system? This question is often asked of attempts to focus on the philosophical and spiritual dimensions of the environmental crisis. It is observed that practical economics compromises even the finest ideals and values. However ecocentric one might try to be in one's own life, given an individual change in consciousness, one is caught within networks of relationships that one did not create. It seems change of the whole system is necessary, but does this not require a change of heart in the majority? How can we expect the majority of people to change their habits, when they are doing all they can just to survive? How can we expect them to act as ecologically and socially responsible producers and consumers?

The market is supposed to be demand and consumer driven, but it is also controlled in many ways. We know that changes in tax and other policies could lead to major changes in behavior. But is such policy change possible, given the power of vested interests? Is it possible to change the structures themselves? My view is that it is possible, and focusing on the issue of not being able to change only prevents us from knowing what changes we need to make. Mainstream culture has little sense of what we must do to save our earthly context. We have not done very well at social responsibility, how can we do any better at ecological responsibility that asks us to consider other beings?

These are challenging questions. It is tempting to try to take on all of them. However, every author has limitations. Here I address the narrative dimensions of Modernism's source of power over us and the spell it casts through its science and technology. The greatest power in a society exists when its people accept its authority and control as *legitimate*; conformity then has meaning tied in with ultimate values. It is easy to become passive recipients of "legitimating" stories. Power generates an aura of authority and legitimacy; organizations which have power work to keep it at all costs. Much of our consent these days, as Chomsky (1988) documents, is manufactured by the major corporate media. Earlier, everyone participated in trans-generational story telling. Passive acceptance of the media stories is disempowering. Becoming critically aware, active agents of social change through understanding these narrative themes, and helping to tell new stories which transmute the old into ecocentric paradigms, is one of the main obligations of those who do ecophilosophy.

"Philosophy," as we use the word here, means the love and pursuit of wisdom, not for power or knowledge of how to control others. Wisdom requires self-knowledge, and self-knowledge depends on awareness of how we *participate* in creating the social reality that we share as culturally interrelated beings. Ecophilosophy is based on the assumption that the ecological crisis is the most serious one humans have ever faced, since the very *context* of human life, the Earth, is at risk as a result of human numbers and magnification of our power by modern industrial technology. This power of our institutions is concealed in the mists of mythological narratives banished with our dreams, for dreams in the modern view are not part of reality. When the West banished the intuitive, mystical, and magical, it also banished its own dreamlife and access to a deeper, tacit, ecological wisdom. It could no longer learn from other beings or from its own subconscious (except as laboratory subjects which it views as objects).

As already noted, the analysis of technology developed in this book centers on the fact that technology is a social practice with four dimensions: cultural, organizational, technical, and environmental. When these work together to form a whole, we have a technology practice. The cultural dimension holds the values and meanings, the organizational, the political-economic and legal structures, the technical the skills and scientific knowledge, and the environmental the source of material and a place to put external costs. Practice is understood on analogy with medical practice. Medical practice is not equivalent to medical science. Medical practice, as it developed in modern Western society, is based on allopathy instead of homeopathy or some other alternative. There are many other *systems* of medical practice available. Each of them is based on observational science. To take another example, forestry, as practiced in Western industrial society, is also not a science. It is a practice and a profession which applies the results of research according to organizational values and aims. Professional organizations exist to promote and further the profession and the interests of their members (not forests). Professionalism in Western society involves the depersonalization of practice and the rise of the "objective" expert and specialist. Disciplinary specializations in Western universities are barriers to understanding the environmental crisis.

Despite the foregoing problems, changes in practice can be brought about in a number of ways, through changes in the values of professional organizations, through cultural changes in values, through economic changes by means of tax and other policies. This book concentrates on the larger meanings of these practices not on such details as economic policies and structures. It assumes that the narrative dimensions of meaning and ultimate values *"legitimates" all* practices which are part of Western industrial culture. However, we do acknowledge the critical importance of policy and economics and so refer readers to recent books which concentrate on these areas outside of my competence. On the economic aspects see the works in the bibliography by Paul Hawken, Herman Daly and John Cobb, and Susan Meeker-Lowry. On the political, managerial, and organizational dimensions see the works by Robyn Eckersley, Andrew McLaughlin, C. A. Bowers, Peter Senge, and Abraham Zaleznik.

Finally, we offer some remarks on how the word "nature" is used in this book. Nature usually refers to the total nonhuman processes which include all other beings and the ecosystemic relationships on which humans depend. The word "nature" in this book refers to this vast assemblage of creation with all of its richness and diversity of beings and ways of life. But humans *are* part of this assemblage even though their cultural life and trans-generational learning through narrative forms enables them to act for or against it. We must realize that we cannot refuse to participate. We can only decide *how* we shall do so, whether destructively, foolishly, irresponsibly, or nonviolently and wisely.

Humans are different from other creatures in nature by being able to create *culture*, a body of practices, tradition, and myth which can become nature destroying by intent. (I personally am willing to grant that other creatures have cultures.) In recent years a form of art has arisen in Japan and elsewhere based on expressing hatred for nature; this is often done by destroying natural entities. Just because nature created us, it does not follow that all the cultures we create are natural. They are more or less so, depending upon their ultimate values, meanings, and practices.

Modern Western culture has waged war on the natural world in an attempt to control it as something other than human. Other cultures have not taken this path of power-over. This power-over approach is shown in the large scale deforestation wrought by Western industrialism. In contrast, the standing ancient forests of British Columbia are natural forests, even though humans have dwelled in them for generations. Aboriginal cultures on the West Coast of North America lived from nature's abundance in harmony with natural processes. Their cultures are created out of nature, and their myths and totems told of their intimate interrelationships with *all* beings. This gave rise to technologies which are *sophisticated* but not powerful in the sense of control over nature. (Power-over can be clever, but it lacks understanding of what it controls.)

If we understand ourselves as part of nature, then we must allow *all* of our Being to express itself in our cultural stories and activities. But modern Western society, as noted above, banished part of our source in nature by suppressing the visionary and intuitive. It attempted to replace all of these elements of self and nature with explicit technical knowledge of principles (science and engineering) which could serve as the basis for creating nature-controlling technologies and human designed places. (See Toulmin 1990) Controlling nature in this way is a dual edged sword, for if we are part of nature as whole beings, then to suppress or repress this natural part of ourselves is to become fragmented and unwholesome. A fragmented self is not healthy. The technologies designed and used by unhealthy selves are usually destructive and unwise. A razor sharp sword in the hands of a fool is dangerous.

To what degree can recovery of our larger visionary self be connected to redesigning our technology practices so that they will be ecologically wise? This book aims to show how understanding the ecological Self, as the larger transpersonal Self, can enable us to revision Christian concepts of destiny so as to give birth to an ecosophic idea of progress, not as power over others and nature, but as cultivation of practices and disciplines which enable us to realize our ecological Self. The realization of the ecological Self has affinities with the teachings of Gandhi and Buddha.

When this transpersonal Self is realized, one is no longer selfishly oriented but is concerned with the flourishing of all beings. Wisdom and compassion are intimately interrelated.

If environmental ethics is confined to extending current utilitarian polity it fails to address the destructive anthropocentrism at the center of our crisis. Here we do not seek a theory or one set of ethical principles. Ethical theories based on principles can be useful aids or guides. In daily life, rules and guidelines can help us to find our way to mature moral life based ultimately upon spiritual realization (in the sense referred to above). Our overarching narratives supply the meaningful context in which these disciplines and our lives are set. These are a main focus for understanding technology. We will show how creative holistic ecophilosophy is practiced by making use of the narrative arts that are available. Ecophilosophy focuses on our stories about ourselves in our relationships, especially to nature. In modern Western society technological development is a major part of this story as we relate ourselves to each other and the Earth.

With the foregoing in mind, let us continue our ecophilosophical narrative journey by considering three stories about technology practices.

PART I

*Historical and Philosophical
Overview of Technology Practices*

Chapter 1

Three Stories About Technology Practices

It is commonly thought that our contemporary world is shaped by the forces of enterprise and science. This belief assumes that the rise of modern science, more than any other single factor, marks the great divide between traditional agrarian cultures that go back to the dawn of recorded history, and the modern technological societies of today. It is also thought that the technological marvels of the twentieth century owe their existence to modern science. While some challenge these beliefs, it is certainly true that our culture is deeply influenced by the institutional activities of science, and that the development of technology is a major force in global and environmental change.

Given these beliefs, and given the widespread concern of scientists and non-scientists for the integrity of ecological processes, it is odd that there is not a more concerted effort to understand technology in a comprehensive and ecological way. It seems clear that we urgently need a holistic understanding of the practice of technology that includes its organizational, cultural, technical, and environmental dimensions. Here our aim is to pursue a comprehensive, philosophical understanding of human *meaning* in technological societies, and the significance of technology in recreation, work, and our relationships to nature.

To facilitate our pursuit of comprehensive understanding, and to help us see practices as whole activities, let us begin by considering three stories about technology practices. Stories and narrative forms embedded in larger mythic contexts provide the most comprehensive accounts of human meaning and purpose. These forms are easily overlooked when we concentrate on the technical aspects of technology, or when we focus only on a specific problem. The narrative descriptions enable us to bring tacit as well as explicit meanings and relationships into the open and enable us to view the larger context in which the technology practices are set. They also enable us to appreciate the personal and uniquely cultural aspects of human technological activities.

Although our culture takes pride in its nonmythic, scientific worldview, this very worldview is part of a larger cultural setting that contains mythic elements, in, for example, its ideas of progress and historical destiny. The mythopoetic dimension of everyday life is the context from which we tell the stories that illuminate the purposes and understandings of our personal lives and of human life in relation to work, technology, and nature. For purposes of the present inquiry, we view stories and narrative forms as the smallest whole units of meaningful context. We resist the tendency in modern disciplines toward abstraction and reductionism which ignores, or even rejects, the primacy of stories in favor of nonconcrete, impersonal theories. Throughout this inquiry we will be reinterpreting our culture's mythic backgrounds, exploring its contemporary stories through concrete examples, and illuminating larger ideals of ultimate values by reconnecting them with our mythic past. With this in mind, let us now consider the first of three stories.

I. *Stonemason*

There once was a medieval stonemason named Peter. One day he was cutting a stone to fit into the wall of a cathedral he was helping to build. He had worked on this particular cathedral all of his adult life, as had his father before him. His family had been stonemasons for several generations. As a stonemason he understood the esoteric symbolism associated with cathedrals (for example, the stone upon which and out of which the church is built). The stone he was cutting was part of a design that embodied this symbolism. The cathedral had been commissioned by Catholic religious authorities, and the designs worked out in consultation with them. As the stonemason was cutting the stone, he was considering its place not only in the overall design of the building but also, symbolically, in the church. A passerby stopped to watch him work. After a while, he asked the mason, "What are you doing?" The mason was at first at a loss to answer, since he was concentrating on the design the stone had to fit into, and reflecting on the symbolism of the design. Without a lengthy explanation he could not tell the stranger about *that* aspect of the activity. So, after some silence, he said, "Cutting a stone for that [pointing] part of the wall."

It is true that the mason was "cutting a stone", but he was doing other things as well. He was helping to build a wall, and fitting a stone into a design rich in meaning. His activity was also part of a much larger undertaking. He would not have been cutting the stone in that way, had it not been for the traditional values, as well as the organization, which made the construction possible. Even if he had known how to cut stone, he could not have taken part in cathedral construction in the absence of the religious and philosophical context that gave rise to the creation of such buildings. Economic factors were also part of this building activity.

The technical skills that evolved in the building trades developed, not only because of technical improvements through practice of the craft, but also through the values that the culture placed on certain kinds of construction, both practical and symbolic. To help build a cathedral was not only a job, but also a dedication to a higher purpose. Other cultures had the skills, tools, and organizational capacities to undertake such projects, but lacking the religious and other values (the esoteric "church") related to such constructions, they built no such cathedrals.

This example illustrates the degree to which technological activity, as the exercise of skills, techniques, and the specific use of materials and tools, is part of an integrated, cultural practice, not all of which is immediately visible. Such practices bring together place, materials, skills, techniques, tools, power, organizational capacities, communal values, and aims. Understanding technology requires an understanding of the interrelationships among these different factors, set within the larger context of place, history, and human activities as natural processes.

But what are we trying to see when we look at whole technology practices? Clearly, if we focus only on the hardware and machines of technological activity, we will lack comprehensive vision. A truck is what it is, as a technological object, because it is used in a context of purposes that define trucking activity. A truck placed in a culture lacking transportation systems and vehicular concepts could be almost anything but a truck for that culture. In the film, *The Gods Must Be Crazy*, when a Coke bottle is dropped among the Bushmen, it becomes many things, but it is not seen for a Coke bottle. Technological devices by themselves, apart from their cultural practices, have no inherent meaning. What they are as instruments is defined by their larger, practical, cultural context. Just as an explosive black chemical is not gunpowder in the absence of the culture of guns and weapons, so a truck is not a truck in the absence of the cultural context that values and uses trucks for hauling and similar activities. Names and naming, like tools and technology practices, are part of a meaningful cultural context. Single concepts do not have meaning apart from such contexts.

II. Zen Monastery

Our second story is set in Japan. Many years ago, a person from the West journeyed to Japan to study Zen Buddhism. After a certain amount of effort, he was admitted to a Zen monastery. He was told to watch what went on, and also to take part in some activities. One day, while he watched the monks go about their routines, it dawned on him that much of their work could be organized more efficiently. He made notes on how the work could be improved, so that the monks could accomplish more with the same effort and have more time for formal meditation.

When the opportunity arose, the young Westerner spoke to a senior monk. He explained his ideas on how they could improve their productivity. The monk listened patiently and agreed with the young man's observations; their work could be made more productive if they adopted his suggestions. He thanked the visitor for his thoughtfulness. However, he then said, "There is only one problem. We do not regard our work as anything other than the practice of Zen. We are not trying to be more productive. We do not distinguish between time spent in formal meditation in the Zendo (place of formal meditation), and time spent working in the garden or kitchen. It is all the same to us." The monk made clear that the aim of monastic life is not productive efficiency. The monks' work is part of their way of life. Their way of life is the study or practice of Zen, and zen (meditation) is their way of life. In not differentiating between the two, he affirmed that their activities were unified by a common dedication and practice (zen) running through all they did. In contrast to modern Western and Eastern technology practices, the monks did not see their work as one thing, their religious devotion and spiritual discipline as another, and their leisure activities as something further. For them, these are all part of Zen. The practice of zen (as living meditation) applies to chopping wood and carrying water, as well as to formal sitting on a cushion in the meditation hall.

This example illustrates how technology practices can be carried on as part of a unifying spiritual discipline. In this case, there is no separation between the sacred and the secular. This is one reason Zen teaches that samsara (the rounds of daily life, death and rebirth) *is* nirvana (the cessation of unsatisfactory life), since spiritual realization is to be found nowhere but in full attention to one's immediate daily life. In the unity of Zen practice there are no dualities, no separation between mind and body, work and spiritual discipline. Such a unified practice is complete in itself, as it is.

In the context of the Zen monastery, then, the idea of pursuing technological progress as something that leads to more power and greater productivity has no point. Although a Zen monk could understand someone caught up in such a pursuit, he or she might see this person as driven by the passions and confusions of the ego. Zen is complete in the skillful practice of zen in daily life, not in looking to the future or in seeking power over nature and others. This story prompts us to examine the defined purpose of pursuing technological development: ever increasing technological power. Attempting to justify this goal leads us to reflect on larger purposes, the meaning of life and ultimate reality. This in turn can lead us to reflect on the meaning of work and how to find satisfaction in ordinary daily activities, such as digging in the garden, as well as in our remunerative occupations such as piloting a plane or teaching a class. In this reflective process we are led to consider the nature of the self.

III. Climbing a Mountain

Finally, let us consider a third story. Several years ago a group of U.S. mountaineers organized an expedition to ascend a high, unclimbed Himalayan mountain. In keeping with their society's emphasis on efficiency and technical expertise, they carefully organized their team so that it included rock climbing experts, ice climbing experts, liaison experts, medical experts, and so on. The climb was conceived as a type of technical undertaking, a technological activity, best pursued by means of a division of labor based on expertise. A member of the expedition later said that they ran into problems as soon as they got on the mountain. They originally planned to have the experts direct those parts of the climb for which they had the greatest expertise. The results were not what the team expected. In brief, the experts climbed for their fellow experts, not for the team as a whole; for example, only those with advanced rock climbing skills could follow where the rock climbing experts led, for these experts wanted to test their skill and ability; and so, too, for the ice climbers. The rest of the party, non-experts, wanted to take easier, safer routes. The conflicts, which developed because of a clash between experts and other members of the team, were resolved when it was decided that the nonspecialists would have a major role in planning the route. The rock experts led on the ice pitches, and the ice experts on the rock ones. The climb went forward as a whole team effort, since all members of the team could participate.

This example helps to highlight how, because of their education and training, people see problems in a particular way, in terms of their own expertise, technical competence, and professional perspective. Technology practices designed by such a division of labor, as an exercise of specialized skills, often create problems for society as a whole, since the resulting systems are built and used by people who do not share the expertise of the designers.

In our society, technology practices are often designed solely by experts. The practices are then simplified to make them accessible for the use of nonexperts, but their technical "sweetness" makes their inner

workings very difficult to understand, except to small groups of technicians. This often results in alienation and disempowerment for the user.
Highly technical solutions to problems that are a result of failings in
whole practices often generate additional problems in part because nonspecialists are excluded from the design process. To go back to the climbing example, the experts' pursuit of technical difficulty and elegance
created additional problems for the team as a whole. These could be
solved only by shifting to a holistic approach. The overall strategy for
climbing the mountain was changed, and in the process an enlarged understanding of the cooperative undertaking, which was necessary,
emerged. This understanding was a result of the group working together
as a community with each member contributing his or her own wisdom
to the decision making process and thereby "owning" the activity more
fully.

These three stories invite us to consider whole practices whose failings are rarely due only to technical causes or problems. Each story calls
our attention to different central features of technology practices, and yet
each is open-ended. Our analysis of them has only scratched the surface
of what they could tell us about technological activities. The last story, in
particular, is useful in helping us to appreciate failures in the way a whole
practice is constituted.

IV. Ecology of Technology

One of the most prominent failings of modern technology practices is
their negative impact on the ecosystems of the Earth. The buildup of
greenhouse gases and other degrading effects on the atmosphere are obvious examples of such impacts. Many now realize that to reverse the greenhouse effect will require large-scale modifications of our technology
practices. A few obvious examples of destructive practices are removing
raw materials from forest lands by clearcut logging methods, the inefficient use of fossil fuels in transportation and production, and petrochemical methods of farming.

We cannot solve the problems created by these bad practices through
technical means alone. Their solution requires that we redesign whole
practices, but before we can do this, we must understand the practice of
technology as an integrated, comprehensive activity and process—we
must consider the *ecology* of technology. Such an integrated approach
based on the ecology of technology is necessary in the designing of new
practices that meet the criteria of appropriateness. These include not only
ecological balance and harmony, but also requirements for social justice
and economic sustainability. Holistically designed appropriate technology

practices would allow us to enlarge and improve our selves and relation-ships. In short, we need a holistic philosophy of technology that appreci-ates all dimensions of technological activity, including the technical, cultural, organizational, and environmental aspects, and how these are interrelated. This philosophy of technology must be ecocentric.

The cathedral builder in our first story was engaged in an art with sacred dimensions. We too need to see the creation of new technology practices as a sacred art, and like the Zen monk in our second story we need to find ways to master the desire for excessive power. These dimen-sions will assist us in using technology practice to become good, nonvio-lent citizens of the Earth. As moral agents we are responsible for designing and creating technology practices that are not harmful. They should cause no needless suffering to other persons and other beings, just because these beings have less power than our technology gives us. Unfortunately, many of the technology practices now being developed, such as the ge-netic engineering of new organisms, represent serious threats to the eco-sphere, especially in the service of immature power seeking. For the survival of all that we love, we have a sacred obligation to understand where these developments could take us. We need to see how alternative practices could avert the potential disasters that are now threatening.

In our reflections on the environmental dimensions of technology practices, we must consider the way in which our modern industrial cul-ture has seen humans in relation to nature. This brings up not only the question of how we have seen nature, but how our perceptions of it are changing. The dominant view in industrial culture has been that nature is a source of raw materials to satisfy human needs and wants. Controlling nature through the use of large-scale applications of technology has been a major drive of this culture. This effort has, more than anything else, redefined who we are, since industrial culture is affecting the natural world in profound ways.

Some have recently gone so far as to say that nature is about to die (Merchant 1980). Others have even claimed that nature has already come to an end (McKibben 1989). The gist of these claims is that human im-pacts have become so pervasive, magnified, and driven by modern tech-nology, that there is now nowhere on Earth we have not altered. The dominant view in the modern West, as mentioned, has seen humans as apart from nature. With the knowledge of science and the power of tech-nology we can now control nature, originally beyond our control. We defined ourselves in relation to this conception of nature as something apart from us. Some now argue, in the light of our impacts on nature and wilderness, that humans must redefine both themselves and nature. In so doing, we will redefine our relationships to nature, since it is being reshaped by our concepts translated into technological activities, and is becoming a human artifact.

While we recognize that our conceptions of Human and nature are reciprocally related, we disagree with the claims of nature's death. To claim that nature has come to an end suggests that there can be no return to natural balance. It is to believe that we cannot restore our own naturalness. This parallels the claim that wilderness no longer has any meaning, since all wilderness must now be protected as defined by our laws, whereas formerly we thought that we needed to protect ourselves from it, since it was something totally separate from us. The early European settlers in North America perceived nature as a wilderness to be subdued. Nature as wilderness was seen as threatening, a place to fear, and a place to be tamed. This conceptual purity implies conditions which in fact did not exist for Europeans either in their native places or in North America. There was no pure wilderness in North America corresponding to *this* concept, when the European settlers arrived. By then, the whole continent was occupied by humans whose ancestors (we believe) had come over from Asia earlier, probably via the Bering land bridge. For the aboriginal people the continent was not a vast wilderness waiting to be subdued. Humans were part of nature, nature was part of them. They made no distinction between wilderness and civilization. In their shamanic worldviews, their ancestors and spirit helpers were kin to themselves and to the animals and plants.

The lesson to be learned from the above considerations is that we need to understand "naturalness" as a matter of degree, as well as an ideal within our stories of human life. In this inquiry into technology practices we recognize that nature is not static. As a creative process it is constantly changing, as are we. For humans, nature is in part concept, but it is also experienced as a creative, evolving process expressing itself in the world and in us. As cultural creatures, however, it is possible for us to distinguish ourselves *conceptually* from nature, and to see it as an object. Modern culture has desensitized us. We often don't hear the authentic voice of nature that speaks softly in our own hearts, for it is drowned out by the noise of our own technological (cultural) activities and artifices.

Our need to reconceptualize nature can be met most powerfully and effectively by revising our dominant stories and myths. Our stories need to appreciate degrees of purity in our concepts of nature and wilderness, and their relationship to civilization. We need stories that give us a clear idea of what wilderness, left to itself, is, so as to be more aware of how and in what ways we are affecting nature. Stories and myths that give us comprehensible ideas of nature and wildness must be an explicit part of our efforts to understand existing technology and to design new appropriate practices.

We have the knowledge and skills, and access to the wisdom necessary to alter the effects of our technology on nature. Restoring nature is often a matter of merely letting it be, but in order to do that we must change ourselves so as to limit our own intrusions on it. This requires some form of spiritual discipline that returns us to our own natural selves. We will say more about this in later chapters. To cite a specific example of needed change, the erosion of farm and forest soils can be halted so that restoration and natural healing will take place. The rate of restoration is directly related to changing our technology practices, guided by a sense of urgency and commitment to ecocentric values. The major form of change needed in all resource industrial activity is toward practices that work *with* nature rather than those that attempt to control it. In order to make this change we must first understand that we are misguided in our attempts to control and gain power over nature and other humans. This understanding comes from developing deeper insight into the ecology of the human self and its cultural and personal mythologies.

A commitment to redesign our practices as a whole, so that they are ecologically wise and harmonious (ecosophic), must include philosophical, spiritual, and practical dimensions, which can be fully expressed only through the narrative power of stories and myths. These give us our sense of meaning as a culture and as individual humans, and they can teach us how to relate wisely to ourselves, to each other, and to nature and wilderness. Like the stonemason, we need to understand the esoteric symbols that reveal the stories we live by. Like the Zen monks, we need to see our daily technology practices as coextensive with a spiritual discipline that applies to all aspects of our lives. And like the mountaineers, we need to see that design of appropriate practices depends on drawing from the wisdom of the whole party, that is, from our whole community, not just from the fragmented activities of specialists and experts. Experts and specialists need to redefine themselves in terms of human wholeness, rather than identifying themselves only as, for example, chemists or engineers. With these changes in attitude, awareness, and practice, we will realize that the sacred is to be found in our secular work. Our secular practice will then become sacred precisely because we will respect, honor, and love ourselves, one another, our homes, and other beings. As a result, all of our relationships will be harmonious. How all of this can be integrated into our work and technology design through a comprehensive philosophy and practice will be outlined in the next chapter and explored in depth throughout this book.

Chapter 2

Definitions and Examples of Technology Practice

The classical Greek philosophers, Plato and Aristotle, reflected on the relationship between moral life and the use of tools and techniques to transform raw material into useful and artistic artifacts. They saw connections between the training of artisans and the development of the whole person. An analysis of the roots of the word "technology" helps to explain why.

The word "technology" comes from the Greek *technologia,* whose roots are *techné*—meaning art or skill, and *logos*—meaning word or study. *Technologia* means the systematic treatment of *technikos* (art object or building) by using *techné* (artistic or artisan skill). *Logia* refers to the systematic study and treatment of a subject or undertaking; it is the root from which we derive the word "logic". If we consider the meanings of the combined root words we can initially define "technology" as: *the systematic organization of techniques and skills, so as to produce some product, by means of reorganizing a raw material or some other appropriate medium.* Given this definition, we would not use the word "technology" to refer just to the products of technological activity, nor to techniques alone. So, for example, it would be a mistake to refer to the hand-to-hand techniques of a martial art as a technology. "Martial technology" is not equivalent to "martial art", for the latter is more comprehensive and includes a whole range of skills, discipline, and training of persons who participate in the larger traditional art using weapons and equipment. Clearly, the systematic practice of *techné* is part of the training of an artisan who undertakes to master an art. Hence, we can see possible connections between this type of discipline and cultivation of character. Such arts do make use of technological *devices* in their practices, but this does not make them a technology *practice*, for a technology practice is an organized activity that includes four dimensions:

- technical knowledge and skill,
- organizational structure,
- cultural purposes and values,
- resource use, raw materials and the environment.

From the above we can see that the word "technology" as popularly used is vague, for sometimes it is used narrowly to refer just to the technical aspect of a whole technology practice, and sometimes it is used to refer to a whole process. To avoid possible ambiguity we will follow Arnold Pacey's use of the term "technology practice" to mean whole technological activities that include the above dimensions: technical, organizational, cultural, and environmental. Pacey does not include the environment as a separate dimension in his analysis, but an integrated, holistic account of technological activities must list it as one. With this modification we define "technology practice" as: *an organized activity that applies scientific and other knowledge to practical tasks by means of ordered systems involving people and organizations, living things and machines; using natural systems and materials; to produce goods, services and other values.* This definition expands the root meanings of the term technology and adds to it the moral and spiritual dimensions of a practice.

As Pacey notes, we can think of "technology practice" as analogous to "medical practice". "Medical practice" refers not just to medical science, but to the delivery and use of all medical knowledge, scientific and otherwise, for purposes of health care. It involves cultural and professional values, economic concerns, organizational, interpersonal, and technical skills, as well as sophisticated devices, scientific knowledge, and pharmaceuticals. The practice of medicine is an art and is not limited only to science. There can be no complete scientific knowledge of human well-being and illness, since both are defined partly in terms of cultural values. We live in a cultural context shaped by a worldview that embodies values and ideals, including an ethos of progress and codes of ethics not based on science. Our science, in fact, is in part based on these usually unquestioned givens. Moreover, humans are capable of creative action and transpersonal awareness, both of which involve freedom to go beyond what is known. Scientific knowledge, by its very nature, is fragmented, specialized, abstract, and too limited to guide our lives by. Its division of labor and its methods lead to increasing professionalization and specialization. In contrast, the *practice* of medicine includes the whole person and it must draw from all of a physician's knowledge *and* sensitivities. A physician needs to consider not just the patient's liver or kidneys but his or her whole being, a being whose health and illness are part of a meaning-rich, purposeful context. As Susan Sontag shows, illness is part of a culture's literary (mythic) understanding of itself. A specific illness is often seen as a metaphor for more general existential concerns.

These, then, are some of the reasons why the practice of medicine cannot be pure science, but, considered as a whole, is an art. In general, the same considerations apply to any whole practice of technology. The above observations help to explain why it is possible to design theoretically complex technological systems that seem attractive on paper, but when applied, their calculated economies disappear in a sea of red ink. The nuclear power industry is a perfect example of this. In theory, nuclear power looks attractive and cost-effective. In reality, however, the application of nuclear power to generate electricity for civilian use has been a disaster whose costs will be borne for generations. Without going into all the details, it is enough to note that problems of quality control and other limitations inherent in the *workforce* have contributed to the escalation of costs in nuclear power plant construction and operation. The quality control and other standards demanded by such complex facilities are far greater than those usually required in the construction and operation of most facilities in industrial society. Delivering such high levels of quality in construction and operation proves to be difficult and costly. In addition, there are other problems overlooked by theory, such as those of waste management, to say nothing of public fear and political opposition to the large-scale use of atomic power. These are all part of the cultural reality in which any technology must operate.

The practice of any technology, then, is like the practice of medicine, and requires the coordinated and harmonious functioning of all four major dimensions we have outlined. If any of these is seriously out of harmony with the others, or is simply not available in appropriate ways, either the practice will not be established, or it will fail. Examples of failures in technology transfers to third world nations illustrate this same point. One of the lessons learned from development aid is that the transfer of a technology practice from one country to another will fail if there are significant cultural differences between them. Transferring techniques and hardware alone will not establish a technology practice, for the cultural and organizational dimensions of the country must mesh with them, if the practice is to be established.

Consider the following simple example as an illustration. The transfer of water pumps and the necessary technical knowledge to support their operation and maintenance seems a simple, straightforward matter. There are many nonindustrialized nations that could benefit from such technology. The designs and concepts are simple and the potential benefits seem great. And yet there are cases where such transfers have not had the expected benefits and in some circumstances have even created serious problems. Sometimes the pumps broke down simply because there was no organizational structure to provide for regular servicing of the equipment. In other cases, the introduction of pumps to existing wells led to alteration of nomadic patterns of life, and this in turn led to overgrazing of arid lands by increasing numbers of cattle. These changes precipitated political conflicts, starvation, and violence.

The question of whether or not technology is value-neutral can be readily answered if we adopt the concept of technology practice, for it includes purposes and values among its essential elements. While a technological device for which there is no context of practice can be said to be value-neutral, such a device cannot be *meaningfully* defined outside of a context that is part of a larger cultured valuational setting. As we indicated in our discussion of the stories in Chapter One, a technological device or artifact totally foreign to a culture, which has no place there, is something that the culture will not be able to define in terms of the object's original purpose. A computer is a computer only in the context of practices that recognize it as such, and in those contexts its design and production are bound up with values in every way. Computers, therefore, are not value-neutral in our culture. They are designed, built and deployed by means of value considerations that operate at every level of their use. The same considerations apply to all technological devices.

The organizational dimensions of technology practice include unions, corporations, consumers and their organizations, professional organizations, economic structures, and industrial organization. Even though we have all these different levels of organization in our culture, and they make possible the practice of large-scale technological activities, the introduction of new methods and mechanisms, for example for handling information, often requires modification of existing infrastructures. Such existing organizational structures are necessary for the practice of ongoing technological activity, but they also enable us to introduce a continuous stream of modifications to existing practices, such as in maintenance and production. Nonetheless, these organizational structures cannot be totally altered; all new devices, techniques, and practices are shaped in various ways to conform to the system as a whole. This explains in part why it is difficult to alter our practices rapidly, even though we might have the technical knowledge and see the need to do so. Let us consider this in more detail by means of a concrete example.

We might each see the need to do something to halt the destruction of farmland, forests, and the atmosphere. However, our means of transport, the way we heat and cool our houses and businesses, and our personal and industrial habits all work against this recognition. Short of declaring a national emergency, it is difficult to see how a government, once it did understand the need, could do much to alter, except gradually, the patterns that are now part of our established technology practices. To be sure, it is not impossible. However, solutions to these problems will not be forthcoming if we continue to think and act from within the existing limitations of our dominant technocratic philosophy. Our imaginations must be freed from the dominant paradigm.

As a further illustration let us consider the current North American controversy over old-growth forests. It is now abundantly clear, given our knowledge of ecological processes, that it would be a grave mistake to clearcut all remaining natural, old-growth forests. Given the greenhouse effect, the importance of standing forests in the carbon and other atmospheric cycles, and the necessity of restoring genetically natural forests (not tree plantations), it is obvious that we should preserve all standing ancient forests and naturally reforest as much denuded land as possible. And yet deforestation is accelerating. Politically, the issue is often characterized as a choice between Spotted Owls and jobs; the outcome of preserving the old forests is seen as eliminating lumber as a building material, and so on. Nevertheless, it can be shown that removing a whole forest by clearcutting is a poor and unwise practice, and although it might provide short-term gain for a few, for the whole economy and for long-term values it is foolish. It is equivalent to dismantling our factories and selling their parts; we are left only with bare ground and have lost most of our productivity. In other words, we are removing not just tree trunks but whole ecosystems with all their many complex processes, diverse beings, and productivity. And yet there are alternative ways to obtain the raw materials we need while preserving the natural forest processes which generate them—at no cost to us!

These natural forests also provide a whole range of other services that we cannot begin to produce for ourselves, such as water quality, flood control, wildlife habitat, atmospheric cleansing, and weather moderation, to name just a few. What folly, then, to remove most of a complex, natural, self-maintaining ecosystem and to replace it with highly vulnerable and unstable tree plantations that provide few of the above services and values. *Yet we do not focus our debate on forest practices!* Instead we debate whether we can afford *not* to cut down the natural forests because without logging them we will lose the use of their raw materials and the jobs associated with this whole industrial process. But the choice is not between old-growth forests and jobs. The choice is between bad forestry practices and ecologically responsible forestry (ecoforestry). The choice is between healthy natural forests and unsustainable tree plantations. A sustainable forest products industry depends on a sustainable forest, and current practices are destroying self-sustaining natural forests. The forests support us, we do not support them, to paraphrase Herb Hammond

(1992). Continuing current practices will ultimately destroy most forest-related jobs within ten years. More jobs and higher levels of economic activity can be generated by adopting alternative, ecosophic forest practices, which would at the same time contribute to ameliorating major environmental problems. Despite these obvious advantages, there is as yet no concerted effort to move in new directions, because of structural and political barriers. Current bad practices also continue because some powerful organizations realize large short-term profits by liquidating forests, just as corporate raiders realize short-term profits by selling off the assets of a pirated corporation. In such a sale, the production skills, capacities, and management capabilities of the existing company are lost, and while stockholders might realize some short-term gains, they and the economy stand to lose more in the long run.

The same sorts of observations apply to industrial farming practices. Farming in North America has become agribusiness. Even though many small farms remain, the scale of producing major commodities is large and capital intensive. The major producers base their practices on the industrial model, and applying this model has many negative consequences. Neither farmer nor consumer ultimately realizes the greatest benefits from current practices, and in addition, these practices adversely affect both the land and ecosystems. Many authors have succinctly described these effects (for example, Berry 1977, Carson 1962, Hyams 1976). Alternative, cost effective, ecologically sound practices have been developed and shown to work (Howard 1956, Jackson 1984, 1985). Moreover, consumers prefer food raised by organic means. And although, all this has been known for some time, there has been very little movement toward ecoagricultural practices. Some say that this lack of progress is a direct result of the entrenched, powerful, wealthy interests that resist change, since it is to their benefit to continue the status quo. While there is truth to this claim, it is also true that the institutional structures developed to pursue industrial goals make change difficult, driven as these structures are by market forces *and* government policies, and influenced by social, political, and other factors.

The history of agriculture in North America reveals a variegated pattern of development. The production trends in every sector of Western economies have been toward increasing scale. This movement toward large-scale production and increased worker productivity reflects the general features of the process of industrialization. This process is not peculiar to agriculture. Agriculture, in fact, has lagged behind other sectors of production in realizing totally controlled, mechanized, industrial organization. The reasons for this are many, but some of them have to do with the difficulties of large-scale control of soil types, land forms, variable weather patterns, and unpredictable biological activity. Even highly mechanized farming today is risky because there are so many variables that cannot be controlled. In contrast to the factory owner, who can shut out the weather and control the space in which the activity takes place, the farmer can control none of these variables. Even when following the most tightly organized schedules of production using highly mechanized techniques, the farmer can still lose an entire year's crop to a hail storm in less than an hour. Farming involves essentially geo-biological processes, and no matter how tightly engineered its practices, it still cannot control these larger forces unless, of course, it becomes greenhouse gardening. The larger biological and ecological context is clearly more evident in agriculture than in manufacturing. Given this, it is not surprising that farmers sought and obtained many forms of insurance, subsidy, and support from large institutions. Politicians, wanting cheap food for consumers and support from farmers, developed policies aimed at satisfying both groups. In pursuing these aims they also provided benefits for other establishments within the economy. They encouraged a whole system of research and development that spurred application of mechanized forms of production to farming. Such efforts continue to this day.

Considering the history and the organizational structures of current agricultural practices, it is not surprising that the system resists fundamental change. Many groups and organizations have vested interests in continuing with business as usual. Even when it can be shown that we would be better off in the long run if practices were changed, it is difficult to alter whole practices, since we often do not understand all the elements of these practices, and consequently have no clear idea of where and how to initiate needed changes. Even when it is clear that alterations of government policies would help to spur needed changes, it is difficult to gain consensus in legislative bodies, since they represent the established organizational power of different interest groups who make competing claims and have different views of what the priorities are and what should be done.

We have illustrated so far the extent to which technological processes must be understood as whole practices, and why technological innovation often does not lead to *new* technology practices, but simply extends existing structures. Since some might think that forestry and farming are not representative of technological activity as a whole, let us consider an example that clearly is. The introduction of computers and software for word processing did not change the basic technology practices of office workers. It increased their productivity and employer monitoring of work stations, but the nature of the work, its aims, basic processes, and its production oriented organizational structures have remained essentially unchanged. The computer, as it has been introduced and operated, represents just one more stage in the long process of industrialization of work.

The forms of organization inherent in most computer software are based on the same underlying models of production and organization as earlier practices. They are not revolutionary.

As a tool the computer is adapted to existing structures, part of a whole technology practice into which it must fit. If, as some hope, the computer does provide a means to free people to work away from offices, unsupervised except for the products and services they provide, then it could lead to alternative technology practices. But to stress a point already made: the alteration of tools and technical knowledge does not in itself change a technology practice, so long as its other dimensions remain unchanged. Revolutionary changes in tools and technical knowledge *can* lead to new possibilities and new forms of production and thus to new practices, but there is no necessity here. There are numerous other counter-examples such as wheeled toys among the Incas, who never applied the principles of the wheel to transportation, or steam engines among the Romans, who made no practical use of this technical knowledge and skill.

The concept of *technology practice* we have outlined requires that we consider the ecology of technology in reflecting on our practices. The word "ecology" is used broadly here to emphasize that we want to understand technology in all its dimensions and interrelationships as both an activity and a process. When we approach the philosophy of technology with this ecology in mind, we will not overlook its four fundamental aspects and the complex relationships among them. These are, to repeat, technical, organizational, cultural, and environmental. When these are carefully described for any given technology practice, and their interrelationships spelled out, then the full significance of the practice becomes clear. We see how the metaphoric and literary, the philosophical and spiritual, the practical and the political, the scientific and technical, the economic and the material interconnect, and how their interaction affects the self, community, and nature.

Technology practices exist within a context of complex relationships. These relationships are part of ongoing processes and activities, part of the self, community, and society, and as such, are also part of the larger ecosphere. To design technology practices in an integrated way so that they are ecosophic (ecologically wise) requires attending to all of these relationships. This is why the design and study of ecosophic technology practices must be transdisciplinary and cross-cultural, including historical, aesthetic, philosophical, spiritual, scientific, and other considerations. The philosophy of technology includes the study of technology practices in this integrated and holistic way, for the ultimate aim of philosophy is *sophia* or wisdom. This wisdom is not mere theoretical knowledge, but practical understanding that empowers us to lead our lives in such a way that we become better humans. In order to do this we must deepen our capacities for learning and loving through deep self-knowledge. As modern humans we are culturally defined by our technology practices, for these, more than any other single factor of our lives, are what make our culture and time unique. These technological processes form part of the ever-present milieu that surrounds us and have become part of almost everything we do.

The technostructure we have created reaches beyond the Earth to the planets; it permeates the airways with the clutter of electronic media and traces of its chemical processes; its satellites are moving stars in the night sky; the odors it produces reach us even in wild places. So, even though one might sit alone in the silence of a mountain retreat far from roads and trails, one gazes into a night sky and sees the moving edge of industrial society, the silence shattered by jets. One catches a whiff of smoke from a distant human-caused fire. One drinks water from a plastic bottle, and sits on a nylon parka. Time is measured by an electronic quartz digital watch. It takes effort and practice to return to the natural mind buried beneath the technological structures that permeate our lives as a result of existing practices. We will return to consider the disciplined pursuit of the natural mind later in this book.

The aim of our description of modern technology practices here has been modest: to describe the concept of technology practice so as to recall things we all *tacitly* know. We have attempted to make these explicit, accessible, and more systematic.

Chapter 3

Approaches to the Philosophy of Technology

For our investigation we will describe the philosophy of technology in terms of six developmental stages. These reflect a deepening understanding of technology during the modern period. Here we will exclude pre-modern reflections on technology. Modifying Rapp's (1981) scheme we will call the six stages the *Engineering Approach*, the *Cultural Approach*, the *Social Criticism Approach*, the *Systems Approach*, the *Comprehensive Analytic Approach*, and the *Ecophilosophy Approach*. (Rapp does not discuss the last two.)

The philosophy of technology was born in Western philosophy during the nineteenth century. Earlier philosophers commented on productive and artistic activities, but they did not see these reflections as a special area. Their observations were made in the context of philosophical questions related to other subjects: What is of ultimate value? How do we become whole persons? The idea that there should be a specific philosophical inquiry into the nature and use of technology came into focus only in the last century because of the increasing dominance of technological development in the West.

I. Engineering Approach

The first modern philosopher of technology was Ernst Kapp. Soon other thinkers adopted his method, based primarily on an *engineering perspective*. This approach focuses mainly on the technical dimensions of technology, and tools and techniques are seen as means to extend the human mind and body. A hammer, for example, is an extension of the human fist; a pair of pliers is an extension of the opposable thumb and index finger. In this approach technology is viewed as a natural outgrowth of the development of the human animal. Human technological activities are explained in terms of pure physical principles, with no attention to their cultural dimensions.

The engineering approach even now continues to attract many popular writers. Basically, it is an optimistic way of looking at technology, viewing it as an efficient way to solve practical problems. This model leaves out the valuational and organizational dimensions of technology, saying little about the impact of technology on nature. *Most importantly*: it unquestioningly assumes that nature should be tamed and controlled for human ends by means of technology.

II. *Cultural Approach*

As noted, the engineering approach fails to appreciate the cultural dimensions of technology, and technology is clearly a product and part of human culture. This was recognized by those whose primary interest is the *philosophy of culture*. Such writers as Ortega y Gasset, Karl Jaspers, Martin Heidegger, Hannah Arendt, and others attempt to understand technology as an expression of the cultural nature of humans and human *Being*. Some, most notably Heidegger, took this examination of culture down into the metaphysical foundations of modern Western society. The philosophy of culture has shown the ways in which technology is an expression of underlying ontological and epistemic assumptions of human *cultural* life. Modern Western culture rests on a worldview characterized by oppositional dualisms, such as wild-tame, self-other, humans-nature, mind-body, male-female. Divisions in the basic integrity of the human psyche and culture are necessarily reflected in the technostructures they create. The cultural approach did deepen the philosophical understanding of technology, but its critics pointed out that it lacked an appreciation for the degree to which technological forces are not *just* expressions of enculturated psychological and philosophical conditions. These conditions are shaped by the underlying reality of the productive system, which in turn is shaped by *economic and class structures*. It became clear that in order to examine cultural assumptions for bias, a critical approach to the philosophy of technology was needed. Perhaps technology has prejudice built into it? It has to do with power.

III. *Social Criticism Approach*

While the school of *social criticism* begins in the nineteenth century with people like Marx, its primary contributions to the philosophy of technology are made by twentieth-century thinkers like Adorno, Habermas, Horkheimer, Schmidt, Marcuse, and Krohn. Although they are not in complete agreement with one another, the general sense of their analysis of technology is the same. It is that the realities of class divisions based on economic structures are *the most powerful* determinants in the development and use of technology. Whereas the cultural approach tends to see technological artifacts as expressions of cultural values rooted in certain philosophical assumptions, the critical school views these artifacts as shaped by the realities of economic life. While they do not deny the influence of other cultural factors, the thinkers of the Critical School believe these are overshadowed by economic ones. The full analysis of these economic factors required far greater sophistication than Marx and other nineteenth-century thinkers achieved. The social criticism approach is not content merely to *analyze* existing structures and lines of power; it critically *evaluates* these structures and suggests alternatives, assuming that it is possible to *evaluate* practices across cultural boundaries. The cultural approach tends to avoid taking this step from analysis to criticism; it is more purely scholarly and does not have the activist inclinations the social criticism approach treasures.

IV. Systems Approach

The *systems approach* developed relatively late in the twentieth century, although there were elements of it earlier. Laszlo, Forrester, Wiener, Illich, and Harich are just some of the better known thinkers associated with this approach, which was applied in the *Limits to Growth Studies* of the Club of Rome, and other cybernetic studies of modern systems. According to systems philosophy the three approaches mentioned so far lack a holistic perspective of technology. They emphasize certain factors rather than others, and mostly ignore the impacts of technology on the natural world. None of them succeeds in understanding technology as a complex, holistic *process*. The systems approach tries to correct these shortcomings.

The systems approach to technological design and development first arose in the field of research and development. As the complexity and cost of modern technologies increased, it became clear that their design and development had to be approached in a systemic way; their planning and execution required a whole range of factors that could be ignored by early pioneers in technological innovation. Technological process and products synergized as a *system* of innovation developed. Modern aircraft, to cite just one example, can be designed and developed only by paying attention to a complex range of issues and *technical* problems, as well as to economic and political dimensions. Aerospace companies, and this is true for other large companies, found that research, design, and development work requires interdisciplinary teams, organized so that no significant details would be overlooked and to keep interconnections working. Such organization requires a coordinated, systematic approach that addresses the *details* of the whole system under development: human, technical, and infrastructural. Theoretic and practical work in cybernetics mirrored industry's practical efforts, and soon the process of information flow, feedback, and output became part of the milieus of research and development in all major industries. The modern desk-top computer fits perfectly into this *system*, and in many ways mirrors it.

When the systems approach is applied to technological processes as a whole, instead of to only one system such as air transport, it becomes clear that we must understand *dynamic interrelationships* if we are to appreciate what technology is doing to us and to the world. Attempts to apply the lessons of systems theory to broader issues were aided by the cybernetic revolution and the construction of powerful computers and software, for these made it possible to construct elaborate models that more accurately reflect the complexity of industrial and global systems. Systems philosophy and its techniques were applied, not only to understanding industrial processes and their economic and social consequences, but also to exploring impacts of these systems on natural ecological processes.

From the standpoint of ecophilosophers the systems approach has one major flaw. Ecophilosophers see industrial technology practices as the primary disrupters of global ecological communities. The flaw they see in the systems approach is that its philosophy of technology and nature employs mechanistic metaphors as the basis of its models. It attempts to make these anthropocentric models applicable to natural systems by making them more complicated so as to accommodate increasing amounts and kinds of data. As useful as these can be, ecophilosophers think that they are *inherently* flawed since humans and the ecosphere are not machines. The machine is a cultural artifact. This is the main reason why ecophilosophers critical of the systems approach prefer to talk about ecological relationships in terms of ecological communities, natural processes, and patterns rather than in terms of ecosystems and other mechanistic descriptions.

V. Comprehensive Analytic Approach

The tools and methods of analytic philosophy, as developed in the English speaking world, have been comprehensively applied to such areas as moral psychology, religious belief, and action theory. Frederick Rapp is the first to apply these methods and tools to develop an overall framework for the philosophical understanding of technology. His book *Analytical Philosophy of Technology* provides the first thorough organization of the major features of technology relevant to this inquiry. His analysis is systematic, logical, cogent, based on extensive study of the literature, historically astute, and of enormous benefit to those who want an overall map of this philosophical terrain. There is, so far as I know, no better outline of the major issues, problems, and structures of this conceptual topography available in English. Rapp hits the target again and again in providing basic conceptualization and systematic lists of relevant features organized thematically. He demonstrates how much analysis can add by way of clarity. He shows the value of analysis when used in an area of "applied" philosophy that many theorists consider "not rigorous". Rapp helps to provide order. His work has been invaluable to me in teaching and research. My own training was analytic.

However, having lauded Rapp's study, I now must say why I think that it is not sufficient for the purposes of understanding technology as a practice which must be made ecosophic, that is, ecologically wise. Rapp's book takes primarily a disengaged approach. This book, however, is more activist in intent. In my view we *must* philosophize not only to understand our practices, but to improve them in creative ways, consistent with the ecocentric values we come to understand as we learn from day to day in the places in which we dwell. This is the core of wisdom realized in everyday life. How must we change our own practices to be consistent with ecocentric values, and how must we change existing social practices? Rapp's approach, in my view, does not give us the *creative imagination* we need. The major barriers to change have controlled our imaginations. We cannot move in a direction we cannot imagine. The media feed us a controlled supply of images and ideas about what constitutes technological development in the existing system.

As I attempt to show later in this book, many of the barriers that we think stand in the way of significant changes in practices to move in the direction of sustainability, are related to the stories we believe, the images and icons we embrace, and how fully we can imagine. Our freedom, or lack thereof, is directly related to our own autonomous imagination. If we do not see the stories we are living out, we lack self knowledge, and if we do not contribute to making those stories, we lack freedom and imagination for active participation. We become passive recipients rather than agents.

Art in advertising, media, and entertainment control our imaginations through mass technologies. This is a new development in human culture. In shamanic cultures every person has their own story that together makes up the mythology of the group as a whole. Each person's integrity is respected, resulting not in chaos, but a surprising order that has no centralized authority. There is order which no one imposes. This decentralized emergence of order occurs myriad ways in primal cultures. There are examples of this in technological society as well.

An unhampered market that reflects all costs of production and use will facilitate optimal order in energy use even though each person makes their own decisions based on the best available information. However, today's market lacks information that should be in the price. The price of energy is artificially low because major costs are treated as externalities. These artificial prices are not determined by the market, but result from control of the market by monopolistic forces working through government, corporations, and the legal and tax system. Not seeing these distortions people think that mysterious *economics* prevents change to ecologically responsible farming and forestry practices. They believe that these responsible alternatives are less competitive, when they are not, if all costs are included.

Ecoagriculture and ecoforestry are actually much more cost effective and have many more economic benefits than the industrial models in use. They are good for long term economic sustainability and development of healthy communities. Healthy communities have other social benefits (that lower all kinds of costs) that the industrial system does not give us, since it destroys nonurban communities (raising costs not reflected in commodity price). The market system is confused with the overall political economic process. But there are simple measures, such as green fees (Hawken 1993), that could work major changes in the whole system. If we free our imaginations of the fixations that come through the media, we see many obvious, small changes which could make enormous differences to stimulate newly emerging practices. New practices will emerge (and are emerging) from the grass roots, not from centralized planning.

As good as Rapp's work is, it leaves too little room for the imagination. What comes from analysis is clarity, appreciation of details, respect for the abstract, but not inspiration and energy for creative change. Rapp's work provides valuable philosophical knowledge, but we need more than this in our current dire situation. This is brought in by ecophilosophy.

Comparative, creative *ecophilosophy* is based on ecocentric values. It examines the concrete stories and narratives, as well as actual on the ground practices and processes that are part of the evolution of new ecosophic practices. In other words, Rapp's comprehensive look at the features and logic of technology concepts is invaluable, but does not go far enough. We need a sixth approach.

VI. Ecophilosophy Approach

The core of the sixth, emerging approach to philosophy of technology is the *ecophilosophy approach*. Methods are integrated with ecocentric values that define technology as practices including the four dimensions outlined in the last chapter: the cultural, organizational, technical, and environmental. This approach is rooted in the work of E. F. Schumacher, Langdon Winner, Ivan Illich, Arne Naess, Gary Snyder, Bill Devall, and others. The appropriate technology movement is a major contributor to a new philosophy of holistic, ecocentric design leading to the application of ecosophic technology practices. (*Ecocentric* means giving priority to values inherent in ecological communities in our design and use of technology practices.)

The ecophilosophy approach has developed a broad-ranging critique of contemporary Western practices and their underlying philosophical assumptions. The aim of ecophilosophy is to understand what ecosophy (ecological wisdom and harmony) is, and to find practical ways to realize it. This in turn requires a recontextualization of human life. There are two main tasks for ecophilosophy. The first is critique, to understand our contemporary problems set within their historical, cultural, and organizational structures. This includes understanding the nature of human self-consciousness as it becomes defined in these contexts. This understanding is guided by an evaluational assumption that anthropocentrism (in the negative sense of valuing *only* humans) is a destructive prejudice. The critique also clarifies dominant power and class relationships, especially as they apply to nature. The second task of ecophilosphers is to articulate an alternative vision of human life free of anthropocentrism and domination hierarchies, a comprehensive vision, a total view that preserves place wisdom and diversity. Not only must we understand the ecology of biological relationships, we must also understand the ecology of the self and of technology practices.

We will explain this approach in more detail, by means of an ecophilosophical analysis of the self using *transpersonal ecology* (Drengson 1989, Fox 1990).

According to ecophilosophy, the lack of a comprehensive understanding of technology is a major problem. We need a comprehensive vision that shows how technology practices affect awareness and sensibilities, and how they reflect certain forms of consciousness. Ecophilosophy aims for ecosophy, that is, ecological wisdom. How can we expand our conscious awareness so as to be *ecologically inclusive*? How can we organize our practices so that they reflect such a deepening and widening awareness? To answer such questions we must include insights that lie beyond the limits of existing academic disciplines. Ecophilosophy takes seriously the insight that nature has wisdom dwelling within it; humans have ideas that can be tested only by considering what nature does. Ecophilosophy recognizes our ignorance and the limits of theoretical and scientific knowledge. Much of our own knowledge and understanding is *tacit*, and needs to be made explicit.

The methods of ecophilosophy are ecological in the broad sense, for it considers *all* significant aspects of the practice of technology and how they are *interrelated*, in context. It uses insights gained from the other approaches to the philosophical investigations of technology. It synthesizes them through a holistic vision of technology practices in their interrelational, ecospheric context. Ecophilosophy unites both the subjective and the objective dimensions of human technological activity. It joins the narrative and mythic with the technical and theoretical. It regards stories as the basic units of comprehensive meaning.

Ecophilosophy draws from the physical and social sciences, the humanities and arts, from studies in engineering, in systems analysis, and from environmental studies. It also draws from major schools of philosophy East and West (creative, comparative philosophy). Its modes of inquiry weave together insights and knowledge from these sources, as well as from practical experience. Its aim is to arrive at a comprehensive and comprehensible vision of technological processes and their relationships to self, community, and nature. Thus, it must ask fundamental questions about meaning and purpose in human life, what it is to be a complete person, how technology practices can hinder or help this development and achievement of harmonious relationships with all beings and nature.

Ecophilosophy examines philosophical traditions to find common elements that give an expanding vision of nonviolent alternatives to destructive contemporary practices. It draws from linguistic analysis, logical formalism, systems theory, hermeneutics, phenomenology, existentialism, and from contemporary comparative studies of religion and mythology. Ecophilosophy also learns from field ecology. The wise practice of technology involves thinking and feeling with living, creative, evolving forms of life, appreciating their interrelationships, contexts, and community structures. Conservation biology and landscape ecology further these efforts.

Instead of analyzing living processes via mechanical and abstract formal principles—using machines as models—ecophilosophy understands *technological* processes via biological, ecological, and evolutionary principles, as expressed in communities of beings living in dynamic interrelationships. Mechanical relationships are simple and unidimensional, whereas living relationships are inclusive and *multidimensional*. They include mechanical principles as lower forms of order and interaction, but they are ordered at higher levels through organizational hierarchies and interrelationships that are communal and social, the latter involving *structures of meaning*. Ecophilosophy shows how social, communal, and cultural forms of order make possible the accumulation and transmission of learning through gesture, symbolism, utterance, and language in interaction with nature and place. Such cultural factors enable organisms to go beyond genetic encoding. Through culture, other expanding forms of order, freedom, and creative action become possible. Stories are layered into other stories; meanings are embedded. For ecophilosophy culture can be understood only by using narrative, storied descriptions that bring together values, meaning, thematic, and conscious purposes.

For ecophilosophy creative freedom exists at all levels in the ecosphere. All beings, not just humans, are capable of creative response; however, certain creative possibilities are realized only by humans, some only by bears, some by ants, and so on. Beings achieve creative possibilities and freedom within their particular ecospheric niches. Culture, however, gives rise to possibilities for creating new *forms* of niche, just as the limbs of ancient trees in a natural forest create forms of space that do not exist in grassland or in industrial tree plantations. In human life moral agency, personal development, and cultural innovation add further niche possibilities.

Finally, ecophilosophy makes use of *transpersonal ecology* (Fox 1990) to illuminate human technological activity. We must explain what is meant by transpersonal ecology. To do so we will focus on the nature of the human self. Socrates observed that personal autonomy is limited by the state, for humans are social animals. However, even in oppressive circumstances, our autonomy is greater than we realize. In reality, our freedom is limited in part by our own imperfect awareness of our ecological Self and powers. Lack of self-knowledge creates fear and loss of confidence; it impedes understanding our possibilities for meaning in the world. We must pursue deep self-knowledge: What is it to be a human self? What is the best life for the human being, one that leads us to realize our greatest good? What is this greatest good? What is full self-realization? And what is the nature of my self?

This inquiry into the nature of the self is not mere autobiographic reflection, but a deep investigation of what it is to be a self-reflexively aware being. What does it mean to be a person? We need both an inward understanding of this knowledge and an outward expression in actions and relationships. Technology practices, for example, externally reveal the inner nature of our selves (character) and culture. Through ecophilosophy we see that insecurity in the self gives rise to technology that tries to gain control and power over others. Ecophilosophy explores self nature through transpersonal ecology, which brings together transpersonal psychology and deep ecology. Transpersonal ecology shows how the ecology of the small personal self (as ego) is embedded in a larger, ecological, transpersonal Self. Let us consider this analysis of self so as to illustrate the ecophilosophy approach.

As adults we normally identify with a narrow conception of self (the ego-self). We seek to make this personal identity complete and secure, but we cannot achieve this by being exclusive and apart. As a result we feel threatened and insecure so long as we identify what we are *only* with egoic consciousness. The ego is like a cell in the body believing it is the whole body; it is threatened from without by the apparent limitations of its incompleteness and the changing nature of the world. It is threatened from within by the emergence of insights from the larger, deeper Self of which it is only a part, and by its own resurfacing repressions of what conflicts with its self-image. What is hidden from the ego in its own shadow is often projected onto what is seen as other than itself (Bly 1988). When it is an object of such projection, nature is seen as threatening, something the ego-self must struggle to dominate and control. In modern industrial society this control is attempted through theories and technology. However, since increases in power through concepts and technology are open to others, the ego's insecurity grows with its technological power. The only definitive resolution to this dilemma comes when the ego confronts its own dark side and created fictions. The outcome of this confrontation is a larger vision that includes the ecological Self. In order for this larger Self-consciousness to be born into an expanding "vessel" the ego must die. But, by undergoing such a death and rebirth, we increase our autonomy through realizing our interdependence.

Saying that technology becomes autonomous implies that it takes on a life of its own. However, it has such a life only as a projection of our own shadows. Technology only *appears* to have its own inner life, dynamic, and logic. In reality it is driven by our own subconscious intelligence, and the crafty ego of its makers. These makers can be unaware that the "autonomy" of technology is only a projection of the shadowy fragments of a larger self. This larger Self is hidden because the small self (ego) is not completely integrated with the whole context and is still engaged in defensive maneuvers.

These matters can be expressed in another way. The human person emerges to self-awareness from a preconscious identification with a maternal matrix (the mother + nature). As self-consciousness crystallizes and the personal self emerges, the person defines his or her personal self through an act of separation from the other by means of an image, the ego. Maturity brings the realization that what the self is, is defined by means of relationships with others. As this awareness deepens, a person realizes that the voice of the narrow self(egoic)-awareness is only part of a larger, ecological (transpersonal) Self (Wilber 1981). The flowering of this full awareness signals the emergence of the ecological Self; one moves to the transpersonal level of consciousness, where self and other are seen as *reciprocally* interrelated. At this transpersonal level autonomy is realized in context and humans can develop a relationship with technology full of new creative possibilities that provide productive solutions to existing problems: technology is seen whole. The causes and conditions of problems are understood and values are clear; new means are created to replace the shadowy struggles between egos and between ego and deeper consciousness. The "separate" ego sees the world in terms of friends, enemies, and heroic struggles. The larger Self *knows* that the world is filled with possibilities for *reciprocal, complementary*, conscious relationships.

The above account of the nature of self/Self, and the relationship between self-awareness, self-knowledge, and transpersonal awareness, is an integral part of the ecophilosophical vision of technology practices we need. Given it, we can say what it is to be a fully mature human exercising the highest levels of autonomy and responsibility, as this involves technology practices.

In modern industrial culture, attempts to fully control children through pedagogy and force distort personal development (Miller 1990). The distresses caused are then internalized and repressed as part of the shadow to the ego, resulting in a deep division within the self and between the self, others, and nature. To compensate for our lack of a sense of integrated personal power, we use technology as a form of power, mainly to try to dominate and control others and nature. Humans desire to transcend the conflicts within the self, conflicts which, under ideal conditions, are a striving for the natural development of transpersonal awareness. This awareness seeks to transcend narrow self-identification in order to open consciousness to the widest possible forms of identification, certainly with nature as a whole, and perhaps even with the cosmos (cosmic consciousness). However, our pursuit of technological power as *compensation* for the lack of this natural development further blocks self-transcendence. Although this block lies within the self, it is perceived to exist outside it. If we understand this dynamic process we are then able to integrate the shadow, and place technology in the context of appropriate practices that are not compensatory but satisfy *vital*, natural needs. When technology practices are no longer a projection of shadow and egoic struggles, then it becomes possible to approach their design and application free of all forms of "power-over" compensations. They can then be used to promote human development and the flowering of human consciousness. They can become truly ecosophic, that is, harmonious with the well-being and thriving of all forms of life.

The foregoing discussion of the processes by which the small self

develops to the larger transpersonal Self has drawn from holistic psychology, spiritual disciplines, psychoanalysis, Jungian psychology, sacred psy-
chologies, cross-cultural studies of consciousness, and from first-hand
knowledge gained through meditation, psychotherapy, and the practice
of such spiritual disciplines as Aikido, wilderness wandering, and shamanic journeying. This ecophilosophical undertaking brings together the
ecological, psychological, spiritual, conceptual, aesthetic, and the practical. All are required for an integrated, comprehensive understanding of
technology practices. We will expand on and apply observations made
here to other contexts, so as to illustrate more fully the multidimensional,
transdisciplinary nature of our ecological, holistic approach. We will explore in more depth the ecology of Western technology and its technosphere.

Chapter 4

Stages of Technology Practice in the West

I. The Need For Broad Temporal Perspective

In order to better understand our current situation, it is necessary to have a broad historical perspective on our technological subject. This broad perspective will enable us to appreciate that we are now in a transition leading to more mature forms of technology practice. This transition will bring to a close the era of the development models that began the industrial revolution. For our purposes we will simplify the complex history of Western technology by organizing it into ten stages, each identified with a significant theme pattern.

Every comprehensive vision of history is based on philosophical presuppositions. Our approach is based on five assumptions. First, we assume that our living heritage requires seeing history as a whole in light of its complete development in the present. Our second assumption is that development involves creative evolution. Our third assumption is that this vision of history involves ecology. Our fourth assumption is that advanced theoretical work in several fields supports a cosmology of participatory co-creation (*cosmogenesis*) and self-production (*autopoeisis*) (Berry 1988, Fox 1988). Finally, we assume that the evolution of autopoeic consciousness can be illumined in part by a study of metaphors and myths. It is an old, primal cosmology.

Historical consciousness, and awareness that we are historical beings, is bound up with the development of our capacity to inquire into technology practices. Historical consciousness is itself conditioned by a larger transhistorical consciousness that seeks a total view. This search for comprehensiveness is the basis of our concept of progress. Here we define progress not only in terms of technological development and stages of technology practice, but in terms of a deepening and widening of evolutionary consciousness. This evolving creative historical consciousness expands through compassion and increasing spiritual power. These are the basis for our ecophilosophic measure of progress.

Throughout history some humans have made the spiritual journey of expanding their awareness. They have moved from the narrow perspective of an embodied, unified, prepersonal self, identified with the maternal matrix, to the wider, personal, tribal self capable of self-reflective awareness. Some have then gone beyond the limits of their cultural boundaries to discover the larger transpersonal Self that cuts across particular cultural contexts and historical periods. It is this global, transhistorical, comprehensive awareness (the transpersonal Self) that is capable of seeing all phases of the human drama with a single eye.

The old television series, Star Trek, gives us an example of this expanded consciousness. It presents a contemporary myth-story made possible by the technology practices of twentieth century industrial society, with its space vehicles, lasers, and electronic communication devices. The Star Trek characters make mythological journeys into different dimensions of awareness, and in so doing they explore the ecology of consciousness. Such journeys, using other mythological forms, were possible earlier. For example, shamanic journeying is another way to explore the ecology of consciousness within a different technological setting (see, for example, Harner 1986).

Since Western culture's technology practices are now spreading throughout the world, it is urgent that we understand them from a historical perspective, which we will describe through developmental stages.

For these purposes, we will define culture as the integrated pattern of human knowledge, belief, and activity that depends upon our capacity for learning and transmitting knowledge and values to succeeding generations through various media. We define myth as traditional stories of events and actions that serve to transmit trans-generationally the worldview of a people and to explain the deeper meaning of destiny, practices, beliefs, and natural events.

Once human beings acquire the important dimension of culture, they can accumulate far more knowledge and skills than creatures without culture. The systematic application of cultural adaptations leads to refinement of technique and improvement of tools. This systematic process of learning and improvement establishes technology practices, which, as we have noted, require raw materials, cultural values and purpose, organizational skills, and technical knowledge, all of which can be assessed and improved through codified methodologies. In nonliterate cultures one of the ways of conserving information and knowledge is through an oral tradition of stories, songs, chants, myths, ceremonies, and the like. This is not to say that the oral tradition serves only this purpose, since it also serves a number of different functions directly related to establishing and expanding cultural relationships of various sorts, many of which we do not understand. One of the major challenges of culture is to acquire, preserve, and pass on important information and knowledge so as to recreate itself from one generation to the next. It does this through stories and myths.

II. Ten Stages of Technology Practice

We will now tell the story of Western technological development through ten stages.

Those ten stages of technology practices in the West are:

- Gathering
- Hunting-gathering
- Hunting-gathering-pastoralism
- Village-agriculture
- Urban-agrarian
- Urban-artisan
- Urban-industrial
- Industrial-technological
- Scientific-information-technology
- Appropriate-ecosophic practices (emerging)

The *Gathering* stage is a hypothesized state of nature in which our human ancestors lived before they became hunters and users of tools. As they developed their skills in making and using tools, their activities expanded to include *hunting*. Humans and their prehuman ancestors possess no innate equipment that suits them to be hunters, other than intelligence. However, given intelligence and the augmentation of their powers by the use of tools, humans became formidable hunters capable of killing any creature found on land or sea. Stone Age hunters were and are highly proficient at capturing their quarry.

As hunting and gathering cultures developed and improved their technology practices, some which were favorably placed made a transition to *agriculture* and *pastoralism*. As our stages indicate, some tribes became primarily pastoralists, some became primarily agriculturalists. Agriculturalists developed commitment and attachment to a particular place; pastoralists, even those who were part of a particular agricultural society, tended to migrate at least seasonally, in search of the best fodder for their flocks. Some pastoralists migrated over large areas, and some, such as the

Tatars, even developed major civilizations. The wandering pastoralist is skilled with animals, and the sedentary agriculturalist with cultivating growing plants.

One foundation of Western civilization in Europe was the culture of ancient Greece. It was formed by merging two distinct cultures, one the wandering pastoral Dorian and the other the indigenous Mediterranean agriculturalists. The merging of these cultures gave birth to a new culture. The vigor of this hybrid pastoral, agricultural, Greek civilization generated major centers of learning and commerce in the ancient world.

We learn from early Greek myths that the first great technological revolution in human life was the control and use of fire. According to the myth, Prometheus stole fire from the Gods and gave it to humans. Hunting and agriculture were the second and third revolutions, and the domestication of large animals and horses was the fourth, with impressive cultural impacts. The introduction and use of the wheel, the invention of the plow, the mastery of simple machines, the invention of the yoke for teaming oxen and other animals, the development of building skills: these and other inventions were part of the spiralling development of technology practices in ancient times. They were usually associated with the development of some form of writing, which is often considered the fifth revolution. All of these came together in ancient times, and nowhere in the West were they more beautifully organized and systematically applied than among the Greeks.

Alphabetic writing, one of the greatest of these revolutions, was developed during the classical period of Greek history. The rudiments of writing were borrowed from the Phoenicians, and both Egyptian and Chinese ideograms were in use long before the Greeks perfected *alphabetic* writing. However, as powerful as ideograms are, alphabetic writing is a more effective tool for mass distribution of information and promotion of literacy. As Walter Ong (1982) points out, alphabetic writing provides new ways to organize thought and systematize information. Moreover, alphabetic writing minimizes ambiguity, which is one of the advantages but also a defect of ideogrammatic writing. With alphabetic writing it is much easier to organize and produce dictionaries, textbooks, and technical manuals. Ideogrammatic characters take a long time to master, but alphabetic characters are quickly and easily mastered so that even young people can be rapidly taught to read and write concurrently. The next major revolution in information and communication technology came much later with Gutenberg's invention of movable type, which made it possible to mass produce books and truly revolutionize communication.

The Greeks' development of alphabetic writing, the hybridization of the older tribal cultures, and the particular advantages of their geography worked together to produce a culture bursting with innovation and a sense of adventure. The Greeks laid the intellectual foundations of Western culture in part *because* they developed and improved alphabetic writing. This development led to major changes in their own outlook, and in the way in which Western humans were to conceive of what constitutes knowledge, political organization, science, and technology. Indeed, it is probably correct to say that historical consciousness was born as a result of the revolution in literacy that happened in classical Greece. The vigor of philosophical creativity of the Greeks can be attributed partly to the transition they underwent from a mythologically based oral culture, some of which was recorded in the Homeric tales, to the literate culture of classical times. Plato is one of the major figures in this transition, and his writings are so fruitful to encounter precisely because he stands between and explores the advantages and disadvantages of both the oral and the literate cultures.

The movement from Gathering, to Hunting and Gathering, and from the latter to Hunting-Gathering-Pastoralism, thence to Village-Agriculture, represented gradual transitions in Western human life. With each subsequent innovation and revolution in technology practices the pace of change picks up. As practices synergize and build on one another the rate of change becomes geometric. By the time of *urban-agrarian* states, such as those of the Greeks and Romans, city states attracted and drew together large numbers of artisans, philosophers, scientists, designers, military experts, political leaders, and workers. These city states became magnets collecting talent and financial resources; some were centers of great power capable of spreading their influence over large areas, as Alexander's armies and the Roman legions demonstrated.

Given the concentration of human talents, numbers of people, and other resources, the agrarian cities provided greater opportunities than had previous cultures for the gradual refinement and improvement of *artisan skills*. The agricultural revolution was mature by the time the Romans and Greeks were in their classical periods. They benefited from the surpluses produced, which freed human energies to run commerce and manufacturing and to field large armies. The urban centers became places where technological innovations could be readily disseminated to large numbers of workers, production could be rationalized, and where large building projects could be planned and undertaken. The building of the Acropolis, with its many magnificent structures, is a prime example of the organizational and artisan skills that cities were able to develop and concentrate. It is not surprising, then, that such urban centers became the primary bearers of culture and civilization, and the primary sources for revolutions in technology practices. It is not surprising that the ancient cities provided the foundations for the feudal cities of the Middle Ages. These, having consolidated gains and achieved long periods of relative stability, were followed later by the great cities of commerce and the Urban-Industrial city, which in turn laid the foundations for the metropolis of today.

The *urban-industrial* city expanded the capacity for concentration of wealth and power. Improving means of transport and communication made it possible for cities to be larger and to provide services for millions of people, instead of thousands or even hundreds of thousands. Inventions such as steel I-beam, the Otis elevator, and the Bell telephone made it practical to build skyscrapers, which in turn made possible the further concentration of human activities on very small areas of increasingly valuable urban real estate. The construction of mega-cities produces a host of problems, not only environmental, but social as well. The separation from nature, which began with eating the fruit of the tree of knowledge of good and evil, became complete in the urban-industrial city. It is now possible to build totally self-contained human habitats with their own internal systems of waste disposal, heating and cooling, artificial light, means of communication and supply of vital services, so that (in theory) one need never leave the constructed artificial system.

With further technological sophistication, the drive to miniaturize systems led to the development of the transistor and the integrated circuit. Just as the agrarian city laid the foundations for the emergence of the industrial city, the industrial city laid the groundwork for the emergence of the *Industrial-Technological* stage. By the time the city had become a totally built habitat, the organization and infrastructure were in place for the transition to this stage. More and more the main occupation of humans became intertwined with tending their technology. The creation of the artificial environment and the development of automated processes enabled humans to devote all their time, if they so chose, to maintaining and interacting primarily with their technological devices.

By the end of the nineteenth century artisan-driven technology practices were no longer the cutting edge of intellectual exploration, especially in the area of new technological development. They had not, of course, exhausted their possibilities, and they continue to be a necessary part of scientific research. But as the twentieth century dawned, science became the leading edge of new technological development, and by the time the century was half over the transition to science-driven technology practices was quite advanced. *Scientific-technological* technology practices are based on scientific knowledge and theory and depend upon sophisticated technological devices and skills. Examples of science-driven technology practices are genetic engineering, hydrogen energy systems, remote scanning and satellite search for raw materials, space travel, nuclear industries, and chemical agriculture. The elaboration of such technologies and the development of integrated systems of information and knowledge, along with better understanding of natural systems and ecological relationships, provide the basis for transcending the industrial forms of technology practice. These forms are, however, still a major part of our way of life.

The Scientific-Technological stage has not yet fully run its course, but we can detect in embryonic form the presence of a new stage of technology practice which, partly following Schumacher (1973), we call the *appropriate-ecological* or the *ecosophic*. Appropriate technologies are ecosophic, that is, they are ecologically wise and in harmony with the way natural processes work. They are low impact, they provide us with the means to satisfy our vital needs, and help us to develop our talents. They are low cost and accessible to all, not just to the wealthy and powerful. They are democratic insofar as they are decentralized and not based on hierarchical forms of management, with the control coming from above. They are human scaled and easily transferred to other contexts. They are highly productive, yet do not generate wastes and toxic by-products. They preserve, and even enable us to restore, the integrity of natural processes and biological communities. They are based on a sophisticated understanding of ecological relationships and of human possibilities, but they are basically simple to use.

What are some examples of such appropriate-ecosophic technology practices? Let us consider two areas already discussed, agriculture and forestry. After decades of development and change, conventional industrial agriculture in the West has come to a dead end as a result of pushing the industrial model beyond its limits by attempting to turn natural biological processes into controlled mechanistic ones. It emphasized farmer productivity and overmechanized the farm. It tried to replace fertile, living soil with chemical stew. Even now industrial agriculture tries to solve the problems caused by large-scale monoculture and soil mismanagement by further applications of biocides and other chemicals to control pests and diseases. Its central objective is to use technological power to control nature, rather than to base practices on an understanding of how to work *with* natural processes. This same course of development has been followed in forestry, medicine, and in other areas. We have extended the industrial model so far that we have lost many of its advantages. Now we are experiencing the pathology of big power and the gross inefficiencies of large-scale production.

Farming, to return to our main example, is not just a science. Like medical practice it is an art that draws from science. Failing to grasp this fact, the conventional industrial approach, in its drive for uniformity and mass production, spawns a host of serious environmental and cultural problems. It destroys the diversity and integrity of both biological and human communities upon which sustainable agriculture depends. With this in mind, new ecosophic, agricultural practices have been designed.

The first dissenters from the industrial-chemical approach were the organic farmers and gardeners who sought to produce uncontaminated food, but there were other persons and groups who pursued ecosophic methods for a host of other reasons. The large-scale application of organic methods has been demonstrated to be productive and sound. (By large-scale we mean farms as large as 300–400 acres.) Different ecoagricultural approaches are interacting with one another, synergizing, and some revolutionary, ecosophic agricultural practices are emerging. These practices range from the do-nothing, natural farming of Fukuoka (1978), to the kind of mixed cropping, rotational methods demonstrated on the Rodale (1985) research farms.

In forestry we can trace a similar line of development. We have gone as far as we can with plantation tree farms based on the industrial-agricultural model. The large-scale clearcutting of naturally forested lands, and the replacement of these forests with monoculture tree plantations destroys the forest ecosystem and devastates the ecological and human communities (see, for example, Camp 1984, Devall 1994, Maser 1988). Such practices are not sustainable. The death of forests in Germany is in part the result not just of acid rain, but of generations of industrial forestry practices that have gradually undermined forest soil fertility and forest community biological diversity.

A main lesson of ecology is that everything is interrelated. Because we cannot know all of these interrelationships, we cannot expect to manage ecological communities better than nature does. No human tree plantations have proven to be sustainable; only natural forests have stood the test of time. Thus, in the philosophy of appropriate technology, we must manage our own activities and design our technology practices so that they complement and harmonize with natural processes. We can do this only by recognizing our ignorance of nature's complexities and respecting its wisdom. In forestry this means learning how to use natural selection (not to be confused with selective logging) methods to get the material we need from forests, methods that do not interfere with the integrity of forest ecosystems and their naturally diverse biological communities. In *natural selection management* (Camp 1984) we can remove from the forest only trees that nature has selected for removal. We must learn to read nature's indicators so as to make these selection decisions. Regeneration and succession are then left to the natural processes of the forest. If by these methods we cannot meet industrial demands for raw materials, then we must satisfy these demands by means of large-scale recycling, conservation, and raw material substitutions. Forests must be maintained as natural ecological communities, which are essential to sustaining human life, the atmosphere, the stability of weather patterns, and even the ecosphere as a whole. These are sufficient reasons to change our forestry practices and lifestyles.

However, there are other, deeper, moral and spiritual reasons for changing our lifestyles and practices so that they are not violent to the Earth. The other beings of this planet have intrinsic worth. Wilderness is good for its own sake; all natural beings are good in themselves. We have no right, only because we have great technological power, to destroy the homes of other beings just to provide cheap paper products to use once and then throw away. As highly conscious beings capable of moral perfection, we have responsibilities to ourselves and to the rest of the ecosphere. It is not our prerogative to manage it, but to manage ourselves, *to act as responsible members of the ecological community*. If we explore our own self-conscious drive for self-realization, we each will find that our completion and fulfillment cannot depend on depriving whole species of other beings of their self-realization. Each of us is inherently good and in our hearts we would rather be knights than knaves.

We have a deep obligation to live in ways that do not destroy the planet and other species. Such nonviolent (in the Ghandian sense) lifestyles and technology practices are possible. They have been already demonstrated in agriculture and forestry. Our challenge is to develop an integrated approach to technology practices that enables us to design ecosophically, and to introduce new comprehensive policy and management tools. For this we must work in collaborative ways with all kinds of different people, from other disciplines, from other classes, communities, and cultures. But to design new ecosophic systems we must ask and answer fundamental questions about our ultimate purposes and values. First we establish our values, then we build our economy and technology from those. We build to allow for our own ignorance; we err on the side of humility and modesty. We also need to create new cultural forms of entertainment, participation, celebration, and story. We need to develop new role models and forms of education for our children. We need to heal ourselves in this process.

For the remainder of this chapter we will switch to narrative forms. We will use story and myth to explore technology practices. We will give these stories an ecophilosophical interpretation to gain insights into human consciousness, spiritual development, and our place. Our ultimate premise: Progress is spiritual and moral development measured by ecocentric values such as frugality, humility, and compassion.

III. Discussion of Stages as Seen Through Narrative Forms

Modern Western culture grew out of the Christian culture of the feudal Middle Ages, which itself was rooted in Greco-Roman and Middle Eastern cultures. We can trace the earliest known Western cultures back to prehistoric times. Archeology and other anthropological studies suggest that all contemporary cultures have their ultimate origins in pre-agricultural gathering societies. The least technologically developed cultures of which we have any knowledge are hunting and gathering ones. However, as a result of studying large primates in the wild, scientists speculate that humans, prior to the rise of technology, lived in much the same way. Gorillas, for example, live in family-based bands that wander about in a home territory. They live by gathering from the bounty nature provides. They do not hunt for protein, nor do they gather and store surplus food. They do not work systematically, using tools to get food. Early humans probably lived similarly in free roaming bands, in areas with mild climates where a diversity of edibles were available throughout the year.

The systematic use of tools developed early in prehominid times, and fossils, which can with certainty be identified as human, are found in association with tools and evidence of their *systematic* manufacture. We know that chimps, gorillas, and other primates, and even birds and other animals use tools from time to time. But none of these creatures has developed tool uses organized as systematic practices that require culture to pass them on. For this reason we do not call their tool use "technology".

The supposition that our ancestors lived in a bountiful state of nature, free from work, is supported by many mythologies about human origins. These myths are remarkably similar across agricultural societies, and all provide some insight into our origins and our relationships to other forms of life. Many of these myths explain why human creatures departed from the ways of other animals and became tillers and toilers. The Old Testament story of Adam and Eve, for example, can be read as a story about our evolution and our ecological and technological development. Let us look at this central Western story about human origins in more detail.

Here is the story as it appears in the Old Testament Book of Genesis in the Christian Bible: Adam and Eve lived in the Garden of Eden, a paradise in which they had no need to labor or struggle. Everything was provided for them by nature which had been created by God the Creator. The story tells us that they live in this timeless state of plenty, free from toil. They feel no separation from nature and can even communicate with other animals, who are not their servants; the animals do not fear them. However, Adam and Eve are given one command by the creator: "Do not eat the fruit of the tree of the knowledge of good and evil." In some versions the tree is called the tree of knowledge. If they eat this fruit they will die. The serpent encourages them to eat the fruit of the tree, saying that their eyes will be opened and they will become like God. Adam and Eve do eat the fruit, become aware of their nakedness and are expelled from the Garden by God. Their punishment includes bringing forth children in pain and toiling to get food from the soil. After their expulsion from the Garden, their son, Cain, who tilled the ground, murders his brother, Abel, the herdsman.

This story has a number of features relevant to our inquiry into technology practices. It describes what is necessary for the development of culture, and for understanding how in the process humans can become separated from nature. In the precultural state humans are not separate from the rest of nature. They can communicate with other beings. They gather their food and do not hunt. They do not kill. They cause no other beings to suffer. This is human life without technology. There is only the gathering of food, which nature supplies; there is no systematic use of tools. Adam and Eve do not make clothes to protect and hide their bodies, and they do not even *realize* that they are naked.

They make no distinction between themselves and other creatures. The snake speaks to Adam and Eve, encouraging them to eat the forbidden fruit. The snake in shallow interpretations is thought to represent Satan, the embodiment of evil. However, from the perspective of transpersonal ecology, Satan represents the shadow of the newly self-conscious beings, Adam and Eve (representing humanity as a whole), for self-awareness newly embodied as ego consciousness does not recognize its own dark, repressed, negative side. As a result, it projects this dark side, its own unacknowledged capacity for selfish action, onto something other than itself, a Satan or some other "enemy". The enemy as projected shadow exists because egoic consciousness is not completely integrated with the whole deeper Self. Moreover, the snake could not have originally represented evil to Adam and Eve, for at first they make no distinctions between good and evil. They have no such *dualistic* awareness. They do not see themselves as apart from nature; only *after* they eat the fruit do they have the knowledge to make such distinctions. Having this capacity, they then are able to separate themselves from nature and from other beings. Here the story symbolizes the emergence of self-conscious humans as a species of persons separate from nature. After Adam and Eve eat the fruit of the tree of knowledge, they can know sin, that is, they lose the original, undivided, sentient awareness that is unified with nature (God). Simultaneous with this, of course, they emerge with individual, personal, self-reflexive awareness (an ego). A new form of consciousness divides the original unity of self with nature and with its own Self.

The story says that if Adam and Eve eat the fruit of the tree of knowledge they will be like God. Why and how is this so? First, they gain a new capacity to distinguish between self and other, subject and object. They are now, like God, apart from themselves as nature; they can conceive of themselves as apart from their "place". Second, God as a Creator, is one who freely innovates and brings new things into the world. After gaining knowledge, they also become creators, and their descendants become innovators; a new power of creation and destruction (technological power as a cultural construction) comes into the world. With this *knowledge* of good and evil, these first humans are free to act, free to *choose between* good and evil. Without this power there is no moral agency and merit. Eating the fruit was traditionally seen as the "original" sin, since this action brought with it the capacity to consciously choose evil. Now all things are different for these first humans. The fall from the original edenic state of blessedness, which represents unself-conscious, sentient life, leads to the possibility of creating a self, a personality, a historical self, through conscious choices, through weighing different courses of action. As a result of their choice they cannot remain in their condition of innocence (edenic or prepersonal consciousness). Self-awareness represents achievement and loss. Moreover, it gives rise to consciousness of mortality and alienation.

Sin, in a nontheological sense, is living in a non-unified state, being out of harmony with the rest of creation, as if the rest of creation did not count. This being their condition, Adam and Eve were no longer in Eden. And where did their journey take them? It took them to a land of toil and struggle, the land of self-conscious responsibility where their fate lay in their own hands. As moral agents what they became would be the result of their own choices and actions. They were no longer the pure products of the Creator's state of nature. In order to survive, they and their descendants turned to agriculture and herding, taking care of their own needs through their own work. They became responsible for themselves. In biblical terms, they must now become good gardeners and good shepherds.

The pastoralist follows the herds and cares for the animals, who live from the bounty nature provides. The agriculturalist cares for the soil and sows seeds, tends the plants, then harvests the results. The life of agriculturalists is fixed to a place and their work keeps their eyes on the ground. Agricultural peoples (represented by Cain) have for the most part had mythologies and deities who were of the Earth, and their principal deities were usually female. Pastoralists (represented by Abel), in contrast, have usually had gods of the sky, and their myths and gods travel with them; they are not rooted in a place. Their principal gods were usually male.

The domestication of plants and animals is often described in myths as taking place in hunting and gathering cultures. When hunting came into a culture it usually became a male occupation, for a variety of reasons having mainly to do with the biological division of labor. Gathering food from plants became principally a female task. In time women learned to gather selectively and began to tend certain kinds of plants, eventually collecting and saving seeds, and planting them. Men developed hunting skills and tools connected with their work, as the women did with growing plants. The female preoccupations turned increasingly to learning about plants and their domestication and those of the men to learning about the ways of the main prey animals.

According to some stories, hunters brought wolf and other wild canine puppies back to camp to eat. However, children like to play with small animals and some pups were not eaten but allowed to grow up with humans. The descendants of these puppies became the first domestic animals, accompanying the hunters on their forays, eventually becoming their helpers. Other gregarious animals, like the ancestors of sheep and cattle, were eventually domesticated as well. It is believed that the hunting cultures, which followed the large herds of herbivores, developed the skills that led to the pastoral way of life and thence to the domestication of the horse.

None of these strands of prehistory can be untangled from speculation and myth. We have no written records of these changes except for the ancient stories and myths handed down by word of mouth and only recorded much later. However, for our purposes it is not necessary to pin down the facts, whatever they might be, for our only interest is in finding a rich and plausible story to bind together the philosophical narrative we have told about the stages of development of technology practices. We want to discover how these stages relate to the stages of evolution and ecological adaptation of human culture and consciousness, especially of modern Western culture. But this requires a larger narrative (story) which ties all of these together. It is useful to retell or reinterpret old stories even as new ones are being fashioned.

Let us return to the story of Adam and Eve and look at it from a New Testament perspective, which gives the story added dimensions of meaning. This story of our origins is usually told in the context of Jewish and Christian religious teachings. There are similar stories in other major religions, especially those with a soteriological structure. By soteriological (from the Greek "soter", meaning savior), we mean the salvational or eschatological (from the Greek "eschatos", last, farthest) dimensions of religious teachings. The soteriological structure of Christianity represents Christ as teaching salvation, the promise of eternal life in Heaven. In my Christian background this story was interpreted as an account of the human fall from a state of grace, a state of blessedness in which there is a special relationship to God. Through human disobedience and defiance of God, we fell from this edenic state. This was the first or original human "sin". Since then humans have for the most part lived in a fallen state, and only with sincere effort can they return to the state of grace. The promise of a future paradise that follows the fall is part of Christian eschatology, with its prophecies of the second coming of Christ. We will consider this story's idea of a fall from and return to a state of grace in the heavenly paradise. This will help us focus on the development of self-awareness and transcendence of its personality-based forms (transpersonal ecology).

Let us look at the story again from this perspective. In the beginning we humans are unified with nature, living a life of ease and plenty (pre-egoic or prepersonal awareness) in the Garden of Eden. But then, as a result of gaining knowledge of good and evil, subject and object, and self and other, we start to live self-reflexively, and, through exercising choice, are responsible for what we become. After leaving the primal edenic paradise, we struggle and work to make our way and improve ourselves. In other words, we differentiate ourselves from nature (original parent) and develop personal awareness. We move from the prepersonal unity of reaction from instinct in nature, to a fully deliberate, self-conscious way of directing our lives. Before the fall, Adam and Eve could not be humble or prideful, for in this prepersonal, unself-aware state there is no shame, no sense that some things are worthy of us and some are not. But as personal beings, as beings with purpose and conscious intent, they (and we) must shoulder the burdens of responsibility along with the freedom. We become capable of being humble or proud.

We see this process of self-conscious development repeated over and over in the separation of infants from their mothers. A human infant is conceived in the state of unified harmony with the maternal matrix (nature), but must separate itself from the mother in the process of birth, not a pain-free process for either. Although the baby must be nurtured and fed by the mother, the child must eventually distinguish itself from her. This development is signalled by self-assertiveness, beginning with shifting some of its affections from the mother to such favored objects as thumbs, blankets, and stuffed animals, for example. The child, if it is to become an adult, must eventually develop a clear awareness that it is no longer dependent but now fully responsible for itself. In many cultures children become adults through the ordeal of an initiatory process. The new adult receives a new name, hence a new identity. In some cultures this rite of passage is carried out by sending the child alone into nature. In shamanic cultures, which practice this return to nature and the source, the journey to adulthood might take the form of a descent into a deep cave, symbolizing the return to the womb of *all* life, the Great Mother. It also signifies a return to the state before birth and conception. The young person goes back to the place before time to receive direction from spirit helpers and a new name, that is, a new identity, leaving childhood behind. In primal cultures a person might go through several changes in personal identity and name throughout a long life.

These basic elements of birth, separation, journey, testing, and re-union are part of the oral tradition out of which the biblical story of Adam and Eve came. Many of the tests that Jesus underwent, in his journeys to the wilderness, his fasting and praying, his working of miracles, and even his death and resurrection, fit into the story patterns of human development that are part of shamanic and other early cultures. People accepted the authenticity of Jesus' teachings in part because they were familiar with stories of those who had journeyed to the lower and the upper world, those who had journeyed to the source and known the spirit world and the Creator.

The soteriological story of Christianity is this: Humans begin their life on Earth in the Garden of Eden; because of their sin, that is, eating the fruit of the tree of knowledge, they are forced to leave the first paradise. Then their life struggle begins. They suffer various trials and woes as they strive to regain paradise. But they do not know how to arise from their fallen state. Life on Earth becomes a burden and a sorrow. They try to return to unawareness. But then Jesus comes into the world, a gift from God, as his only begotten son. He is the one chosen to lead (show) humans to salvation and back to God. Through him they can ascend from their fallen state and return to a state of grace and blessedness. They will then know eternal life and bliss in *Heaven* (not Eden). The teachings and sufferings of Jesus show what is involved in the transformation of Jesus (the earthly, profane historical awareness) to Christ (the sacred or holy consciousness).

Let us now apply this story of the human fall and salvation to the evolution of human consciousness and the development of technology practices. The human person and humanity as a species began life in a state of prepersonal and sentient unity with nature, symbolized as the mother, or the edenic state of grace. The fall from grace is a fall from the state of innocent ignorance. As a result we humans are born into a state of *self-conscious* existence characterized by moral and spiritual trials. The burden of this self-conscious life is the awareness that we have separated ourselves from nature. This conscious separation gives us the power to act upon nature in systematic ways. We are able to objectify our own native powers by extending our organs and minds to embody them in material form in tools and machines. With tools and technology comes increasing power and the world becomes "our oyster", ours to control and manage through technological power—to such an extent that we have gained the possibility of destroying ourselves and the world. This power, gained through separation, creates a sense of loss, for we not only have the burdens and blessings of responsibility, we also lose our capacity to identify with other beings. We lose the sentient harmony with nature and others we earlier enjoyed. But now we are challenged to accept responsibility for ourselves and our actions.

In our struggle to confirm ourselves as separate from nature, we suffer the pain of alienation from the ground of our own being. Only by maturing fully do we realize our larger ecological Self. Then we know that we have the capacity to be in harmony with nature and other beings, if that is our conscious choice. The resulting unity is not a return to prepersonal unity (Eden), but emergence into transpersonal awareness (Kingdom of Heaven), where all our relationships with nature and others become I-Thou instead of I-It. Rather than treating the other as an object, as in I-It relationships, we treat the other as a subject just like ourselves with feelings and an inner life that counts for us.

Thus through actions they themselves undertook, humankind emerged from the state of nature. The fabrication of tools and their systematic use changed us forever, and it changed our relationship to the rest of creation. But is this all there is to human life: to be born out of the primal unity, only to struggle in separation, never to regain the original edenic bliss and harmony? The salvational story of Christianity (and of most major religions of agricultural peoples) says "No"! There is a higher state, the Kingdom of Heaven (Nirvana), which has been revealed by those who have undergone a transformation from personal to transpersonal consciousness. Jesus and Siddhartha, for instance, exemplified what it is to *complete* the human journey that began symbolically with the bite of the apple, and ended on the cross or under the Bo tree. They became, in the process, Christ and Buddha. Jesus and Siddhartha are the names for the historical personality, while Christ and Buddha are names for transhistorical consciousness. Thus, Christ and Buddha are not proper names. They are not owned by any particular historical person, nor do they represent particular personalities. The Christ or Buddha nature is shared by all of us. It is the universal or shared awareness.

This movement to more complete consciousness (what we are here describing as transpersonal consciousness) is a movement beyond historical personality. The personal is the historical, linear, temporal, egoic awareness; the transpersonal is the sacred, timeless, holistic consciousness that unites all beings. The transpersonal level transcends personality, transcends the tribe, transcends culture, transcends the historical, transcends place and time, and it transcends human-centeredness and anthropocentrism. To realize this transcendence is to experience a new state of grace or blessedness, conscious oneness with nature and others. Going through the limits of the ego-boundaries can be a painful experience, filled with shadows and terrors. To go beyond these boundaries is to die and to be born yet again, for a third time. It is to leave the security of the known for the great mysteries of fully transpersonal consciousness. Those who have taken this journey and realized the transpersonal can authentically say that they are in everything and everything is in them. Their actions are characterized by wisdom and compassion, because they realize how we are all interdependent, how each of us is part of the other; how, for example, our grief as persons is bound up with the grief of all suffering beings. They understand the meaning of our suffering and the reasons for it. All other beings confirm or illuminate this larger Self.

At this point, let us focus on the historical level, so as to elucidate stages of technology development. Human actions to change the world depend on our brain, opposable thumb, and extension of our powers with tools and technology (culture). But these actions deepen our division from nature, just as they give us identity and power. However, since we are from nature and to nature we each eventually return, we mourn this loss as a loss of innocence. We long to reach a state of unity and bliss, free from struggle and the burden of time. This can be an immature longing for the prepersonal state with no responsibilities, or it can be an aspiration to transform ourselves to an extended state of awareness, as we indicated, to allow the evolution to an expansive consciousness, one that opens to all of reality once more. For humans this represents *transformation* because we will have passed through the egoic, personal stage. We long for paradise and see it as a future *historical* fact, something to be realized some day. But this hankering for future bliss can be blind to the possibility that the perfection we seek is available now in the present as an ongoing activity (or non-activity). How do we react to this hankering without such full awareness?

A surface rendering takes the Christian soteriological story as a *literal* account of what will come to pass in time as foretold by prophecy. To many people in the Middle Ages Christianity promised a second coming of Christ; and with this future event there would be the dawning of a new earthly paradise. But it also promised Heavenly bliss after death, provided one lived according to the requirements of the church. As secular culture emerged in the modern West, it cut itself free from the soteriological structure of religious Christianity. The loss of this innocence of the Middle Ages, with its simple Christian faith, brought a period of vast changes in human life in the West, changes driven by the emergence of commerce and powerful technologies. The changes were driven initially by the fact that the systematic applications of the power of artisan crafts were freed from religious constraints. This reality was soon transcended by the development of modern science that became part of a new myth and religion (of secular society and economic order).

In place of the religious story the secular culture substituted its own story of human progress, which would come about through our own efforts. Powerful technologies would transform the world into a human built paradise (Utopia). Progress would be measured in terms of increasing technological power over nature. One finds unrestrained optimism in the writings of people like Descartes and Bacon, a human hubris, that science will create a new order, a new paradise, superior to nature! But this will be a material, not a spiritual paradise. Modern scientific culture rests on the preconditions of Christian theology, even though the two were embroiled in conflicts as science emerged. Modern culture begins with an act of separation from the authority of the church by the assertion that reason can establish the validity of belief in God and knowledge of the world independent of biblical and religious authority (revelation and tradition). Therefore, science, which is applied reason, and technology, which is applied science, become the new means to salvation. The Christian soteriological promise of salvation, of a blissful paradise, is transmuted into the quest for control through perfection of technological power. All human "problems", suffering in flesh and mind, insecurity, discomfort, old age, debility, infant mortality, unhappiness, lack of power, and even mortality, would be solved through technological transformation of our world. In the earlier ideals we purify ourselves; in technotopia we purify the world.

As the mythical story makes clear, we cannot consciously act upon the world *without* transforming ourselves; when we change the world, we also alter ourselves. When we use power to transform the world through technology, we necessarily transform our culture and ourselves, usually in ways not anticipated or desired. The degree of our responsibility is directly proportional to the amount of power we have, regardless of its source. Since, through technology, we have made ourselves the single most powerful species on the Earth we must now face the challenge of becoming the most benign and compassionate of beings. This is nothing less than the obligation to realize the transpersonal level, as this has been exemplified by the transpersonal ecological interpretation of the Buddha-Christ transformation stories. This transformation would reclaim the spiritual truth at the core of the soteriological story we have been examining. It would apply its profound lessons to the way we develop and practice technology. We have reached the stage of development in which the old models and paradigms are no longer appropriate and we must now create new ecosophic technology practices suitable to the Age of Ecosophy. In the next chapter we will examine how the idea of the technological imperative is relevant to this process.

Chapter 5

Technological Imperative

We must cultivate appropriate ecosophic technology practices and transform our consciousness if we are to halt the destructiveness of our current technology practices, and the global disasters they are leading us to. We are haunted by the twin threats of instant annihilation from atomic weapons, which still exist in large numbers despite the end of the cold war, and the slower death of the biosphere and nature caused by industrial technological processes. The existence of serious social problems, the inequities in the system, the widespread abuse of drugs, the corruption of civil authorities, the selling of politicians, the drivel of popular entertainment on TV, species extinction, environmental degradation, — these, and a host of other negative results of our modern economic and social system show its inherent shortcomings. Many believe that it is foolish, naive, and stupid to expect anything good to come out of such a system. Those in power will not allow any major changes in the status quo, and so "business as usual" continues to exploit humans, consume the Earth, poison the air and water, and depends on ever-increasing consumption and waste.

Thus we see that technology practices are not always progressive, where "progress" is defined not in terms of increasing profits and/or power, but in terms of ultimate moral and spiritual values related to the highest good that can be realized in human life. There is much wrong in our current situation, but it can be changed. We each have a responsibility to work in our own way to bring about needed changes. History is not a straight line. The development and refinement of technology practices is not fixed. We must keep hope alive so as to make genuine progress toward ecosophy. We believe that humans have access to the knowledge and skills required to create new, wise technology practices. The issue is whether we have the vision, determination, and moral and spiritual fortitude to undertake the needed transformation. The structures we need to change are actually cultural *processes*.

An alternative vision to our ecocentric one is based on the following beliefs: Technological processes have become self-driven. They have taken on a life of their own, with their own inner logic, regardless of the political and economic system. Technology has become an autonomous force. The powers we have unleashed cannot be controlled; they have become more than human, transcending class, race, and culture. There is nothing we can do to prevent the development of ever more powerful technologies, even though we know these will ultimately destroy human life. Some go so far as to suggest that humans are merely the evolutionary means to create new forms of intelligence, new artificial "life" forms, which will not be limited by our carbon-based biological flaws. Machines, as genetically engineered hybrid artifacts, will take over the world, and the development of artificial intelligence, super computers, and nanotechnology provide the means for this transition. This technological process will run its course, no matter what we do, and the whole world will be shaped and finally controlled by it. The Earth is becoming an artifact of human technology, an object being reshaped by the technological imperative that drives us to extend technological control over every object and process in our world. But humans in turn will be made over by an autonomous technology, and then they too will be replaced.

This view is a serious challenge to our positive vision of the emergence of ecosophic technology practices. Such an autonomous technology would destroy all hope. If we lack hope, we will be defeated and unable to act at the outset. The alternative technotopic vision is disempowering. In order to avoid this trap we must examine the idea of the technological imperative in more depth.

A major drive spurring technological development gives rise to a process of continual refinement, improvement, invention, extension, application, and transfer of technology practices everywhere, to all aspects of nature, and to human life. There are many reasons and motives for this ongoing drive for expansion of technological control and efficiency. Some have to do with basic human nature, some with the logic of the process itself, some are social, and some are economic. This expansive technological imperative is often seen as leading to autonomous technological development, in other words, development that is self-driven, that feeds on itself independent of human intentions. Since there is no point at which technological perfection and development can be said to be complete, this process is an ever-expanding spiral. Technological practice and development, however, *is* a human activity. As such it explicitly reveals implicit features of our cultured character structures and their fundamental modes of being. Like human desires, technology is capable of limitless and continuous expansion. It mirrors in material form and order the basic elements and dramas of the Western human self. It is the material, technical embodiment of both our past and current awareness.

Throughout Western history there have been gradual but drastic shifts in our view of our relationships to nature. In the primal view nature is the creator of all things; agrarian civilizations see an external being (a God) as responsible for creating nature. The scientific-technological worldview is that nature has no creator; it is a self-organizing machine. In this view humans create machines, which reflect the laws of nature, to control nature's machinery. More recently, technology is designed to mimic the thinking processes of humans. Today some think that the technological process has become autonomous. It less and less reflects the conscious decisions of its creators; clever machines will reproduce and maintain themselves, completely replacing nature and humans. With this view, modern Western technology has become totalizing, and it will eventually replace human and natural processes to suit *its* imperatives.

Let us consider the above thesis by focusing on the assumed metaphors used to describe humans and machines. We are dealing here with a story, not a scientific hypothesis. The story metaphors have been literalized to seem like substantive accounts of the world as it is. Here is what took place. First natural processes were explained on analogy with machines. Then the machine metaphor was applied to humans. The metaphor literalized says that both nature and humans *are* machines. Let us consider a recent example of this story. The developers of the computer and cybernetic systems made use of analogies and metaphors. First the computer was described as like the human mind; it was said to have memory, make decisions, and so on. And then the analogy was turned around, and the computer itself was used as a metaphor. This process is reflected in descriptions of the human mind as a biocomputer, on analogy to the computer. Finally the metaphor was literalized as: humans *are* sophisticated machines whose brain is a complex controlling biocomputer. The implication is that we do not need the machine analogy to understand the whole "system", for the human body simply *is* a machine with a built-in biocomputer (mind), with hardwiring and programming.

Analogy and metaphor can be useful even when literalized, but once literalized they can also blind us to our own clever pictures, which are then taken for how things are. We then come to see the world *through* our own limited conceptualizations. However, the structures of these concepts reflect not necessities in our stars and the world, but self-created ideas that trap our understanding and imagination by means of the seductive pictures they create. Misunderstood human autonomy becomes projected onto our technology, smuggled in by means of concealed metaphors. Once the machine and the computer become part of an entrenched, literalized metaphor, these linguistic devices are no longer seen for what they are: useful fictions, or human artifacts produced by our own imaginations and technological activities. The images and pictures of the literalized metaphor filter our perceptions, and these filtered perceptions then create the impression that technology has a life of its own. The idealized images created by our own literalized metaphors conceal the true nature of our world and activities with false pictures of the way things are. When we recognize literalized metaphors for what they are, we see them as some of the many available empty thought forms, which are sometimes useful. The closed possibilities and boundaries they create when held on to dissolve only when we see *through* them, much in the way that sleight of hand magic loses some of its appeal and illusion when we know how the tricks are done. When we see through the pictures our literalized metaphors create, our whole situation appears quite different. A larger space opens to us. The process of becoming spellbound, bewitched by our own literalized metaphors, can blind us to our own complex activity of constructing metaphors, analogies, models, and analyses (Wittgenstein 1953). This in turn can lead us to project human autonomy onto technology. We give up our freedom for the destiny of the technological imperative.

Let us examine this idea of the technological imperative and the supposed autonomy of technology from another angle. Culture is an adaptive organic process utilizing technological activities and tools to create technology practices which are used to provide necessities and abundance. We can single out these practices and study their history, see how they evolve through time and continue to change. We see that they outlive their inventors and seem to change independently of their users' original intentions. Hence, they seem autonomous, since they seem to have a life of their own and are not controlled by any one person or group. However, if we consider all factors, including the tacit, historical, and collective ones, we see that technology practices provide an observable example of *whole* human activities seen through time measured in decades and centuries. As objects of study, we can subject their practical, technical, and cultural details to systematic analysis. We can then see, for example, that imaginative artistic play with technological elements is one source of technological innovation. Art, play, and drama rehearse and anticipate technological changes in daily life. We realize what we first imagine. Science fiction, film, and comic books illustrate this cultural process. As fields for the free use of imagination, play and art are always ahead of our technical abilities. Significant technological innovation would come to a halt without imagination and conceptual play. Seen from this angle, then, the idea of the technological imperative is an objectification of the creative imagination of human beings.

There is another level beyond the imaginative that we must consider as we seek to understand the technological imperative. Humans are psycho-physical, imaginative, but also spiritual beings. Their self-reflective cognitive and imaginative capacities enable them to engage in free-flowing conceptual play. It is this play, and the serendipity and novel discoveries associated with it, that feeds technological innovation and change. Thus, the ever-changing character of our technology reflects a restless spirit coupled with our powers of imagination and creation. These do not have to find their main outlet in technological power. That they do is a matter of cultural values and choice. The technological imperative, from the transpersonal perspective, is a material expression of our underlying need to perfect and realize ourselves. If this need is deflected from self-development, it will find an outlet in substitute gratifications and compensatory pursuits. However, the restless human spirit finds tranquillity only in completion of its natural development. According to the great spiritual teachers, our mission in this life is to transform ourselves by expanding to the utmost our capacity for love and understanding. In other words, the ego strives for a completion that can be realized only by going beyond egoic concerns to the transpersonal dimensions of spiritual life. This transcendence is not an escape into fantasies of permanence in another worldly realm. It is nothing less than coming into full consciousness in our present daily lives. This human completion has been exemplified by the great spiritual teachers who fully realized the transpersonal dimension of human life. This is the human mission.

Progress, as already noted, can be measured meaningfully only by moral and spiritual values. These values are what the human spirit aspires to, after all material and social needs are met. Indian philosophy identified the categories of human spiritual needs many centuries ago through an analysis of four main kinds of human desires: for growth and pleasure; for worldly success; for service; and for complete liberation and spiritual completion. The fourth desire is for perfection with three features: *sat-chit-ananda* — unconditioned being, wisdom, and bliss. Satchitananda corresponds to Heaven in the Christian soteriological story, (and also to the Buddhists' nirvana) as a way of being, realized here and now. It cannot be attained by building a material Utopia, but only through reaching complete, total consciousness (Christos) in our present lives. In our technological society this natural human desire for completion and liberation, which is a deep spiritual need, is not perceived as such. The desire for fulfillment of this need is misplaced as a quest for completion through material accumulations and power. This is why we fail to perceive the true nature of technological power, which conceals this underlying raison d'être. Moreover, technological power is placeless, whereas ecosophy grows out of spiritual bonding with a place.

Understanding a whole technology practice is akin to understanding a martial art, as a spiritual discipline. One cannot understand the art as a whole, by focusing only on technique. One cannot succeed in defense against a sword by focusing attention on just the sword. The martial artist must take in the whole situation, including spiritual dimensions. Likewise, to understand technology practices we must be able to see the whole practice, including its misdirected spiritual aspects, while being aware of its complexity and details. If we look only at certain technical details we might get an impression of imperative determinism, and conclude that technology is autonomous. However, as we have seen, this imperative is a projection of our failure to recognize our need as moral and spiritual beings to transform our lives and realize ourselves in harmony with others. If this need is frustrated and hidden, it will find expression in compensatory ways. When it is hidden in the details of the technological process, as well as through forms of projection in our shadow, this imperative comes to be dimly seen through literalized analogy and metaphor as a technological imperative. The imperative then is misperceived as an autonomous technological force that we are powerless to control. But the source of autonomy is actually in us. Only authentic understanding of our spiritual and moral depths and our psychological and social relationships will help us to unmask the many disguises of our shadows projected through literalized metaphors.

As Socrates pointed out, unless we have *self-knowledge* there is no way to attain *objective* knowledge and wisdom. The two are reciprocally interrelated. When we are self-ignorant, we are prone to self-deception and confusion. We then fall victim to our own conceptual creations, and the fantasies and illusions they generate. We become captives of pictures we ourselves make and project. We then do not see the world *as it is*, or our *place* in it. We do not know what we can genuinely become through the practice of transformative spiritual disciplines, which deepen our self-knowledge, broaden objective understanding, and bring wisdom. In the next chapter we will expand on these themes by exploring eight attitudes toward technological development, as these reflect levels of understanding and maturity of self related to technology practices, social life, and nature.

Chapter 6

A Spectrum of Attitudes Toward Technological Development

I. *Examples of Relationships Between Technology and Cultural Forms*

That the pace of cultural change is driven by the rate of technological change is a common assumption. In some analyses, material conditions, and especially technological adaptations, are seen as the primary forces of cultural transformation. And yet, evidence from studies of nonliterate, technologically simple cultures shows that cultural change can be quite dynamic without corresponding changes in technology practices, and vice versa. This is true in part because technology practices are part of a culture's character, and changes in those practices usually signal that the culture is changing in other ways as well. That sweeping changes result from the introduction of new technology practices into cultures is easy to demonstrate. For example, most of us are familiar with the changes brought about in Aboriginal plains cultures of North America when the Spaniards introduced the horse. A whole new way of life developed, centered on the horse and its domestication. Nonetheless, one can also think of cases where adoption of new technology practices has resulted in only minor changes in a culture. As Marx and others have pointed out, cultural change is a complex phenomenon, and different aspects of culture can change at different rates and in different ways, even though they are all interrelated. The attitudes, beliefs, and habits found in a culture can be fairly uniform or quite pluralistic. Generally, small, technologically uncomplicated and relatively stable cultures are less internally diversified. Modern technological societies are usually very diverse. Even those that appear monolithic and have an official political orthodoxy, such as the former Soviet Union and China, can be quite diverse.

In complex, modern technological states, rates of change vary, depending in part on such internal factors as educational institutions, freedom and openness of the media, and dynamism of the economy. In any modern democratic state, it is well known that people are diverse in their attitudes, beliefs, and lifestyles. Of course, all societies have some diversity associated with different levels of maturity, resulting from demographic patterns and age distribution. Certain features of human life assure that this will be true in any society. Humans are born in total dependency, and must spend much time developing into mature persons capable of taking care of themselves.

The more complex and diverse a society is, the more time young people must spend becoming adapted to their adult roles. In agrarian societies children worked with parents of the same sex to learn the skills needed in their adult roles. By the time they were sixteen or seventeen, they knew most of what they needed to take their place in the society. This is not true in advanced technological societies, where the complexity of technostructure, fragmentation of specialized work and the relationships of the family to work, require that children go through a long period of formal training in schools, if they are to contribute significantly to the society.

The public school systems in emerging Western industrial society were created in part to replace the home training of the earlier agrarian society, which was no longer appropriate to the industrial realities. The apprenticeship training process for the artisan crafts also waned as industrialism advanced (see Rorabaugh 1986). The changes in these two forms of training of traditional agricultural-artisan society led also to significant changes in social structure and in the relationships between generations. As apprentice training and home farm instruction both declined, displaced farm workers and artisans moved into urban areas, searching for a place. Attitudes toward work changed, and children lost their traditional place in the work force. Most could not learn farming from an early age, and there were fewer and fewer masters and journeymen who trained apprentices in their homes and shops. The machine factory production of shoes, to mention one example, employed a new kind of worker, a laborer who had to learn only a few simple skills. He or she was not an apprentice who would learn a whole trade from raw material selection to designing, and constructing and finishing the final product. Such a whole art could in fact be seen as representing life as a whole. This is not true of machine tending. When children could no longer find positions as apprentices or farm workers they became footloose in the cities. The public school system was organized with at least a twofold purpose: first, to provide a steady stream of trained persons for the work force in the new industrialized society, and second, to get adolescents off the streets. The

public schools became the primary source of enculturation and job training for young people, now defined by a period called "adolescence", a
time of long transition from childhood to adult life.

Public schools, and especially high schools, have often been criticized
for their preoccupation with social life and activities such as sports. But
these activities are an important part of our enculturation processes as a
society. School is the logical place for this process to take place, for where
else would young people in industrial society learn to be adults, except
to play at being adults while in school? Our society has few other institutions to provide this learning. Most families today are either single parent
families, or they are families in which both parents work. Hence, few
children have adult supervision throughout the day at home. Few families
are equipped to educate their children at home for today's technological
world. Even if they could provide supervision and education throughout
the day, they would not be able to provide *enculturation* experiences
which come from associating with a large number of children of different
ages. The public school system is a logical counterpart to the industrial
culture we have created. By studying changes in technology practice and
associated changes in cultural forms, we can appreciate the close interconnections between the two, which until fairly recently has not been
fully appreciated.

II. Technological Change and Changing Attitudes

The technology practices in industrial societies are one of their most dynamic features, and changes now taking place constitute yet another technological revolution. Some believe that this revolution is moving us to a
new type of social order based on small-scale technology practices, small
institutions, and global networks. Large political entities are breaking up,
old alliances are coming apart. Ethnic and other minorities are reasserting
their identities. Some think that the new technologies will provide opportunities to destructure industrial society by replacing large industrial organizations with new, small-scale technologies. Daniel Bell (1979) talks of
"post-industrialism". Ivan Illich (1970) talks about deschooling and
decentralizing society.

Cultures, like individual persons, can go through various stages of
development and maturity in their attitudes to, adjustment with, and use
of technology. In our dynamic and diverse society, a whole spectrum of
attitudes exists. Some people reject technological development and try to
prevent it; others champion any type of technological innovation whatso-
ever; still others express attitudes of caution. And there are those who
have gone through all of these stages and changes in attitude to reach a

mature view of technology. They recognize its promises and hazards; they fully accept their own responsibility for its wise design and use. Recently, wide public approval of technological innovation has been tempered by greater caution, since in recent decades some "advanced" technologies have created *significant* problems resulting in some *very* costly failures. Many of us know how often the experts (who suffer from tunnel vision) can be wrong. Given the risks associated with some modern technologies, such as PCBs, dioxins, nuclear wastes and so on, it is easy to see why caution is growing. Perhaps soon a majority of North Americans might prefer that many industrial products are not manufactured.

Our relationships to technology practices are in part a reflection of our attitudes, which in turn reflect our level of maturity. Let us take, as an example, the different attitudes a person can have toward a martial art. People are attracted to the study of a martial art such as Karate, Judo, or Aikido, for a host of reasons. Perhaps they want to be able to defend themselves, or maybe they want to be able to win over and beat other people. They work hard to learn the various tricks and techniques. However, as time goes on, if they continue to practice, they might begin to discover that the martial arts, at least where they emphasize the *chivalrous way*, do not readily enable one to defend oneself or to win over others. This is not their primary aim. The person who continues to practice begins to shift his or her attention away from preoccupation with techniques, to a study of the philosophy and ethics at the heart of the Japanese Budo (martial arts) tradition. So, while they might have begun their study with a desire to attain a certain kind of power because they felt insecure, as time goes on, their fears might subside. They begin to discover that training in Budo leads to purifying the self of fears and also of the desire for victory. They discover that there are deeper meanings to Budo training, and that at least some Budo are spiritual disciplines. In Japanese culture the development of Budo, training in the way of respect, salvaged some of the values gained through training in the older warrior tradition (Bushido) associated with feudal Japan and the era of the samurai.

The transformation from Bushido to Budo represents a maturing of attitudes toward the martial arts in Japanese culture, and also in the individual who begins to understand the deeper meanings of Budo. So today, young people might be attracted to Budo, thinking it is Bushido or violent warrior training—as represented in the movies—but through ongoing practice discover that it is not. If they stay with it long enough, they will lose their fascination for warfare in its various forms. Note that we are not claiming here that the whole of Japanese society turned to Budo and dropped interest in Bushido. The rise of Japanese militarism that led to the Second World War in the Pacific showed that a large number of

Japanese had not by that time learned the deeper lessons of their own Budo traditions. Our example is only meant to illustrate different attitudes toward technical power and its development, and to show that there are different levels of maturity in its practice.

Without using sophisticated polling and survey instruments, we cannot say precisely how public attitudes toward technology break down into the eight categories we will describe. We are not here making exact empirical claims, merely conceptually identifying the range of attitudes toward technology in our society. Readers should ask themselves whether any of the attitudes described fit their own experience. We will now describe eight attitudes toward technology, explain their relationships to one another, and how consciously changing our attitudes could facilitate transition to ecosophic technology practices.

III. *Spectrum of Attitudes Toward Technology*

Within dynamic Western industrial-scientific-technological society there are many attitudes toward technological development and change. Our investigations lead us to identify eight different attitudes toward technology, running from technological optimism to technophobia, an outright fear and rejection of technology. One caveat needs to be added in relation to this spectrum of attitudes: we do not claim it is exhaustive. However, we believe these attitudes represent the main stages of response to technological change. The eight attitudes are:

- technological ignorance,
- technological anarchy,
- technological optimism or technophilia,
- technological autonomy,
- technological concern,
- technology rejection or technophobia,
- technological moderation and reappraisal,
- appropriate ecocentric technosophy.

We will now examine each of these in more detail.

Technological ignorance is the state of a person or culture not self-reflectively aware of its own technology. The person or culture sees it merely as part of the reality of everyday life and the fabric of culture, not as something apart. Technology is not questioned. It is not extolled. Any discoveries that lead to technological change are purely by chance. There is no active cultivation of innovation. There is neither fear nor love of technology. In much the way that a child takes for granted what is part of its home, the person who is in a state of technological ignorance simply takes the culture's given technology for granted. There is no pro or con attitude, merely on acceptance of what is there, a neutral attitude. There is no conscious evaluation of technology, no critical judgement about it.

Attitudes are expressions or reflections of value judgements. They are self-involving and turn on one's identification with or separation from the thing toward which the attitude is formed. In the case of the complete ignorance we are describing, there is no explicit attitude. We can speculate on the state of our early ancestors, their approaches to tools, and their eventual development of technology practices. Adam and Eve, as primal human archetypes, lived in nature in a state of innocent ignorance. They were not self-reflectively aware enough to have attitudes that would engender shame; hence, they did not think of covering themselves. They did not hunt; hence, they gave no thought to weapons. Weapons and tools and their conscious fabrication go together and are interdependent. They are progressively developed only when certain cultural awarenesses and attitudes are present. Suppose then there is a dawning realization that techniques and tools, carved sticks and chipped stones can be systematically improved. They are seen then not just as natural extensions of the self, but as separate entities to be perfected, carried around, used, and cared for. At this stage we can certainly identify specific attitudes.

We surmise, then, that with the rise of self-awareness a cultural consciousness of technology as something to be cultivated would also arise. Technology would be seen as something that could spell the difference between survival and death, power and humiliation, meager life and abundance. The pursuit of powers obtained by using devices such as tools and weapons gives rise to techniques and skills, and with these powers certain attitudes and cultural practices arise. These new powers naturally become something that can be consciously pursued and perfected. This pursuit, of course, involves the use of ritual, ceremony, and even festival to seek the approval of the gods and the participation of the spirits of nature. From dim awareness of tools and the nonexistence of technology, there gradually emerged a conscious cultivation of toolmaking skills and the development of techniques and artifacts that are passed on from one generation to the next, a technology. With this discovery there also emerge conscious judgements and values related to technology.

The new pursuit of powers dependent upon or augmented by technology gives rise to exploration and *anarchy*. Anarchy refers to the attitude that any technological discoveries are worth looking into, and all possibilities should be tried, ruling nothing out. We can find a number of junctures in history where such attitudes of anticipation and hopeful search are present in relation to technology. This attitude characterized the West in the early stages of the industrial revolution.

As discoveries are made and successes realized, there is a shift in attitude toward *technological optimism* and a love of technology (*technophilia*). This is like the first love of adolescence, filled with optimism and unrealistic dreams. The disappointment following its loss can lead to caution in future relationships. Prominent attitudes toward technology in the industrializing West in some ways exemplified this. Even as late as the nineteenth century, we find statements of unbounded optimism and complete fascination with the new technologies, with emphasis on the promise of a new world resulting from the coupling of science and technology. Many today still feel this optimism. On the other hand, since the nineteenth century and even earlier there have been dissenting voices urging caution, and some that expressed a downright rejection of the brave new technological world.

A starry-eyed optimism toward technology avoids a realistic assessment of what technology can do for us; it ignores the inherent risks associated with increasing technological power. This enchantment sees only the positive aspects of this bewitching power. But all power carries risks. As Lord Acton once remarked about political power, "All power corrupts, and absolute power corrupts absolutely." We can say the same about technology insofar as every increase in its power carries risk of decreases in our *personal* power. It can lead to disempowerment and de-skilling. Moreover, every increase in power brings social changes we might not want. Finally, every increase in power carries increased environmental risks.

Every significant technological breakthrough and development has both positive and negative aspects. Optimists emphasize the positive aspects, pessimists the negative ones. Even the control of fire, as we see from the myth of Prometheus, had both positive and negative consequences. The greater the power, the greater the risk that it will be misused. The grave environmental degradation we witness today is directly related to the use of powerful technologies. These negative consequences are now impossible to ignore. Thus, an unbounded optimism and love for technology can give rise to a great disenchantment, as can any romantic enchantment. When expectations are high, and the possible negative side effects and risks are ignored, we run a risk of deep disappointment. Today many in technological society hedge their bets, as a result of disappointments in the past. They try to be realistic, by stressing the possibilities of failure. And when a project succeeds, they can be both relieved and pleasantly surprised! If it fails, they have already prepared themselves to accept this.

Since the beginnings of the industrial revolution, the active pursuit of technological power in the West has had strong elements of technophilia and optimism, facilitating the development of great technological power in institutions and with this, the rise of the sense that there is a technological imperative. This optimism, as we have seen, has led to the belief that technology has an *autonomy* of its own. The fourth set of attitudes stems from the belief that technological development is an independent, uncontrollable force. It is seen to have a power, a momentum with which we must not interfere. If we are optimistic and believe that things will turn out for the best, that technological development is an inevitable, progressive, evolutionary force, then we will cheer this autonomy. If we are doubtful about so-called inevitable progress (as equated with technological change), we will be guarded about this supposed outcome. We might even be alarmed at the thought that technological development is something autonomous and beyond our control. Projects, once under way, have an inertia that is difficult to control or stop. Furthermore, once various infrastructures are in place, we are left with the consequences of "development", which then might require large expenditures of money and human energy to rectify. Consider, for example, the nuclear power industry. Even if we phased out all reactors and shifted to solar power today, we would still have to deal with the large costs and problems associated with the facilities and the waste products that are the result of the industry as it has existed.

The perception that technological development is a mixed blessing fraught with certain risks, and that it appears almost autonomous can engender concern and fear. *Technological concern* and fear naturally arise when certain forms of technological development are not understood, or when their hazards are clearly seen. There are many reasons for opposing technological change, not the least of which is the belief that the development threatens one's livelihood. The Luddites were not blind opponents of the technological development that industrialized weaving in England. They were reacting to the personal economic and other threats posed by the introduction of the new textile machines, threats they correctly perceived would limit both their freedom and income. They saw that the new machines would undermine the practice of a craft that was a way of life, that gave artisans a measure of independence and dignity, as well as a fair return for their work. The development of the textile machines and factories meant that they would no longer be self-employed artisans, but would become supervised and low paid machine tenders and shop workers. The early textile factories did indeed become infamous industrial sweatshops exploiting indentured children.

Fear and the associated attitudes of concern and caution can lead to the stronger reaction of *technophobia and rejection of technological development*. The Luddites' attitudes went beyond concern, and their fear led them to action. They burned factories and smashed machines. They did not go so far as to reject all technological development, for *technophobia*, as we define it, is not the fear of *all* technology but the hatred of the technological development that threatens tradition and the status quo. To be sure, this fear can involve a rejection of the status quo as well. It could take the form of trying to go back to an earlier phase of technology practice. Some persons or groups have tried to go all the way back to Eden, to take off their clothes, eat only raw food, throw away their artifacts and live wild in a state of nature. But this course of action is rare. More commonly, we find groups who accept technological development up to a certain level. For example, they might refuse to use electrical devices, farm only with horses, use only hand tools, wear only homemade clothes, and reject telephones. The Back to the Land movement of the late sixties and early seventies revived earlier rural technologies and farm practices, such as using horses for farming and logging. A religious group with an older history, the Old Order Amish, recognize that their way of life will be destroyed if they modernize their farms. By holding on to the horse agriculture of an earlier era, they have maintained a good standard of living with small mixed farms, and have increased their numbers while doing so. Their resistance to technological change, however, is based on religious principles not just a fear of technology. These religious principles inform their attitudes toward farm practices and livelihood.

Technological moderation and reappraisal arises in a culture when sufficient numbers of people have gone through the changes in attitude associated with earlier stages of technological development. A typical shift might take people from optimism and love of technological development to concern and finally to rejection. They might then try more primitive technologies, and after some experimentation might reappraise their attitudes and relationship to technology once more. As a result they come to a more moderate attitude, recognizing that one must be discriminating and choose more wisely as not all technological development is bad. They might then try to articulate a more comprehensive philosophy about technology as they come to a realistic and mature attitude toward development and changing practices.

Given a mature attitude, technology is no longer seen as savior and saint, or as enemy and devil; it is not seen as autonomous. The creation of *appropriate, ecosophic technologies* is understood to depend upon the wisdom of the designers and users. The key to sound technology practices is seen to lie in solving problems of environmental pollution before they arise, at the design stage. Those who adopt this attitude aim to design and develop technology practices that do not generate unwanted, hazardous waste products, and that are not destructive. While developing forms of transportation that do not produce excess greenhouse gases, they try to minimize the production of these gases by the present inefficient forms of transportation. They change their forestry practices, increasing productivity by reducing waste; they end the foolish practice of clearcutting, and develop selective ecoforestry practices. They pursue the same sorts of objectives in agriculture. Farming is done so as to increase the fertility of the soils through ecologically sound practices that increase the flourishing of the biological communities. Designing practices to harmonize with nature's processes becomes a primary guiding purpose of a mature attitude toward the practice of technology.

IV. Final Reflections

Reflecting on the spectrum of attitudes toward technological development can deepen our understanding of our own relationships to technology practices. It enables us to see how our attitudes toward each other, technology, and nature condition our perceptions of technological development. It leads us to such questions as: What is our personal relationship to technology? What is our communal relationship to it? How are these connected with our relationship to nature? The attitudes we take toward technological development reflect our level of maturity and can help or hinder our ability to create ecosophic practices. We have to examine not only our role in technology practices, but also the interrelationships between their technical, organizational, cultural, and environmental dimensions, along with our attitudes toward one another and nature. Only then will we begin to have a comprehensive and integrated understanding of technology. Through an examination of our own attitudes we gain deeper self-awareness, since our attitudes toward technology reflect what we currently are and how we are in the world. These attitudes are reflected in our technology practices. For example, the pursuit of the technological "fix" as a panacea and cure-all for our problems is possible only because we deceive ourselves, through self-ignorance and ignorance of our condition, about the true nature of these problems. Carefully examining our attitudes toward technology can help us to see through this deception to gain a deeper understanding that enables us to change our relationships to technology. Freeing our attitudes also frees us from the compulsions of the technological imperative. The way is then open for us to take control of our technology and to design new practices that will both protect the planet and benefit us.

Chapter 7

Major Characteristics of the Age of Technology

We have discussed so far how major forms of technological change affect culture and nature. We have examined the roles and character formation of the cultured human subject, and the process whereby humans become self-reflectively aware beings. We have examined some of the mythic, narrative accounts of the three main phases of mature human development: *the prepersonal, the personal, and the transpersonal*. We have considered the different stages of Western technological development and the cultural values, purposes, and attitudes associated with evolving Western technology practices. We have considered the impacts of technology practices on the environment, and we have described the features of some of the instruments, techniques, and tools that are used to change the world. We have investigated the idea of the technological imperative and its influence on our conceptions of history and human relations to nature. Finally, we have described some of the material changes accomplished by different technology practices and their associated attitudes.

In surveying the features of technological development it is clear that there is an irony in the drive for total technological control. It seems the more control technology gives us, the less we control technological change, and the more it appears as an autonomous force. The drive for technological control of the world, which has been extended to virtually every aspect of modern technological society, was motivated in part by trying to increase human autonomy. Instead, we seem to have become prisoners and technology has sway over us. This is a result of the original drive for power in the worldview of the modern West. It is echoed in the interconnected nature of the problems in the systems of technological control we have constructed.

In this chapter we briefly draw together some of the main characteristics of these technological systems as manifestations of the Age of Technology. The characteristics which we describe show the degree to which the organizational structures of technological society fit the demands of the type of technology practices we have designed. Research and development of modern technological systems requires a complex infrastructure, not only of goods and services, but also of expertise, skills, and intellectual organization. As Ellul (1964) and others have shown, the drive for control by means of technique and system leads to a totalization of society by the technical domain. The cultural backgrounds of our technology conditioned the emergence of practices unrestrained by moral and religious limitations. The center of our activities shifted away from building a rich culture to building complicated organizational and technical structures. From research funding, to final application, modern technological systems have been designed by specialists who do not appreciate the larger context, including the ecological requirements of sustainability.

A balanced technology practice is one which all practitioners can understand. It is one which is guided, not by technical considerations of what is possible, but by what is vitally necessary given overall values and spiritual meaning. Many of our films and novels are metaphoric and allegoric commentaries on this situation. However, psychic numbing, denial, self-deception, and other defensive strategies enable us to go on working according the system's functional demands.

When looking at professional journals in university libraries one is struck by the shortage of critical reflection on this whole system of technological structures. It is important to know what the main features of these are. We will now describe them. Let us consider first, however, the major characteristics of the Age of Technology itself.

I. Characteristics of the Age of Technology

The pursuit for perfection and increasing power in technology practices, and the spread of technology throughout our culture, have now become so pervasive that it makes sense to call the twentieth century the Age of Technology. As Rapp (1981) and many others have pointed out, the Age of Technology is characterized by:

- constant technological alteration of the natural world,

- substantial alteration of daily human life through technology,

- continuous global expansion of Western technological processes.

Everywhere we look, we see the impacts of human technology, in every aspect of daily life, in every place we go, and in everything we do in our professional and working lives. When we fly across the North American or other Western settled continents, almost everywhere we see the effects of modern technology: large-scale clearcuts, roads, highways, freeways, buildings, airports, large-scale irrigation projects, machine cultivated farmlands, power grids, dams, and blazing lights at night. This alteration of the physical landscape, which continues at an ever-accelerating pace, and the pervasive character of technology in all aspects of our lives, are intertwined. There were large landscape changes in earlier history, but these did not have the global consequences we see today. The ongoing transformation of the physical world, the technological organization of social life, and the global magnitude of these developments indicate that we are preoccupied by technological activity. It has become our be-all and end-all; it permeates our vocations and avocations; it is part of both leisure and work.

More than any earlier people we define and see ourselves in terms of our technological activities and artifacts. In art, fiction, films and entertainment, work, leisure, care of our homes and preparation of meals, physical conditioning and recreation, and everywhere in advertising, there is a pervasive application of devices and techniques, and the ever-present influence of the technostructure. These features are all aspects of the industrial revolution's dynamic, ongoing technologization of the world. And now increasingly we see the creation of technological artificial worlds, built environments, manufactured experience in "virtual reality", genetically engineered, cloned, human-created, new organisms. All these are part of the Technological Age. This technological context shapes how we think and perceive, just as the typographic revolution led to ascendence of text forms of thought (Ong 1982, Bowers 1988).

The intrinsic dynamics of this process of technological totalization involve several major factors. (See Zimmerman 1990, Winner 1977, 1986). Here are just some of the main ones:

- the creation of *objective measures* of progress defined as increasing efficiency and quantity of output, using common denominators,

- the *accumulation of technical gains* used to further other technological gains,

- an intensifying *systematization of technological process* that produces greater standardization and uniformity, including an operational definition of qualities such as sound and sight in terms of abstract formulas and digital codes,

- ongoing *refinement of research and development methodology*, with increasing emphasis on forms of methodical innovation and development to yield new technological processes,

- a *redefinition of basic concepts and legal codes* to allow the patenting even of living substances for the purposes of exclusive market rights (exploitation).

The Age of Technology is increasingly dominated by corporate, science-driven, technological development. The emergence of this technology is based upon a number of intellectual factors that help to further define this age. Rapp (1981) beautifully summarizes these widely recognized factors to include the following:

- objective means for evaluating work,

- agreed upon ways to measure increased efficiency in management and production,

- powerful incentives for technological creativity,

- widespread agreement about standards of rational inquiry as defined by "value-neutral" objectivity,

- objectifications of nature by applying Baconian-Cartesian mechanistic models so that it can be treated as only a source of raw materials,

- application of abstract logical and mathematical models capable of simplifying the world into sets of functional instrumentalities,

- experimental methods of inquiry and development that are constantly refined and applied to widening circles of problems.

Looking through this list we can see that crucial to the emergence of the Age of Technology has been a desacralization and objectification of nature. The modern worldview ushered in by Descartes and Bacon gave nature as machine to secular commercial forces. As the Age of Technology develops, all politically powerful measures of value are reduced to costs and benefits that can be assigned dollar values and divided among competing interest groups. Under this regime the mechanistically defined world becomes primarily a storehouse of raw material and a source of power for the engines of industry to turn out commodities and services for the market.

II. Views of Nature

Many different views and attitudes toward nature have emerged during the long history leading to the Age of Technology. The background against which all views of nature rest is nature *as it is in itself*. Humans, such as mystics and Zen meditators, who come to perceive nature in this way, could be said to be aware with no-view or no-mind—to use a Zen phrase. They have gone beyond, or let go of, conceptually conditioned experience to enter holistic spontaneous awareness. Their mind or consciousness is pure, free of judgements; it is like a dust-free mirror. It is empty of attachment to distorting, limited concepts and views. This awareness is rarely mentioned in modern Western philosophy and culture, although it can be found in our traditions especially in phenomenology and mysticism, and in spiritual disciplines in the East. Instead, the dominant modern view of nature reflects a shift from the Middle Ages—when nature was viewed as sacred because it was God's creation,—to the deistic view that nature was created by God, who then lets it run by itself. Nature was seen by some modern philosophers as God's gift to humans who could get power over it if they learned its laws through science. They believed that knowledge for the sake of power did not necessarily require that we *understand* nature or the inner life of natural beings. For Descartes and some other modern philosophers, nature was seen as a machine lacking any inherent consciousness or soul and thus void of intrinsic value. According to them, we can do with it and its beings whatever we desire and have the power to do. The aim of science is prediction and control of natural processes and materials so as to satisfy our needs and desires, and to help us become the "masters and controllers" of nature.

The Age of Technology requires that nature be viewed as a storehouse of raw materials to provide the stock and power for the machinery of industry and the wealth of commerce. These materials can be turned into valuable commodities and services by applying technology to them. This technology, to be most effective, must be based on scientific knowledge of natural laws. Through the philosophy and activities of the industrial revolution, and into the twentieth-century Age of Technology, nature becomes gradually redefined in social, legal, and economic terms. Old natural entities like ancient forests become viewed as decadent, in need of replacement by superior, human-engineered tree plantations. Wilderness becomes an artificial creation defined by legislative acts. We think of nature, not as something with a life of its own apart from us, or as something with its own values independent of us, but as something we circumscribe and set aside for our benefit as defined by statute, tradition, and contract. In the modern era nature was first controlled through concept and theory, then through technical and technological means. We classify the wilderness, study it, organize it, zone it, and decide its fate by compromising it to competing human interests and activities. Wilderness and all other natural spaces, entities, and living beings are, for example, "endangered species", "game animals", and "predators"; they become circumscribed by anthropocentric human values, theories, laws, and politics. These become powers made possible by the Age of Technology, and they are part of the conceptual background that modern philosophy helped to create.

III. Negative Effects of Machine Metaphors

The increasing power of technology has done increasing damage to the human spirit, to other beings and to the Earth's ecosystems. Recognizing this, we began to reach the limits of our modern industrial philosophy, and are now seeing more clearly that its machine metaphors have, except in limited cases, outlived their usefulness as major guiding paradigms. Nature is not just a machine and only raw materials; it is living, creative, and evolving communities of beings. The dawn of ecological consciousness is signalled by our coming to see the Earth as just such a being, and ourselves belonging to its *life-created* ecosphere. We see our fate intertwined with its ecological communities and processes. At stake is not just our physical survival, but also our spiritual and psychological well-being. Our larger ecological Self suffers the pains of innocent beings over which our technological power runs roughshod. If we think and feel deeply enough, we come to see the arbitrariness that infects our anthropocentrism, the view that only humans have inherent worth, for this attitude is at the center of the instrumental-resource view of the natural world. The deep response is to feel and affirm that nature has *inherent* worth, that natural beings must be treated with respect, as subjects with an internal life and intrinsic values. Great spiritual traditions have expressed this attitude as: all beings have Buddha nature; all creatures are part of the body of Christ; the Great Spirit is in all beings. Supporters of the Deep Ecology movement realize that humans have no right to interfere with the flourishing of other forms and communities of life, nor with the natural evolution of life on Earth.

Ecological consciousness leads us to see that we have the right to satisfy our vital needs, and that we must find the ways to satisfy these needs that are the least disruptive of other forms of life. Changing our technology practices is essential to this shift. The emergence of the Deep Ecology movement facilitates this way of seeing nature and leads us to see how we can create ecosophic lifestyles and communities—ones that are ecologically wise and harmonious. The awareness that nature is endangered by our technologies is the beginning of a transformation signalling the transition from the Age of Technology to the Age of Ecology, which itself is a way station on the path to the Age of Ecosophy. The perception that human activities and technologies now threaten the survival of planetary ecological communities and processes can lead initially to Shallow Ecology responses. Shallow responses are motivated primarily by our own small self-interest. But as the Age of Technology runs on, reflections deepen and many begin to question its values and our attitudes. We ask deeper questions and seek self-knowledge and ecological insight. This search leads us to see that our hard-won cleverness and our gift of natural intelligence must be put to more acceptable, *nonviolent* ends. If we would see ourselves as the most highly evolved consciousness on this planet (a major prejudice especially of Western industrialism), then we must work on ourselves so that we can be nonviolent, compassionate, and wise in all our relationships.

Being able to crystallize the main features of the Age of Technology has helped us to see more clearly the cultural paradigms that are its foundations. We have been able to do this in part because the imperative development of technology has led us to extend the industrial models to their limits. Being at these limits represents great dangers, but also fine opportunities. If we seize the positive opportunities, we can salvage a great deal from the knowledge and techniques we have acquired. They can provide us with useful tools to redesign and refashion our practices, to help us move toward the Age of Ecosophy. In Part II we will explore the different elements of this new philosophy of design being drawn together by creative people to help us imagine in a practical way a new era guided by ecological wisdom. It will be an era in which technology is no longer our main preoccupation, for we will no longer be dominated by but will have mastered the imperative of development. Our good work will focus on spiritual and communal values, on communion with other beings, on learning to live by the wisdom of the Earth, and on working to restore the damage we have caused through our intoxication with and addiction to the power of technological supremacy. In the chapters ahead we will explore spiritual disciplines that could help to give birth to this ecosophic transcultural vision of technology practices, and the human place in nature.

PART II

A Vision of Technology Practice as an Ecologically Wise, Spiritual Discipline

Chapter 8

Technological Limits and Forms of Innovation

I. Main Categories of Limits to Technological Development

Two notable conclusions have come out of the studies of technology in the last few decades. One is that *all* techniques have limits, whether translated into material forms or not. The other is that, at advanced levels, technology tends to generate problems faster than solutions. Technological power tends to generate problems in direct proportion to further increases in power. Many of these problems have no technological solutions; they are not themselves technological ones. Those who are promoting alternative or appropriate technology, as discussed in chapters 4 and 6, are aware of these objections to further technological development. One solution they offer is downsizing and simplifying technology, making it smaller, more elegant, and less complicated.

There are limitations to technological power, and we will discuss these under the four basic categories suggested by Rapp (1981):

- the structure of the natural world,
- available intellectual resources,
- material resources,
- social conditions.

These are not mutually exclusive for they do overlap, and yet it is instructive to deal with each separately.

When we consider the limitations to technological development set by the *structure of the natural world*, four features need to be considered:

- the laws of nature,
- human psycho-physical structure,
- the principles of ecology,
- the principles of logic.

In many important ways, these are interrelated conditions inherent in any whole natural system.

Technology is a product of human culture, reflecting not only our naturally endowed capacities and their use, but our culturally acquired habits and practices. In traditional cultures technology clearly reflects the mind-sets created by the cultural context. Even primitive stone tools are marked by the identity of their cultural source. It has been argued, however, that modern industrial technology is less and less shaped by cultural influences and is no longer a reflection of culture or place, because it has become global, and because it is shaped by abstract principles and values, formally derived from the most general *laws of nature*. One of these principles is that whatever is theoretically possible is materially possible. A logical consequence of this belief is that theoretically there are no natural limitations on technological power since resources are a result of human ingenuity interacting with available material. The supply of iron ore, for example, might dwindle, but science and technology make it possible to utilize other materials for the same purposes. A widely held belief in modern technological society is that because of engineering, basic science, and human imagination, there are few limits on what we can do—if a task is theoretically possible, given enough time and money we can do it.

It is true that the decline of a resource in nature has historically led to the creation of substitutes. Industrial culture has been very adept at this process. However, industrial culture is only a few hundred years old, if we date the foundation of modern philosophy at about 1600 A.D. Yet, many ancient cultures, which thrived for far longer periods, declined because their agriculture and forestry practices depleted the fertility of the soil, altered climates, and changed crop lands into deserts. They fell victim to the invariable laws of nature. Modern Western European culture, having followed the practices of these ancient civilizations, was given a new lease on life by colonizing other places such as the large continents of North and South America, which had great expanses of uncultivated land, uncut forests, and other abundant resources. Today, industrial cultures are destroying these forests, grasslands, and croplands faster than nature can repair them. But have we not reached the limits of these lands today and are we not also bound by the same laws of nature?

Let us look again at the contention of modern culture that technological innovation will always provide ways to solve problems of critical shortages caused by dwindling resources. This might seem true if we focus on rather simple types of shortages, such as a shortage of iron for tool manufacture. Obviously, such shortages are now more easily overcome, since we know more about materials and how to process them, and even how to design and develop new materials. But shortages resulting from degradation of farm and forest lands pose problems of far greater magnitude and indicate that there are ecological limitations to technological power. We will consider these limits in more detail later.

It is evident that modern industrial technologies intrude upon the natural world in more complex and large-scale ways than the technologies of traditional societies. The birth of the chemical industry in nineteenth-century Germany, for example, moved modern culture into new dimensions of destructive impact on nature. Since the conceptual dawn of the industrial revolution, the aim, as stated by Bacon and Descartes, has been to master and control nature. One of the cornerstones of modern industrial philosophy is that we should learn the laws of nature so that we can make "her" do our bidding. As we have seen, this attitude is one basis for the technological optimism that swept through our culture as it began its pursuit of total technological power.

This optimistic faith in part represents a translation into technical form of the older mythological dreams of power which were pursued through esoteric formulas and incantations. Supposedly, the secret formulas enabled their possessors to order the spirits and powers of nature to do their bidding. The modern form of this faith was early infused with the tradition of magic and esotericism associated with alchemy. These mythological tales of power can throw light on our modern relationship with technological power. In Tolkien's *The Lord of the Rings*, a modern mythological tale, the token that is the source of power—the ring—has an ambiguous nature. If the ring of power (technological skill and knowledge) falls into the wrong hands, it can wreak havoc upon innocent people, but even if it falls into the hands of someone who means well, the possessor of this power and those close to her or him can be destroyed by it. The use of the ring's potentials, as of technology's potentials, is fraught with risks. We usually appreciate this wisdom about power in political, not technical contexts, and yet in mythology humans have always appreciated the wisdom that there are risks in having power, whatever its source.

The mythological view is that those who seek to have complete power and domination over others and nature will in the end be destroyed by this very power. Ancient Greek myths, for example, told stories about mortals and gods who overreached themselves, and who for their hubris were humbled by the gods, the powers of nature, and the universe. These are powerful cautionary tales for those who believe that even the laws of nature can set no limits to the growth of technological power. In the mythological world, as long as each being obeys the "laws of its kind", it will thrive and flourish. But if it oversteps its natural boundaries, it will sooner or later be brought down. The insight in mythological wisdom is that there *are* natural limits to seeking power, and that the unlimited hunger and thirst for power is self-consuming. Power always has two faces.

To live by the philosophy of extreme technological optimism, that technology has no limits, is to risk ignoring our own nature. This philosophy encourages the pursuit of power over others, placing high value on power as providing control and a sense of self-worth. But the power of any person or group is always limited. A person who identifies with power as a way of defining the self, could feel incomplete because this power is not great enough; such a person will always hunger for more power as a way to completeness. This hunger can become an addiction, but limited power can never fully quench the thirst for completeness as total control. As a result, such a person, group, or culture will be on an endless treadmill. The more they seek power, the more completeness eludes them. They can never catch up with or realize their desire for completeness as power, since to achieve this end, their power would have to be infinite. Unless they go to the roots of their desire and understand the source and reason for confusing completeness with power, they will never find completeness and harmony. Human beings must recognize that we can expand our powers only so far, and we always have enough power if we know how to work within our natural limits. The capacity to use our own naturally endowed powers for personal development is realized by fully unifying ourselves to attain a mature understanding of our *vital* needs, sources of fulfillment, and means to self-realization and completion. To fail to understand these as a result of self-ignorance gives rise to pursuing compensatory satisfactions, and such impossible aims as unlimited power. This is only one of many dangers inherent in the pursuit of total technological control. Here we have described one type of limitation to technological development — that set by the laws of nature.

This leads us to consider the limits to technological development set by *human psychological and physical makeup*. In many instances technological development has reached the physical limits of humans. One example of this is the way in which the capacities of jet fighter planes stress the pilot's body to the point of "blacking out". Pressurized suits and other modifications to the human system then become necessary. Technological development has enabled us to extend human artifact presence to areas not compatible with human presence, such as distant planets and the ocean depths. If we consider the human body as part of an ecological context, then other "body" limitations become apparent. Industrial forestry, agriculture, mining, and manufacturing can degrade the context to such an extent that the human organism can no longer function, or functions only marginally. Machines can be designed to function in almost any situation, but the physical makeup of humans limits their use and effectiveness. For example, the demands of electronic processing and decision making, given current computer speed and complexity, can exceed human capacities. This in turn "requires" delegating more "decisions" to the programs and machines, creating a vicious circle, since computer programs can be so long and complicated that there is no way to adequately test their reliability. Failures will occur, and some of these might be catastrophic.

We have already discussed some psychological limitations. We underscore here, however, that human psychological limitations are more culture-specific than physical limitations. The attempt to transfer technologies across cultural boundaries sometimes encounters psychological barriers. These are deeper than just different habits, for they involve attitudes and values that have been inculcated from birth onward. Such things as taboos and sacred groves, for example, have psychological elements associated with them. Since local technology practices are integrated around local attitudes and values, their practice creates no psychological dissonance. But the introduction of "foreign" technologies can be psychologically stressful and can cause fear, anger, and hostility.

Psychological and emotional stability in a culture is a function of many factors. In industrial-technological-urban culture the earlier traditional structures and values, (associated with place and productive practices that are individually empowering) have been undermined. The industrial paradigm of development is based on monoculture, uniformity, speed, and abstraction, all of which run counter to the natural inclinations toward place-specific wisdom, diversity, accumulation of tradition and values, and sense of community, self-worth, integrity, value and meaning. The symptoms that major psychological limitations of industrial culture are being stressed are found in a whole series of interrelated problems of dysfunctional relationships, violence, alienation, and sense of meaninglessness. All of these characteristics, which are functions also of Modernism—the philosophy that supports the industrial development model—signify cultural crisis.

Our culture has lost its sense of meaning and connection to intrinsic values of human life and nature. Modern industrial culture is breaking down because it is placeless, has lost a sense of connection with a larger dimension of value and sacredness. Rejecting these values gives modern industrial culture its power, but this power has an Achilles' heel. Dysfunction follows from pursuing a model that tries to restructure the world by imposing the alien values of industrialism on everything, to create an impersonal world of uniformity, dominated by instrumental, commercial values. There is no place in this model for a living planet with diverse

human and biological communities. Industrialism attempts to turn everything into a human artifact, including animals, plants, humans and forests. This is psychologically alienating and undermines human integrity
and community.

What about the limits set by the *principles of ecological communities?*
Here we are dealing with forms of relationship and organization so intri-
cate that we do not even know what they all are, let alone understand
them. They are far more complex and subtle than any of our technological systems of organization. Even our most complex super computers do
not begin to match the complexity of natural ecosystems. Despite our
ignorance, we do know that the products of industrialism have profound
effects upon ecological communities; we are only beginning to appreciate
how these impacts adversely affect us as well. The depletion of the ozone
shield, the greenhouse effect, the rising rates of human cancer are only
some of the consequences of industrial culture's impacts on nature
through complicated causes convoluted through ecological processes.
Consider, for example, the greenhouse effect resulting from consumption
of fuels and other chemicals that stress atmospheric and ecological processes. This activity is complicated and involves cutting and burning forests, burning fossil fuels in transport, using CFCs in aerosols and
refrigeration, the production of methane as a by-product of certain processes, and so on. The consequences of the buildup of certain gases and
chemicals are large-scale. We do not fully understand them, and we cannot directly control them, but can try to mitigate the negative effects by
better management of our own activities. We have to work on these problems on several different fronts. We can shift to other sources of energy,
use conservation and other means to lower consumption, restore forests
and stop clearcutting and burning them, change the chemicals used in
refrigeration, and so on. The greenhouse problem requires a multidimensional approach, including changes in lifestyle—and even then we cannot
be sure we have solved the problem. There is no simple or single technological fix for this complex, large-scale disruption of the ecological principles of balance.

Next, consider the limits to technological development imposed by
the *laws of logic* and the consequences of inconsistency. Consider, for
example, how the "war on drugs" fails to attend to inconsistency, thus
making it impossible to find a solution to the problem of drug abuse.
One aspect of the problem is as follows: on average North American children see or hear around four thousand ads a week; many of these ads tell
children that when they suffer from some woe or pain, all they have to
do to get immediate relief is to consume some substance, often a drug.
Alcohol, tobacco, and caffeine are socially acceptable drugs, readily available and until recently all heavily advertised. In the light of the above, it

is foolish to think that a few anti-drug messages in the vast sea of media ads, coupled with law enforcement, is going to solve the problem vaguely defined as "drug abuse". There are confusing inconsistencies and mixed messages here. Moreover, consider that governments in all jurisdictions raise revenues from the sale of legal drugs, which (as we earlier noted) are more costly in terms of social problems, disease, and death than all of the "illicit" drugs put together. The government benefits from these sales. So, the media and our culture are filled with conflicting messages about the use of substances that alter human consciousness and affect the way we feel, look, and perform. Given these and other inconsistencies, it is not surprising we make little headway in solving these problems.

There are other inconsistencies. We constantly emphasize the prime value of freedom and the free enterprise system (and in many ways the illegal drug business is a form of pure capitalism); at the same time we expand police power and infringe civil liberties in order to deal with the "drug crisis". Politicians refer to drugs as a great threat to national security. And yet, even if we turned all of North America into one large prison, we would not solve the "drug problem", for after all drugs are readily available in existing prisons! Realizing this, some people say we need to place more emphasis on educational and rehabilitation efforts. But this ignores the reverse educational impact of the daily media with their thousands of pro-drug, feel-good ads. A careful consideration of the inconsistencies in policy, cultural practices, values, media hype, and existing laws would help us to see more exactly what the problems are and how they might be dealt with. Failing this, no amount of technological power or technical fiddling is going to solve the ill-defined problems that have led us to wage our various "wars on." Perhaps we should ask why we think we need an enemy, an adversary. Now that the cold war has ended, we no longer have the communist "enemy". Are "drug pushers, drug lords, and drug abusers" to be our new enemies and scapegoats? And what is the psychological and economic logic in all of this? Do we still have a shadow that we feel the need to cast on some other social group or thing? Is this scapegoating just a way of avoiding our real problems? The failure to examine these inconsistencies in a logical manner might be a result of our own denial and a refusal to face our own shadow (as a culture and as individuals). The above examples show some of the ways in which the structure of the natural world sets limits on the development of technical power.

The *intellectual resources* at our disposal make up the second category of limitations to technological development. These limits are imposed by the current state of our scientific knowledge, skills, techniques, and settled practices. Much literature devoted to extolling the wonders of technological progress has staked our fortunes on the possibility of making discoveries *in the future* that will solve problems caused by *current* practices. Let us look at nuclear power as an example. Experts knew at the outset of atomic power plant construction that reactors would generate highly toxic, radioactive, hot waste. They did not know how to dispose of these wastes, and proposed storing them on site until a more permanent solution was found—although they had no idea what the solution would be, or whether there was one. Instead of waiting until they found a permanent solution, industry, with government urging and subsidy, forged ahead with the construction of nuclear power plants. The result today is that nuclear waste disposal has become a major technical and political problem. The nuclear power industry is now in a state of decline, and taxpayers are going to have to pay enormous costs for disposing of the wastes. The U.S. government has commissioned many studies to find an acceptable solution for this problem. One proposal is to build a permanent depository underground in some arid location. However, people are justifiably wary of what the experts suggest, for they have been wrong in the past about nuclear power and other complex technologies. Major accidents in several countries have been extremely costly. Given these facts, it is no wonder that nuclear power has little popular support.

Both the problems and the costs generated by the nuclear power industry are partly a result of failing to heed *what we do not know*, that is, recognizing the limitations of our intellectual resources, which include our understanding of society and nature. We can be so impressed with our own technical knowledge that we lose sight of the large areas of ignorance and uncertainty surrounding the development of complex technologies. We cannot bank on removing all of our ignorance, since as human beings we know we are limited. In the case of projects with great risk, we need to temper our enthusiasm by reminding ourselves of how much we do *not* know. To embark upon the construction of new technologies with high hazards and costs, on the assumption that we will be able to solve major problems in the future, is foolish and irresponsible. We must, in such cases, provide for wide margins of safety. In the case of nuclear power and its waste products, we had no certainty at the outset that we would be able to solve all problems, and although decades have passed we still have no clear solutions. The magnitude of the hazardous waste problem will remain with us for thousands of years.

Another aspect of our intellectual limitations, one not so readily recognized, is the nature of our current modes of thought and problem solving practices. Unless we can find a way to escape from our current thought patterns, it is difficult to see that there are other ways of approaching problems. Some ways to bring about this shift might be to shake up one's paradigms by engaging in cross-cultural studies, participating in shamanic journeying, in Sufi dancing, or Zen meditation. These and similar activities, outside our normal patterns, can help us to realize what limited perspectives we operate from, by helping us to break free of them.

The limitations posed by *material resources* partly overlap some of the limitations already discussed. Here we take "material resources" to mean not only raw material, such as iron ore, clay, wood fiber, and so on, but also energy, machinery, labor power, and environmental resources. Environmental resources include such things as oxygen needed for reduction processes in steel manufacture, and rivers and other bodies of water to transport ships or to carry away unwanted waste materials. Environmental resources also include solar energy, prevailing winds, tidal power, availability of wild animals, plants, and trees. By labor power we mean the power of human energy and activity, its availability, capacities and potential for organization and focus.

Each of the elements we have mentioned has certain limitations. Humans can only work so hard, and put in so many hours a day. A highly trained, specialized work force cannot be easily turned to new tasks, unless workers are retrained. Existing plants with their equipment, tools, and machinery have certain built-in limitations. For example, it is difficult to convert a semiconductor plant to the manufacture of automobiles or boats. Existing tools and machinery represent substantial investments, not only in capital, but in the way the labor force is organized for work.

Any given location has its advantages and disadvantages in terms of the environmental factors present. A location far from any major seaports, located in a remote desert has few resources to support most productive enterprises, and yet it might be ideal for some highly specialized activities. As already noted, "resource" is a relative term, and material resource limitation partly depends upon the proposed activity and available knowledge and skills. Nonetheless, generalizations can be made. Despite the potential power of genetic engineering, animal size and growth rate must function under certain natural laws and environmental limitations. Despite new forms of conditioning and diet, humans also have psychological limitations that set upper limits to productivity. Availability of raw materials can be a serious limitation in production, and although substitutions can be made, they are often more costly and can require significant modifications of existing processes, equipment, and work force.

A common cost in all production is energy expenditure. So central is energy to the industrial production of goods and services that it would make sense to do our accounting on the basis of energy budgets. Such budgets would provide valuable information on more of the costs of doing business, including environmental ones. They could also help to directly cut production costs, since energy saving investments continue to pay off, especially as energy costs rise. The substitution of petroleum-powered machine energy for human and animal muscle power has been one of the major ways of increasing human productivity in industrial society. This widespread use of petroleum (and other fossil fuels) has enabled us to reduce the percentage of farm and factory workers in the total work force. Given cheap sources of energy with minimum environmental impact, labor costs can be cut even more by using more machines and fuel. Whereas horses and humans are psychophysical beings who can get ill and balk at work, machines and petrol have no such limitations. They do not organize, malinger, or go on strike. Human efforts, then, are greatly magnified and multiplied by machines using petroleum fuels. The two main limitations here, however, are environmental impacts and fuel costs.

Even with the high productivity of industrial societies, there are definite limits to the amount of food, fiber, goods and services current technology can produce. Increasing production of any one of these items will result in increased costs. Raising global consumption levels to equal those of industrial nations would be impossible, if only because of the environmental and material resource limitations we have discussed. Of course, we can *imagine* alternative modes of production that are less wasteful, more efficient, and that use solar power. These could (theoretically) increase our productive output while lowering environmental and other detrimental impacts caused by current modes of production. While designing such alternatives is challenging, actually changing existing practices runs into even greater obstructions such as institutional inertia, conflicting government policies, worker intransigence, management opposition, and resistance from various levels of professional organizations and bureaucracies. These fit into our last category of limitations.

Social conditions obviously can seriously limit the way in which alternative forms of production and consumption are developed. These conditions include such factors as market mechanisms, political and legal restrictions, social and cultural limits, religious and spiritual values, cosmology, and philosophy.

Let us look first at market mechanisms. Since virtually all economic activity is shaped by existing policies, laws, and corporate activity, there are almost no truly laissez-faire markets. In many countries, such as Japan, for example, market mechanisms are intertwined with older traditions of trade influenced by family lineages and other tribal connections. In the U.S. and Canada the market is shaped by political and economic factors. In Canada, for example, marketing boards have regulated the supply and price of farm commodities. In the United States the Federal Farm program artificially lowers prices on some commodities and raises them on others. The European Common Market, NAFTA, GATT, and other international and national bodies exert similar controls. Subsidies, tax advantages, legal restrictions, patents, and copyrights all shape and limit the forms of production and their profitability. Existing tax policies favor industrial forestry and agriculture over small scale, decentralized, alternative approaches. Moreover, there are often conflicting policies within government. While one government agency might try to discourage smoking, for example, another might support tobacco producers and help them to sell their products overseas. In the forest industries, the government Forest Service might establish policies that undermine the efforts of another agency, such as the Environment Ministry, to preserve habitat and plant and animal species. Congress or Parliament might pass an endangered species act to protect certain animal and plant species, and then enact legislation that forces agencies to increase forest production beyond sustainable limits. The result of the second legislation is to decrease wildlife habitat, degrade the environment, and threaten species survival, in conflict with the first act. Some government policies might encourage a type of farming that causes soil erosion, while other agencies are trying to prevent its loss.

These conflicting policies in part reflect the pluralistic values of our multiracial, multiethnic, culturally mixed societies, committed to democratic processes. They reflect competing economic interests: consumers vs. farmers, management vs. labor, environmentalists vs. timber companies. They also reflect confusion about our basic values and aims and about our worldview and conception of our place in the scheme of things. Modern industrial culture exalts individualism and encourages enterprise. It fosters and promotes competition to get ahead of others and to try to be "number one". Television programs and movies are filled with themes of conflict, violence, competition, revenge, greed, and conspicuous consumption. At the same time our society gives lip service to fundamental Christian values. Serious disagreements about the performance of abortions, and whether to use aborted fetuses in experiments reflect conflicting values, and sometimes confusions about the ultimate purposes of our society. While we carry on a costly "war on drugs" in the inner cities, we ignore other conditions that promote the abuse of drugs. As we have already noted, the messages of the dominant media promote drug use as a quick fix, a way to solve personal problems by getting high or seeking thrills. (Part of the "high and thrill" no doubt comes from violating social mores.)

The social limitations we have mentioned are related partly to the large, complex, multicultural character of modern industrial societies. The very structures of these societies create serious problems that are difficult to solve. Just as there are size limits to effective government and how far political power can extend without military force, so there are limits to the size societies can attain, without becoming fraught by increasing social ills and problems. In industrial culture mass production and transport have enabled us to greatly increase city size by providing effective communication, transport, and skill in high-rise building construction. However, the social and personal costs are high, and point to limits of urbanization. The urbanite has been cut off from nature, which is our source, and has been surrounded by an artificial environment that is increasingly polluted, subject to violence, disruptive noise, and dehumanization. The large industrial city is not at all conducive to wholesome family life, and it has become increasingly difficult to govern.

It is almost a cliché in our spiritual traditions that humans live not by bread alone. We are incomplete beings, whose completion requires a sustained effort toward physical, moral, and spiritual development. We cannot accomplish this development in isolation from other people, for our personal work of realizing ourselves as social beings depends on others. As cultural beings we tend to reflect the conflicts and confusions of our milieu. It takes considerable effort and good fortune to rise above social conditions which are rife with violence, confusion, and conflicting values. Clearly, attempts to solve such problems as the so-called drug crisis or environmental crisis by technical or enforcement means alone will continue to fail. Education for responsible living and action is difficult in the face of the powerful contrary messages that saturate our society. Much popular culture encourages immaturity, thoughtless consumption, needless competition, and the idea that there is a quick fix for anything we do not like or that ails us. So we have bread and circuses, cheap food and entertainment, but neither nourishes our deeper needs.

There is no easy solution to the way modern social conditions limit technological development. As we have seen, these conditions are influenced not only by conflicting policies and confusions about values, but also by such things as lack of skills, low levels of literacy, and lack of adequate health care (reflecting not only shortages of trained personnel but also inadequate health care delivery systems). Attempts to transfer technological development to "undeveloped" cultures have often failed because of the types of social limitations mentioned here, more than from the other categories of limitations we have discussed.

Technological development has a different meaning in highly industrialized nations than in nonindustrial nations. We assume that bringing our highly industrialized technologies to less developed nations will help them industrialize. This is not necessarily so. If the aim is to stimulate indigenous development of new appropriate practices, this is not the route. The challenge is one of helping them to create technology practices of an appropriate cultural and environmental scale. For example, a society might benefit more from wheelbarrows than from huge, expensive earthmovers; improved hand tools might provide a better means to increase productivity, while maximizing employment and minimizing social and economic dislocations. Although the problems of technological development in advanced industrial societies are obviously different from those in nonindustrial nations, the categories of limits we have described apply in both contexts.

II. General Reflections on Technological Innovation

Much attention has been focused in recent years on the problems caused by the ever accelerating rates of technological innovation. Given the social and cultural dynamics of industrial society and the dynamism of market systems, even with the limitations we have described, the pace of technological change will continue to increase. It is astounding that there are many people in our society who were born before there were automobiles, planes, televisions, telecommunications, computers, nuclear weapons, space rockets, artificial satellites, genetic engineering, electric hot-water heaters—and this is just a partial list! Another sobering fact is that over 90 percent of all the scientists and engineers who have *ever* lived are alive now. Considering the vast amount of time, money, energy, and human talent devoted to research and development and to increasing the pace and diversity of modern production, it is not surprising that the rate of technological change is accelerating.

Although change has been rapid, it is logical to assume that the basic *form* of change has remained the same throughout the industrial period. We have simply applied the basic models of machine technology to more and more areas of human activity, while continuing to improve the power and sophistication of machines and to increase their output and efficiency. The computer-information revolution, according to this line of reasoning, is not significantly different from the revolution in textile production that displaced older craft work with machine production. The computer is merely doing to white-collar work what already has been done in blue-collar trades. Now the goal is to replace skilled human experts with "expert systems" utilizing software based on digital systems of artificial intelligence (AI), which will emulate the way experts make decisions and reach conclusions. On this view, then, innovation is primarily *translation*, not *transformation*. Technological innovation is primarily the continued translation of the metaphor of the machine as a basic model of reality and society into ever increasing material and intellectual activities. The computer is just a calculating machine that uses electronic switching in place of mechanical levers. It might be faster, quieter, more efficient, and able to do far more than any mechanical device, when processing and transferring encoded information, but it follows the same principles and logical steps. Since the cutting edge of technological innovation and development is dependent on utilization of information, the computer has itself become an important tool in furthering technological innovation.

Each new tool and technique pyramids with existing knowledge, skills, and machinery to increase technological power even further. This synergy seems arithmetic in its power to process information, but it proliferates problems geometrically. When the two curves cross, the problems outrun solutions. Given current models governing industrial activity and social life, some would say we have already reached this critical point with respect to the environmental and other limits on production and consumption. More of the same kind of innovation will not save us.

It is advisable, then, to see if it is possible to find basic forms of innovation that would *transform* existing practices. The movement from ecologically foolish and destructive activities to ecosophic ones would be such a transformative process. It would involve not merely a change in the *amount* and *speed* of activity, but a change in its *nature* and *quality*.

When we contemplate changing any activity, whether in production or in personal habits, we need perspective on what and how to change. We need to be able to "dis-identify" ourselves from that which we want to change. If, for example, we want to change the violent logging practices that are destroying forest soils, stream quality, and forest ecosystems, we need to distance ourselves from these practices in order to see how they can be changed. Very often people directly involved in a specialized activity, as in industrial forestry, are so close to it, and have so much at stake in its practice, that they are reluctant even to imagine that it can and should be changed. They often have their personal identity invested in it and it is a source of security and meaning as well as income. Even when alternative practices might be better for them economically in the long run, they resist change because of habit and a sense of who they are. This is an understandable human reaction.

Because we so often resist fundamental change, we must find ways to break free of existing identifications if we are to *understand* the nature of our own activities. If we succeed in breaking free we are also able to envision alternatives. Once we see alternatives we can design and test new practices. If they are validated, then we expand them, while continuing to monitor them. We can share the results with others. All this is possible only if we can step outside ourselves to gain perspective.

III. Two Modes of Consciousness

Human consciousness works in two basic modes, which Heidegger called meditative and calculative thinking. Some people strongly criticize calculative thinking, taking it as the model of rational, intellectual activity. They claim that this type of cogitation must share major blame for the damage wrought by modern industrial cultures, damage resulting from an overdeveloped calculative intellect depressing our intuitive side. Some have gone even further, claiming that this assertive force represents a division in the human psyche that began with agricultural civilization, especially that of the Greeks. Hunting and gathering (primal) cultures, it is claimed, were (are) not riven with dualism and division, not fragmented, and had (have) no hierarchies of domination and control. There was no patriarchy. With the rise of agricultural society in the West, particularly in ancient Greece, hierarchies of domination and control arose. The values shifted to those of patriarchy, with emphasis on heroism, power, and calculative thinking. In modern industrial culture the calculative mode of thinking (or consciousness) is dominant, exhibiting its basic elements in both the self and society.

The meditative mode of thought (or consciousness) is associated with intuitive capacities and the ability to see things as a whole. Its basic emphasis is on states of being, rather than control and having. Even though the calculative side of our nature is dominant in industrial society, the meditative power of human consciousness is not altogether absent, for it is the primary source of creative imagination and visionary power. However, there is no sustained cultivation of this holistic power in our culture. The overwhelming bulk of our activities and educational processes promote development of the calculative, controlling thinking that drives technology and thereby helps to feed consumptive "power-over" behavior. We need holistic awareness to get beyond our dead ends.

Insight comes when there is a pause in ongoing calculative activity. When we let the mind rest, stare into the fire, sit by a river, or watch the stars without engaging in calculative thought, then insight comes. When the mind runs free and we play, meditative consciousness surfaces. In storytelling, in improvisation, and in spontaneous action, we sometimes find ourselves in a unified state of being that *is* meditative awareness. The march of innovative activity in industrial culture is marked by two forms of change: change that is the result of extending existing models to other areas; and a change in quality represented by the introduction of new models, new ways of seeing things, shifts in paradigms and their associated perceptual gestalts. The play between these two basic forms of change is the play between calculative and meditative modes of consciousness.

Consciousness itself has no fixed form. It is ever changing and flows like a river. But conscious activity can take many forms. Realizing the inherent nature of consciousness to be formless (although one can say it is both form and formlessness) requires not that we *do* something productive, but that we refrain from a narrow identification with doing. There are disciplines that train us to allow the meditative mode to be present in self-conscious awareness. These disciplines can seem threatening, for they enable us to let go of our usual identification with egoic consciousness and its many forms of activity, from which the small self derives a sense of meaning and security. Moving to the transpersonal level of consciousness transcends this egoic form of awareness in important ways. It undermines self-created boundaries and the limits we place on extending our capacity to identify with things and beings beyond our ordinary sense of who we are. This is not a movement into psychosis or a regression to a pre-egoic state. It is a development beyond egoic awareness to a higher state of integration and consciousness, the realization that wisdom is not the product of calculative thinking. Wisdom has no personal ownership. Calculative thinking has a valuable but limited place in our lives. Even in monasteries which emphasize cultivation of meditative states, someone has to make plans. Organization and order are needed. These involve the use of calculation. Such activity, then, is not the be-all and end-all of spiritual work in monastic life, but only a useful element in the cultivation of the whole person within a spiritual community.

To see technology as a whole practice we must see it as more than productive and economic activity. If we are to transform our activities to ecosophic ones, we must see the practice of technology through meditational consciousness. If we are to transform our technology practices, we must transform ourselves, and the way we are in the world. All designs reflect the level of awareness and the moral and spiritual perfection of their designers, who are the source of both good and bad innovations. Good innovation comes from meditational consciousness and draws from our whole being; clever change comes from calculative thought. When calculative thought is embedded in and disciplined by meditative, holistic awareness, *wise* innovation becomes possible. Let us now consider the main forms of innovation in relation to technology practices.

IV. Forms of Technological Innovation and Mastery of Design

For our purposes let us consider the four primary forms of technological innovation as:

- minor modification,
- technological hybridization,
- technological mutation,
- technological mastery as design of whole practices.

By means of a series of *minor modifications* carried out over a period of time, a technology can be slowly improved and technical problems solved. The same gradual improvement and refinement can be applied to production processes and the organization of work, as well as to the marketing side of technological innovation. A product can be designed, built, and readied for market, but unless there is preparation of the market for its introduction, the product could be an economic failure. Modifications of technical design processes, alteration of the product and the production process all influence and are influenced by markets. Change by minor modification is the easiest form of innovation to identify in the historical development of technology in the twentieth century.

As those of us who read novels and comic books know, many of the major products of twentieth-century technology were conceived long before they became technically feasible or economically viable. The submarine, the airplane, the automobile, and space vehicles all appeared in imaginative conceptual artistic form before they were built and introduced into our culture. Film and television have played and still play similar roles of providing ideas for new forms of technological design. Although not commonly recognized, artists, novelists, and cartoonists often lead the development of technological culture. Not only do they lead as heralds, but they also help to prepare the culture for the introduction of such new technologies, much in the way that imaginative play helps children to ready themselves for new experiences.

Despite this preparation and conceptual exploration, the actual process of design and production of practical technologies follows a much slower route. It is marked by gradual refinement and piecemeal solutions to problems that only become evident when design passes into prototype, and then a product for mass production. Many things can go wrong in this process and major problems often arise. These problems can lie in the technical details of design and production; they can lie in limits to worker skills; they can lie in marketing; they can lie in servicing and use of the product once it has been distributed; they can lie in environmental impact, which becomes evident only when the product has been in use for a while. To anticipate all of the possible problems in the design phase is difficult, even though they can often be categorized. It did not dawn on the designers of early cars that the automobile would eventually be implicated in widespread air pollution, acid rain, lung cancer, and a host of other harmful side effects. The problems anticipated by designers tend to be in such practical areas as device reliability, efficient production and successful marketing.

Automobile technology provides fine examples of minor modification. The earliest cars were clearly seen as extensions of horse-drawn buggies. In design they looked like them. They used the same brake systems.

They were even called "horseless carriages". The power of the engines was rated in terms of "horse" power. As time went on the production process and the design of the car gradually improved. Problems with brakes and clutches were solved, materials and designs were modified for greater durability, the production process was rationalized and made more efficient, and eventually the assembly line and mass production of parts came together through organizational structures that still exist. Over time the process and organization were refined so that by now we have become very good at manufacturing, distributing, servicing, and using automobiles. We have an infrastructure for them. We got here through a process of gradual innovation, involving countless modifications of the basic designs, processes, and techniques of auto use and manufacture. This was an evolutionary, not a revolutionary process.

Technological hybridization involves applying the knowledge and skills learned from one form of production and technological development to other areas. Such hybridization might apply the techniques of biotechnology to a nonbiological process. It might marry two technologies to produce a new form of technology practice, such as applying the steam engine pump to a wheeled vehicle on rails to produce a locomotive. The ongoing process of technological development involves a great deal of cross-fertilization, synergistic interaction, and experiment with how technologies can be applied to areas outside those for which they were originally designed. This process attempts to combine the usefulness and power of different technologies to yield new combinations. It is not just pouring old wine into new bottles.

Much research is devoted to exploring ways in which technological hybridization can solve technical problems. For example, designers have brought together aircraft, automotive, and bicycle technologies to produce a prototype human-powered car that is practical for commuting on the highways and roads in all kinds of weather. Some have designed hybrid engines for cars, combining solar photovoltaic technologies with hybrid propane-electric car engines. The application of space technology to sailing vessels provides yet another example. In selective breeding, hybridization has long been used to modify and "improve" animal and plant production. Biogenetic engineering techniques to produce new plant and animal forms is one application of this practice.

In nature, hybrids are often sterile, as are the products of human selective breeding. This is not so in the technological world. Hybrid technologies have been very successful in spurring development of new technology practices. By applying lessons learned from two or more fields, designers have stimulated technological innovation, change, and development in others.

Technological mutation is the transformation of a technology to some other form, or for some radically different purpose. For example, the Chinese invented and used gunpowder for fireworks and entertainment. The Mongols and then the Europeans transformed this technology and used it not only for armaments and warfare, but also as a tool in the construction of roads, tunnels, dams, and mines. Another example is the program that developed the fission nuclear bomb in World War II. It was a short-term crash program with a narrowly defined military objective. Although the theory was based on scientific hypotheses, the bomb had not been demonstrated to work under controlled conditions. Scientists working on the Manhattan Project, as it was called, had to overcome both theoretical and practical problems before they produced the bombs that were dropped on Hiroshima and Nagasaki. The work of these scientists laid the groundwork for the later development of "non-violent", "peace-time", forms of nuclear technology such as electrical power generation and medical applications. The bomb technology was "mutated" into peacetime use by combining it with the technology for generating electrical energy by steam turbine. The new hybrid-mutant was then installed in electric power networks.

Last, let us consider the process of innovation we call *the design of whole technology practices*. These practices are based on the mastery of a holistic design process that includes appropriate human, spiritual, and ecocentric values. All of the forms of innovation mentioned so far require mastery of rules and techniques for design and development, but they depend primarily upon staying within the established concepts of practice and progress, that is, within the confines of the dominant industrial paradigm of humans and nature.

But the process we are speaking of, designing appropriate technology practices, is a process of innovation that involves whole system design. Its emphasis on technological mastery and creation requires the capacity to transcend technology and much of our dependence upon it. It opens possibilities that were not there before. To master such an art (for it is an art), we must rise above our fascination with techniques and rules. In just such a manner, the master poet who has fluency with language, writes with freedom and spontaneity; she transcends the rules and techniques used in teaching beginners. This mastery of an art leads to creative, spontaneous, and relatively autonomous activity. To be masters in the design of appropriate technology practices, we must transcend the "necessities" that seem to dictate a narrow range of possibilities. Consider an example.

The saying, "We cannot solve our energy problems, unless we move into nuclear power generation in a *big* way" became the refrain of many designers. But they approached the problem with the assumption that *centralized* production and distribution of energy was required to meet continuing increases in consumption. Two important dimensions were overlooked: the possibilities for energy efficiency and conservation with appropriate changes in lifestyle, *and* decentralized, small-scale, one site generation of energy for cooling, heating, and production. Once designers stopped thinking in terms of large-scale, on-site generation, and rising consumption curves as future necessities, all sorts of alternative solutions suggested themselves. One of the reasons designers often do not see such alternatives is that they tend to suffer from the tunnel vision of specialized experts. For other reasons they tend to resist solutions that might alter current structural relationships and the economic status quo.

The processes and activities of innovation, which we describe as technological mastery and creation of technology practices, imply the possibility for self-mastery. Attaining a deep understanding of the laws of nature and the principles of ecology would enable us to avoid seeking control of nature to get power over other beings. Such a mastery would facilitate the self-discipline necessary to harmonize with natural communities. We could then give more of our own energy to realizing ourselves and our highest values without tyrannizing other humans or other beings. As we have seen in previous chapters, we now face the threat that human life will be dominated by technological necessities. The end of this domination lies *beyond* technology. It will be found through actualizing human potentials to master the whole technological process so as to *subordinate it to higher values* that transcend the present transient and ephemeral ones of industrial culture.

The design process that deals with whole technology practices honors ecology, respects all humanity, develops creative community and the self, and promotes communion with nature. In short, the design of whole technology practices will be conducive to the realization of ecosophy. Our overarching purpose would be to realize ourselves, a perfect human community, and achieve communion with nature. To develop ecosophic technology practices that facilitate these purposes is to realize *technosophia,* that is the wisdom to design and use technology practices in harmony with nature and spiritual values. We will say more about the criteria for *technosophic* technology practices in Chapter 11. Next we will consider the role of art, imagination, and the sacred in technological society, and why spiritual disciplines are needed for the wise design and use of technosophic technology practices.

Chapter 9

Art, Imagination, and Sacredness in Technological Society

I. Creative Imagination and Technological Innovation

Although we might not normally associate imagination with technology, we know that artists and novelists, calling on creative imagination, have often provided the conceptual and aesthetic inspiration for technological innovations. Jules Verne novels and Buck Rogers comic books are a striking example of fantasy preparing for reality. But what is this imagination that we all take for granted? Much philosophical literature has been devoted to defining it. Some see it as dealing with the unreal, a form of fantasy and play. Others, more pragmatic, consider that objects of imagination are drawn from ordinary experience, and that the imaginative process is one of merely rearranging familiar images and ideas. Still others, closer to the definition we will work with, see imagination as a significant capacity necessary for human freedom and creativity.

Let us see how one modern philosopher illuminates the faculty of imagination in his analysis of mental functions. Kant (1963) shows that imagination is central to the development of human self-conscious awareness. This form of awareness depends upon a complex process of conceptualization, that in turn involves an interaction between reason, sense perception, and imagination. As he pointed out, our raw sense experience *appears* to be a fragmented series of perceptions lacking unity and continuity. However, imagination and reason provide this vital continuity by enabling us to recall past experiences, identify them as our own, and re-identify them in the future. Without imagination, we would be aware of successions of sensations through time, but would not be aware of them as being ours. In short, we would not be self-aware. We would not be able to imagine ourselves in other settings or to project our intentions and plans into the future. Far from being the faculty of unreal fantasy, then, imagination is an important function of consciousness, necessary for self-conscious, rational life. It is deeply involved in the actual *constitution* of our sense of a coherent self, identifiable through time. Without it we would not be able to project ourselves (as constituted) through time. Language enables us to conceptualize ("He's John", "I'm Alan", and so forth), but without imagination we would not be able to *visualize*. Modern technological society tries to control the flow of images by manufacturing experience. But this whole process presupposes the imagination of some human person. Control a person's imagination and you control that person.

We can see from this analysis how important and necessary imagination is to the innovation and design of new technology practices. Without the capacity to envisage how things might be different, or what it would be like to be in entirely different settings, or to accomplish things now beyond our capacities, it is difficult to see how we would ever progress beyond our present stage of development, except as a result of changes forced on us from the outside. If other beings, in contrast to humans, do not act upon their world to change it in radically different ways, part of the reason must be that they have not developed a capacity for focused imagination.

But here we need to go beyond philosophical speculation and look more deeply at this important faculty. Our experience tells us that imagination is a two-edged sword. This same faculty that enables us to create, also enables us to destroy. The same capacity that enables us to imagine Utopia and a future paradise, also enables us to imagine future hells and new forms of torment. An active imagination that is negative and self-involving can produce paranoia, if we fail to understand how we can project our hidden, shadowy, "dark" side.

In many cultures the source of all power for both creation and destruction is regarded as the realm of the sacred. In Hindu mythology, for example, many gods are shown as having at least two faces, one destructive, the other creative. This connection is also found in the Garden of Eden story: If we have knowledge to become like God, we will have the power to create and destroy; and with this power goes *moral responsibility*. Creative imagination, as we define it, participates in this quality of the sacred. Thus, it is a power that must be used with care to follow strict moral guidelines. To alter our technology practices in revolutionary ways so as to create a new order, is to destroy an old one. Insofar as we vest our sense of worth and belonging in an existing order, we gain our security there, and so we see threats to the old order as threats to our own existence. Technological innovation, then, can be both attractive *and* threatening. Hence, resisting such change can be seen as a form of self-defense. At the same time, our secular culture does not recognize the sacred, self-transforming power of truly creative activity. As a result, technological innovation continues without spiritual constraints. The resulting loss of values causes profound personal and social problems.

The awesome transformative power of creative imagination should place the activity of design in the circle of the sacred. This would in turn require a show of respect appropriate to the extent of the power involved. With such an awareness, designers would purify themselves before taking part in the process of design. To undertake serious design activity without such purification would involve high risks to themselves and others. They could cause a host of ills by unleashing powers they are not able to guide. For example, research in genetics, which is fascinating and challenging to scientists, is fraught with danger when applied to genetic engineering of humans and animals. Innovation in the service of profit often ignores the downside, seeing only the imagined benefits. The more power involved in an activity, the greater the responsibility one assumes in participating in it. This is one of the reasons why those teaching martial arts (Budo) techniques emphasize the ethics of respect from the outset. The techniques of Budo are extremely powerful, not only physically, but also mentally and spiritually. A student who does not internalize correct values while acquiring this power can harm him or herself and others by acquiring technical power, without the corresponding increase in responsibility and a sense of appropriate and respectful action. The same should apply to all techniques involving power.

When undertaking the design and development of new technologies, our society has no comparable spiritual discipline with the necessary ethical dimensions. But clearly, given our cultural crisis, we do need one. As it is, we train people in specialized technical fields with no attention to spiritual dimensions, and with scant attention to the ethical requirements such power, skills, and knowledge demand. Current training fails to educate the whole person. As a result, we have people with powerful knowledge and skills who sell their services to the highest bidder, with no concern for their responsibilities to the community, to society, or to the natural world. This incomplete training and education also results in the design, development and use of technology practices that are *destructive* of most values, such as human health, freedom, community, and culture. These destructive technology practices are inequitable and give unwarranted power, control, and wealth to a few, wealth often taken from future generations through government programs. In addition, many of these same technology practices destroy the ecological integrity of soils, forests, watersheds, hydrological cycles, the atmosphere, and oceans.

Their impact upon the natural world and their cost, in terms of all values, to present and future generations are enormous. So we see that applying imagination to technological development that truly serves humans and the natural world requires binding to the sacred.

II. Art and Technology

Let us look more closely at the role that art and imagination play in technological development. Engineers, scientists, designers, and various craftspersons make essential contributions to the development of technologies. Artists include painters, graphic designers, poets, musicians, writers, and filmmakers. They have a profound influence on our culture's values and imagination, and the way technologies are developed, marketed, and viewed by the public. Clearly, engineers and designers have deep moral and spiritual responsibility for the kinds of technology they produce and the uses to which these technologies are put. However, the complexity of modern society presents obstacles to connecting the conception with the application of technological development. The intellectual and physical division of labor, the fragmentation of knowledge, and the highly specialized functions workers play can make it difficult for those who take their moral responsibility seriously to control the results of their work, and the way their creations are used. Scientists might dedicate their energies to the production of genetically engineered new species of bacteria and fungi, but lack the competence and knowledge to predict and control the effects of these new species when they are released into an ecosystem. To give another example, scientists can apply their genius and technological skill, in an isolated way, to the design and production of chemical pesticides derived from nerve gases. However, these same scientists are unlikely to realize the devastating effects such products can have on the environment—partly because they have no ultimate control over how their discoveries are used. These are some of the structural obstacles to personal responsibility.

Some believe, however, that the current misuse of our technological power is not the result of structural flaws but of human depravity, greed, selfishness, avarice, and sin. They attribute this depravity and lack of responsibility to our having turned our backs on the Creator. Or, religion aside, others conclude that the technicians and scientists who work to develop new *destructive* technologies know very well what they are doing. They are seen as cynical people who just do not care about the consequences of what they do. The agribusiness moguls, for example, know full well that current practices are undermining the fertility of the soil and that the food produced is contaminated with chemicals that can cause cancer, but they simply do not care, since they are after short-term profits, and believe they and their families will not be negatively affected. The forest products industry executives and many of the industry workers know full well that they are destroying the forest ecosystems to derive short-term profits, but they do not care, so long as they enjoy their current largess at the expense of the public. Perhaps many in power *are* cynical. There are people who take advantage of the system to line their own pockets and increase their own power. However, such greed and cynicism have a source; they are not part of our original nature.

Confucius observed many centuries ago that the leaders of a society must set an example of propriety and proper conduct, and believed they were capable of doing so. He believed that if they, above all others, did not adhere to the highest ethical and spiritual values, the whole society would be plagued by confusion and corruption, since all look to the leaders as examples of what is best in a society. Because of their position, we look up to our leaders and emulate them, just as children imitate their parents. This imitation itself involves a certain visionary power. However, once corruption is present at the top, it tends to spread throughout the system. This makes even more difficult the attempts of artists, scientists and others to act with the moral and spiritual responsibility appropriate to the power of creative technological innovation.

One of the most pervasive technological developments in our society is television. It is instructive to analyze how art, technology, and imagination have all contributed to creating this medium, which has had such profound influence in changing our culture. Before and during the Second World War, the main forms of public information were radio, newspapers, and film. Few people went to a movie more than once a week. Radio and newspapers were the daily sources of information and entertainment. All three of these media followed logically from the older oral tradition. Radio drama was built around a text, but listeners were free to use their imaginations to fill in the visual and other details. But TV gradually shifted away from the oral tradition, working more with visual images. Today it leaves almost nothing to the imagination. It has become part of a cultivated atmosphere of manufactured "experience".

As television developed over the last 50 years, it has had its share of critics and analysts. Marshall McLuhan (1964) was one of the first to note how this new form of communication creates a *new* context, with his now famous phrase, "The medium is the message." In other words, the impact of TV is more the result of its nature *as a medium* than its content. Jerry Mander (1978) claimed that TV, regardless of its content, is detrimental to the human values necessary for community and freedom. Still others have held that neither the form nor the nature of the medium matters, only its content. They said TV is a powerful but neutral medium which, if used properly, can be a positive force in our society.

These opinions make clear that TV *is* a powerful medium. If we consider just its content, we can see that it is a very effective tool for shaping and influencing our attitudes, often subtly, through associations and images. It conditions our imaginations. Further advances in the technology are bringing us closer to actually manufacturing "experience". By controlling imagination a medium becomes an unacknowledged means to control us through controlling our visionary capacities.

Let us examine this process in more detail. Engineers and scientists give us the power to create mass media. Skilled workers enable us to build the hardware. Businessmen provide the marketing skills to sell and distribute these products. The creative artists and artistic technicians shape the form, content, and themes of media, that feed our cultural appetite with a diet of images and ideas. Looking at the content and nature of the messages in programming and ads, Phillip Fandozzi (1979) wrote: "Art in a technological society easily succumbs to this process, i.e., it tends to serve a function (relaxation, entertainment, therapy) and artistic labor becomes mere personal expression."

Art, in this context, is no longer considered a sacred pursuit, a way of knowing, a way to unification of the human person, and a way to discover the true nature of the world. On the contrary, in industrial technological society, as reflected in its media, art is a mere function, an instrument, a way of making things more palatable or pretty; it is just technique used for entertainment or perhaps for therapy. It has no intrinsic value. The main reason we invest money in art is that it serves these marketable functions. As we have seen with the example of TV, art and imagination play a major role in technological development and use. The technology itself complicates our capacity to decide whether this role serves our highest purposes. But what are these "higher" purposes, and are they revealed by the media themselves?

III. Shifting Consciousness

The latest imaginative collaboration of artist and technician is in creating the experience of "virtual reality". Computer software programs allow users to create and experience various forms of reality "from a human to a lobster to a comet to a robot capable of disposing of hazardous waste." Essential to the conception and design of these systems is imagination. But the systems themselves control and depress our imaginations. If we surrender our imaginations to the media we surrender ourselves. What we value and respect is in part related to our capacity to extend our sense of self, to expand our circle of concern. This process is in part a function of imagination and the ability to shift our modes of consciousness.

As William James (1902) remarked, all around us are other forms of consciousness separated from our ordinary awareness by the flimsiest of screens. Learning how to shift consciousness from one state to another enables us to control and alter at will the *character* and *quality* of our experience. We can, with certain kinds of training, project ourselves into other "realities". This is something that Viktor Frankl learned, when he was in a concentration camp in World War II.

Frankl (1959) was a physician and psychiatrist, trained in orthodox medicine and Freudian psychology. In his book *Man's Search for Meaning* he explains how he came to question the models of human consciousness he had previously accepted. During his long reflections in prison he saw that Freudian psychology does not go deep enough. Uncovering and dealing with repressed conflicts can still leave a person feeling that life is unsatisfactory, even though one's health and general situation are excellent. Frankl found, in the prison camp, where conditions were appalling, that some people (including himself) were able to transcend their misery and find joy in seeing a sunset, for example. These experiences led him, after the war, to develop a whole new approach to psychotherapy, which he called *logotherapy*. This therapy is, in simple terms, a way to help people find *meaning* in their lives. The basic problems and questions of human life, Frankl saw, are not solved after we have overcome our psychological problems and our problems of security and success. Even if we develop a well-integrated personal self, we still long to transcend this self to find meaning. Here we have referred to this larger meaning as embracing the transpersonal dimension. Meaningful experience is not what happens to us, but *what we do with* what happens to us, as William James observed.

The archetypal story of Buddha's life supports Frankl's theory. Siddhartha (who became Buddha) was raised in the best of circumstances, with love, wealth, and position. Despite this abundance he felt something lacking in his life. This dissatisfaction led him to set out on a journey in search for understanding. He eventually received enlightenment under the Bo tree and thereafter was called Buddha, meaning one who is awake. The story of Siddhartha becoming Buddha is archetypal in that it symbolizes what each of us must do to realize and complete ourselves fully.

Another psychologist whose work supports Frankl's idea that we discover and construct meaning is Stanislav Grof (1976). As a result of his experiments with LSD, he concluded that traditional Western models of human consciousness are incomplete. They do not illuminate the "altered states of consciousness" he observed in his patients. Moreover, he and other researchers found that there are other, nonchemical ways of revealing the same structures of consciousness, other ways of visiting alternative "realities", such as yoga, meditation, and breathing techniques. Grof's findings support the general theses of transpersonal psychology and the studies in the ecology of consciousness that gave rise to *transpersonal ecology*. The model of human consciousness that emerges is a holistic one. It reveals the intimate interconnections between human imagination and consciousness, and all other conscious beings. The work of Grof and others suggests that human consciousness is not unique. Its depths are revealed by the capacity to re-experience our entire evolutionary history as well as to identify with other life forms.

Many alternative ways of accessing and altering our normal modes of awareness were developed by the meditation traditions of Eastern cultures, mainly those of India, Tibet, China, and Japan, although elements of some indigenous practices, such as Shamanism, have often been interwoven with them. They are found, too, in some forms of Western mysticism. These methods are increasingly being used in the West, and there is a growing participation in Shamanism. Of special interest, in our technological age, is the revival by Michael Harner (1986) of older shamanic practices for psychic journeying and exploring consciousness. He calls this contemporary revival *Core Shamanism*. Many native peoples in North America have kept their shamanic practices alive, despite attempts by the dominant industrial culture to suppress them. Through the use of imaginative projection, chanting, drumming, rhythmic breathing, meditation, marathon walking, sweat lodges, rituals, ceremony, and other forms of discipline, humans are able to experience the multifaceted, multidimensional character of consciousness in the world.

When we consider the foregoing ways of accessing other levels of awareness, it is clear that technological society can only *seem* to appreciate the inherent capacities of the human person and the multidimensional nature of the world, *if* technological humans get access to these through *technical* means, that is, through chemicals or through the technological aids of software and hardware. Just as our sense of reality is conditioned by the technostructure with which we have surrounded ourselves, so our escape from this structure *seems* to come by way of pushing the technology itself to its limits, where it then opens to "virtual reality", then perhaps the multifaceted nature of reality itself. However, the technological aids themselves are just a product of the power of an imagination that reaches far beyond *ordinary* consciousness. This is the imagination that William Blake said could open the doors of perception to the infinity in a grain of sand, and the eternity in an hour.

Let us consider how human imagination transcends technology. Humans can now, through interactive "virtual reality" programs, experience "being a tree". However, this is not the only way to access other levels of awareness. For eons humans have been able to do this without technology. Most important: this ability is *required for the existence of technology*. History depends on the words and images that came before technology. Language and imagination are inherent in us as beings capable of moral and spiritual development. Technology depends upon self-reflective awareness.

The source of awareness is the source of creation and destruction of our experienced world. In nonsecular cultures this source is the creator—of the same stuff as the Great Spirit. But modern technological society conceals from us (its users and creators) our own open, flowing, *spontaneous nature*. It takes control of cognition and visualization, reason and imagination. It tries to give us one story, but reality includes manifold stories and also no-stories. We must discover this for ourselves. This is knowledge of the *sacred transformative power*. Let us consider an example of this power as used in ceremony.

Some years ago I attended a workshop, led by Michael Harner, in the use of shamanic journeying to connect with the spirits of nature. In one of the exercises we sat with a tree of our choice. We could study it, hug it, try to identify with it. After some time, we all returned to a drumming circle and were instructed to close our eyes, be our tree, and stand together as a forest. Three drummers began to circle around through the "trees". We experienced ourselves as a forest community, and we felt as trees, rooted to the ground, swaying in the wind. The drums sounded like wind, then rain and thunder, then a river. We could hear birds, feel the sun and then the darkness. Then the journey leader said, "Here come the chainsaws!" The drums changed tempo, taking on a frightening, whining sound. A collective fear swept through the "forest". Trees began to weep and fall. We were all deeply shaken and profoundly moved by this exercise. The setting and aids were a darkened room, three drums with beaters, and drummers skilled in the art of shamanic drumming. This was not the "virtual reality" produced by technological means. It was not playacting or pretending. It was more like a trance or lucid dreaming, in contrast to our usual vague, confused dreams, which often have no sense of reality.

What we experienced could be described as moving into a state of transbiotic or transpersonal awareness through the power of imagination for creative visualization, and the capacity to extend and alter our identifications. Practices such as these from the Shamanic tradition, and similar ones from Eastern meditation traditions, can take us back to our whole Self, our larger ecological Self. This in turn can help us to attain an enlarged sense of meaning and connection in our lives, beyond ego self. This is what Frankl described; it is also part of enlightenment as attained by Buddha.

IV. A Fundamental Question of Technology

Given the power of our imagination and the largely untapped resources we have for experiencing other forms of awareness, we might ask a major "question of technology". That is, to what extent does dependence on its instruments enslave and conceal from us our own essential meditative nature? Heidegger (1977) claimed this is its greatest danger. The ever present popular media feed our imaginations with an impoverished diet of images and incitements, and the technostructure isolates us from nature and other beings. Our means of getting, spending, and consuming, with their attendant industrialization of life, reduce wild and free beings to components in a factory production system. We also come to be like the battery chickens of industrial agriculture. In such conditions as these there is no hint of the divine or of possibilities for self-transcendence. The imagination becomes imprisoned, and with its externally imposed control, we ourselves become trapped. Our own activities and technological entanglements conceal holistic consciousness from us by keeping us so busy that we neglect sitting contemplatively, hence forget how to meditate, how to pray, and how to just be.

Technology catches us in *calculative* thought and prevents us from realizing the home and completion we seek. Achieving this completion would end our restless searching and the compensatory use we make of artificial powers to control ourselves and the world around us. However, perhaps we had to lose ourselves in the technological pursuit, in the quest for the magic wand, for the ring, in the search for the secret formula, so that we could find *ourselves* in the process. For sooner or later we realize that the search for "power-over" is an endless treadmill. No matter how powerful we become we will never sate our hunger and quench our thirst, for this hunger and thirst are not for power but for self-realization and fulfillment through compassion and wisdom. This can be attained only if we sacrifice our craving for power, having seen through its allurements and recognized its limitations. When we realize our original nature, when we realize our kinship with all beings, when we give up power for love, we come home to an acceptance of the human condition as it truly is.

Here we are in the sacred realm, the ground of the holy, the kingdom of spirit. To say that humans are spiritual beings is not to claim that we are disembodied, ethereal wisps, but that we are embodied beings who can only find a sense of meaning in this world through following a spiritual Way that sanctifies and perfects our relationships with all beings. This meaning is not found in possessions, power, fame, in satisfying curiosity, in glamor, in thrills, in addictions, but in learning to love unconditionally, and from this love to understand and then to serve and help other humans and other beings. This means being in harmony with nature and the cosmos.

The concealment of our essential spiritual nature by technological pursuits and the technostructure (which also conceals wild nature) is not a new problem. It goes back to the foundations of modern society. When metaphors are appropriated and their creative use controlled, depth is concealed. For example, the literalized metaphors of the machine left the spiritual dimensions out of modern Western science and philosophy; in the same way, the earlier literalization of the metaphors of spiritual teachings by religious institutions reduced such teachings to mere shells of their deeper meanings. The process of literalization in religious interpretation came before and laid the foundation for the literalization of metaphor in philosophy and science. Modern society technologizes the word and manufactures experience, banishes the wild and free, tries to eliminate depth and in the process hides the human Self.

Humans, and all other beings, have the need, desire, and drive to realize and complete themselves, to fulfil their destiny. This need is expressed in our restless search for something that will give meaning and genuine satisfaction. It is found in our explorations of space and the Earth. It is evident in our attempts to alter our consciousness and to discover and create new things. When this core need is frustrated and we are unaware of it, we seek compensatory gratifications. But nothing short of ultimate realization will satisfy our desire for completion. But more than *finding* a good place (ecotopia) we want to *create* a good place through imagination (utopia). What we actively imagine we also create in terms of an experienced world. This is a key to the transformative power concealed in the Self and alluded to in sacred teachings. It is this that modern technology subverts, monopolizes, and takes over. *It tries to control story making*—a primal creative power.

The longing for lasting bliss, unconditional love, and permanence which we all experience, could be a longing for what we missed in childhood. However, it is also a longing for realization of our divine nature. The Greeks, Plato in particular, recognized that our desire to be powerful and immortal is, in fact, a desire for the divine. We desire the Kingdom of Heaven, but we do not find it in ephemeral satisfactions. Thus, we project it upon a fantasy world, something beyond this life, beyond this world, beyond this universe, not of *this* reality! But this world *is* reality. Once the spiritual becomes separated from embodied life, it is first an imaginary vision and then becomes an abstract idea. It rides concealed in the modern idea of progress. But the stories of the great spiritual traditions have depth. They teach that the Kingdom of Heaven lies within our now ongoing embodied life. In Buddhist language, "Nirvana is Samsara"; in Christian sayings, "The Kingdom of Heaven is within."

In Hindu traditions, as we have already noted, humans are perceived as layered beings. The key to understanding the stages and the ultimate completion of human development lies in analyzing the nature of our basic desires. We desire to avoid pain and pursue pleasure. We desire to survive and to grow. We desire to be loved. We desire to be accepted by others. We desire to stand on our own and to make a success in the world, to have power, to achieve something. But beyond that, when we have matured and completed ourselves in these ways, we feel something is lacking and we work to be of service to others. Even as we serve we become aware of the desire for liberation or *ultimate transformation*. This liberation is the last stage of individual human development. The realization of this liberation (or *moksha*) is characterized by *satchitananda*. "Sat-chit-ananda" is unconditioned being, wisdom, and bliss. To realize satchitananda, for the Hindu, is to complete our mission in life. Here nothing is hidden. The insights of Frankl and Grof, the examples of Christ and Buddha, and the Hindu explanation of life, make it apparent that we can *know* what our goal in life is in the context of a larger sense of meaning.

The priests, in the old societies, held the keys and knew the means to higher realization and ultimate transformation. The means to higher realization are difficult to follow and cultivate. They are sources of power that have to be learned in a gradual fashion, just as learning a martial art is a gradual process. The body has to be gradually strengthened, the mind disciplined, the spirit unified, the proper ethics and respect internalized. The teacher cannot give the beginning student the most advanced teachings. The students must discover bliss and satchitananda for themselves, by means of their own effort—no servant, technological animal, or human can do it for them. "Follow your bliss," said Joseph Campbell.

For various political and military purposes one can restrict access to bliss, for example in surrounding sexual intercourse with guilt, so that through a certain kind of conditioning people will be divided within themselves about their own most fundamental drives for bliss. If the frustration and repression are too strong, individuals become self-destructive. Or perhaps the repressive shadow falls not upon oneself, but upon some other external "enemy" or scapegoat. Racism, sexism, and ethnocentrism are typical results. They destroy our bliss and nature's! The attempt to turn consumers of "illicit" drugs into pariahs is a way to divert attention from more serious problems requiring changes in technology, stories, social practices, and economic realities.

But in a society that has lost contact with the sacred in daily life, in which religion has been reduced to fairy tales, where spiritual disciplines are replaced by job-training, and in which frustrated needs are exploited to push commodities, it is not surprising that the technological imperative would seem to become a most pressing demand. Its simplicity gives it center stage. To embark upon the technological journey we are told, is to embark upon the "greatest adventure of all time". We seek a new Eldorado in the imagined utopian technostructure, and yet in our fiction, in *Star Trek*, for example, the vision of the technosphere becomes only a metal and plastic place, where the same immature conflicts are carried on. We become caught up in fantasies and material pursuits, when there is a world crying out for commitment, sacrifice, dedication, and meaningful work. We have within the power to solve our problems, to regreen our society and to release creative human energies for benign, ennobling actions and purposes. Yet we believe that the system and its structures enable us to act by changing the world and ourselves to conform to its shallow monocultures. Our freedom is shrunken because our imagination is impounded, imprisoned by the sheer number, variety, and direction of images generated by mass production, mass education, and the mass media. It is important to recognize that the supposed sense and autonomy of technology is a reflection of an imprisoned human imagination and ingenuity. Guided by one story it created, it perpetuates modern technology. Beyond the limits of the technological imperative lies the open freedom for self-realization and a transcendence whose realization changes our whole lives, our technology practices, and even our whole culture, to abide in ageless *ecosophy*.

V. *Spiritual Discipline and Faith*

We have assumed throughout this chapter that it is necessary to understand spiritual disciplines and practices. Spiritual practices contain elements of the divine or sacred, and give us ways to transform consciousness and unify the Self. We will explain now what we mean by spiritual disciplines in relation to the usual conceptions of religion and the self.

As explained earlier, the emergence of the modern Western worldview—which underpins scientific philosophy—led to the loss of psyche (see Berman 1981, Drengson 1989). The psyche, as defined in terms of soul or mind by Descartes and others, seemed eventually to relegate the thinking conscious being to the status of a "ghost in the machine" of the body. When the body came to be seen as a fully determined machine, attempts to explain human behavior shifted away from invoking creative free will to invoking deterministic physical and psychological principles and causes. Human wholeness vanished into fragments of the self.

Western art and literature mirrored a self shrunk to a tiny, hollow voice. Just as the natural world was desacralized, and its mysteries and powers ignored or hidden under mathematical formulas, so too the human Self was reduced to a minor and insignificant "self", tossed about on the winds of determinism, having no larger possibilities, no genuine creative freedom, no possibilities for transcendence and realization of a larger Self. In this sense, imagination was subordinated to a singular worldview, but that very view was itself created and sustained by imagination, a key to finding sacred power.

In Western religion the same patterns prevailed. We still had the wisdom texts, the recorded spiritual teachings of the master guides of the Way, but few understood them, and generally our culture did not glean from the texts the practices that are the means to ultimate transformation. Some Eastern religions did not suffer the same fate—their holy teachings retained their power. But in Western intellectual circles religion was explained away as primitivism, or in terms of its social functions (psychological, economic, ordering force, and so forth), or in terms of its phenomenology of experience.

If one reads the holy texts in a way that reveals the underlying processes of transformation implied by the sacred teachings, one cannot easily reduce religion to one or more empty categories (see, for example, Streng 1985). The stories become simply fairy tales without this depth. In the absence of authentic spiritual teachings, modern humans lack significant personal power to transform their lives. As a result, as we have seen, they look elsewhere for their bliss, to external sources of personal power, to politics, fame, wealth, technological power, thrills, and pleasures, all of which are dependencies. They are not the realization we seek.

This failure to recognize the inner or esoteric meanings of sacred teachings as revealed in some of the holy scriptures is understandable when we consider the standard analyses of religious language as including only *three* functions: *descriptive*, *performative*, and *emotive* (see Hick 1983). The descriptive function of language is used for such purposes as characterizing experiences, giving an account of rituals, or recounting religious history. In its performative function, language is used to accomplish an action which it also announces or reports, as in a wedding ceremony when the priest says, "I now pronounce you husband and wife." The emotive function of language is to evoke and express intense or subtle feelings, as, for example, with symbols and liturgy in ceremony. However, these three functions do not exhaust the field. Another most significant use of language in spiritual traditions is the *transformative function*. Here language is used as a means to facilitate transformation of consciousness. It helps us to transcend the usual limits of language and concepts and our attachment to them. The transformative function is illustrated by the use of language in mantras and chants where the repetition and quality of the sounds alter awareness and put us in a meditative state. Zen koans are another example of such transformative devices. Imagination is crucial to all of these functions.

This analysis of religious language needs to be supplemented by considering the four major elements of religion as described by Streng (1985):

- religious phenomena,
- religious personalities and activities,
- religious doctrines about human nature and the world,
- spiritual practices of ultimate transformation.

This network of elements taken together reminds us that *authentic* religion always includes a transformative spiritual practice. Recognizing this enables us to illuminate the nature of faith. Faith is not *just* propositional assent or unfounded belief in dogma. It is not just ultimate concern, or merely devotional feelings. It is not just having a certain experience such as mystical ecstasy. It is not just *willing* to believe that we can attain salvation.

It is commonly acknowledged that faith embraces the first three categories of elements listed. However, its essence lies in the fourth category, spiritual practices that bring about ultimate transformation. These practices are esoteric and often identified with mysticism. In reality the mystic does not take occult flights *from* reality, but through spiritual practices, becomes more grounded or centered *in reality*. A mystic, in a spiritual tradition, is a person who devotes his or her *total* energies to practicing disciplines of ultimate transformation. These practices are enlarging and open our hearts as embodied beings within a larger world of sacredness. Practicing these disciplines purifies us of ego-oriented control. They open our whole being to the ennobling completion of our spiritual mission here on Earth.

Mysticism is not a technology of consciousness. It is a living, creative practice, the concrete realization of philosophy in daily life. Authentic practice brings forth the Kingdom of Heaven (full-bliss-consciousness), which is already at hand within us. The practice of spiritual disciplines authenticates the Way that leads to or realizes the Christ or Buddha (consciousness) right in this very daily life. Mystics in this sense are not tuned out of daily life, but fully and wholly present to and in daily life, honoring and serving all their relationships to the highest degree. They fully experience and totally live their human lives, realizing their highest potentials.

VI. *Transformation and the Way*

Both Buddhism and Christianity are authenticated as spiritual Ways by the transformation of Siddhartha and Jesus from historical, limited selves to fully conscious, transpersonal, transhistorical beings (Buddha and Christ). Given this completion Jesus and Siddhartha could both say, as Christ or Buddha consciousness, "I am the Way, the Light and the Truth." They were living revelations of our own sacred, divine nature. They exemplified the Way that leads to the full realization of the human being. The Way is that which transforms the human person from fragmentation and discord to wholeness and cosmic harmony. As spiritual beings no one else can take up the Way for us. We each must take it up and come to realization through our own efforts. If we follow the teachings of Buddha and Christ, it is the daily practices that transform our ordinary human consciousness into its Buddha-Christ nature, making manifest all of its latent powers and possibilities. The personal becomes transpersonal. The conscious personal self expands to realize it is only part of a large transpersonal Self that identifies with all humanity, with all sentient beings, with all beings, and ultimately with all of creation. When one realizes this all creation is joyful.

When spiritual disciplines become corrupted to rules and used as means to gain power over others, whole systems of prohibitions are erected on what is considered the negative side of abstract logical dichotomies. There are then "bad guys". This separation leads *away* from unity of being to fragmentation, and to a hatred of that part of one's self that is negatively judged. It then becomes part of the subconscious shadow that is projected outward. Thus, Jesus asked in the Sermon on the Mount, "Why do you see the mote that is in your brother's eye, but fail to see the beam that is in your own?" And Buddha admonished, "Be a light unto yourselves."

The stories of both Buddha and Christ (and similar stories from other traditions) present in archetypal form the cycles of human development from the preconscious to the personally conscious and then to the fully conscious, complete and mature being who radiates compassion and healing power. This consciousness, in its perfection, has no shadows, has no enemies, loves all beings, feels no divisions, lacks nothing. This healing consciousness is holy, for it makes and is whole; it is our true (Buddha-Christ) nature. It is not something we need from outside ourselves. When we read the stories of Buddha and Christ, we are moved, for we feel there is something deep in them, something that touches our own core. We see ourselves reflected in them. But often we cannot identify why we sense their depth or what this depth is. One of the reasons is that our true nature is obscured by the busyness of current technological pursuits, which lead us to think that our destiny is to control evolution, create new forms of life, and manipulate humans through technological means. This thinking catches us up in calculative, linear, fleeting, historical mind awareness. It cuts us off from meditative, timeless, holistic consciousness.

The technological imperative we sense from the limited calculative perspective turns out to be the imperative of the insecure ego, with no opening to the spiritual. The ego tries to substitute technological power for the realization of authentic spiritual power through self-transformation.

Our destiny is not to be the controllers of life on planet Earth. Nor should we be its destroyers, as irresponsible producers and consumers. It is our duty to perfect ourselves so as to realize our highest form of awareness in daily life. Such a consciousness must certainly be one which is compassionate and wise. To live wisely and compassionately on Earth as self-conscious beings is to transcend our egoic tendency to strive for power over others. We can turn these same energies of control to the spiritual transformation of our own lives, so that we become ever more deeply and expansively aware. In this direction lies the source of freedom and creative power to transcend all *calculative* imperatives, including control by technology.

In the light of the observations made in this chapter let us note that the systematic application of techniques, hardware, and manufactured substances to alter consciousness, to experience "virtual reality", is usually in our culture in the service of egoic calculative thought. Such techniques do not constitute the practice of a spiritual discipline. They do not lead to ultimate transformation. Transformation is not merely an ephemeral alteration, but a process of change and development that expands awareness through the exercise of our spiritual and moral capacities. It releases us from the crippling effects of our egoic psychodramas. It enables us to cast light upon our shadow. Transformation is a process of making whole, thus it is a *holy* process, a process whereby we come at last to a realization of being at home in the cosmos. This coming home is ecstatically experienced as "satchitananda". It cannot be induced by technological tinkering. It requires spiritual work, consciously undertaken, for it involves a transformation of our mode of being. It completes our conscious evolution as humans. The human individual does not achieve fulfillment with physical maturation, or with completion of formal education, or with the assumption of a profession, or upon taking on family responsibilities, or with retirement from a profession, but only through the transformation of the fragmented personal self in the realization of full consciousness and transpersonal fulfillment. Mystical or visionary experiences, during which this larger world streams into our being with light and joy, are realizations of this deep transformative consciousness. They reveal that the transpersonal ecology of the self is embedded in the larger natural Self that is the kin to all beings. This transformed consciousness is open to every human who chooses to follow an authentic spiritual discipline.

To take up an authentic form of spiritual discipline is to follow a sacred Way, the holy life, a Divine Way with heart. On this path, by fulfilling our desires and needs and perfecting ourselves as spiritual-moral-psycho-physical beings, we actualize the compassion and wisdom to which this life here and now is open. To lose track of the Way, or not to know of the Way, is to be condemned to wander aimlessly in dreams and illusions. It is to live without direction in a personal universe that lacks meaning, rather than in a cosmos filled with meaning, harmony, and light. The cessation of what Buddha called "dukkha", that is, the unsatisfied, incomplete life of hunger and craving, is realized through practice of an authentic spiritual discipline or Way that puts one in harmony with nature. We will say more about the Way later.

Chapter 10

A Redefinition of Progress in the Practice of Technology

I. A Quantitative Concept of Progress

We have seen how, in the Age of Technology, we can be seduced by the technological imperative to feel that we have no control over the techno-logical "beast" we have created. Another idea that can bewitch us is that of "progress". Progress is highly revered in our society. It is akin to heresy to oppose it. Let us examine this idea in more detail in the light of our earlier discussions. We will redefine "progress" by features that are nor-mative and qualitative, and not just quantitative. Let us first consider an example of a quantitative concept of progress.

Many years ago I managed a men's clothing department in a store that was part of a large retail chain. The store I worked in had several departments, most dealing in dry goods—a shoe department, a women's clothing department, a jewellery and notions department, a housewares department. Each department had its own head, and in some cases had several employees in addition to the department head. The store had an assistant manager and a manager.

Each Saturday, before opening time, the sales staff and managers gathered to discuss the last week's business, the specials for the weekend, and the prospects for the next week. The manager always told us what the gross sales had been the year before for the same week about to end, and what they had to be this year, so as to realize a gain of 10%. The management of the store and the chain as a whole, used increasing gross sales as a primary measure of progress. A salesperson's commission, that was over and above a set salary, was based on reaching a quota calculated on past gross sales for that department. As gross sales increased, the quota was adjusted upward. Those who had been heavy "producers" in the past (mostly women) set a standard for themselves that they had to exceed, if they were to get the same total commission. By manipulating the quotas in this way, management supposedly provided us with an incentive to "do better, to excel, and to improve".

At our Saturday meetings the manager gave us a pep talk, somewhat like those given by coaches in locker rooms before football games or during a halftime break. The subject of the discussion was mostly on how to "move" (that is, sell) the merchandise we stocked. The aim was to sell as much as possible to every customer, or at least to sell something to everyone who walked through the front doors.

Here is an example of a system using gauges and rewards as an easily quantified means for measuring performance. There was no mention in these measures of such things as customer service, or satisfaction, or human contact and cooperation among staff members. There was no mention of ways to improve the quality of goods sold, and no discussion of prices to the customer in relation to those of other outlets, and certainly no discussions of ecological responsibility. The main goal of the employees, managers, and workers was increasing the gross sales over the amounts for the year before, both personally and for the store as a whole. I should add here that within the chain individual stores were classified according to their location, so that our store was compared for purposes of evaluation to other stores of similar size in similar communities. Given that the aim of this business was to sell goods to make a profit, and that the stockholders and board members wanted to see increased sales, expansion of operations, and increase in market share, it seems reasonable that quantitative measures of "progress" would be the basis for judging the quality of employees and operation of the store as a whole.

Have businesses always thought of progress in terms of continuously increasing gross sales? Have Western humans always thought of progress as inevitable, driven by continuing developments of technology and expansions in speed and productivity? The answer, of course, is no. In the ancient West ideas about progress related to historical development were at best obscure. Some scholars of the philosophy of history say that the dominant outlook among Greek thinkers, and many other ancients as well, was to see the world in relation to a past golden age. Following the golden age everything was in decline. Plato gives this impression in his stories about Atlantis, in his account of the decline of the Greek landscape and forests, and of Greek character and leadership. When he describes the Utopian state in the *Republic*, he is usually interpreted as describing an ideal state, a perfect state of being, a condition exemplified by pure archetypal, nontemporal forms, which necessarily decline to imperfection when embodied in material earthly life. Although other interpretations of Plato exist, this is certainly the traditional one. Plato is seen as an example of an aristocrat who bemoaned the coming of democracy, for it brought on government by the lowest common denominator; it did not ennoble the lower classes, but de-nobled the gentry as they lost their power.

Our purpose here is not to examine interpretations of Plato, but only to cite a standard example of how the ancient world often saw history. The ancient view lacked the aspirations of progress that gradually began to emerge through Christian eschatology. In the early years of the Christian era, the life and teachings of Jesus looked toward the future and the promised second coming of Christ, which would start a millennium of paradise, the Kingdom of God on Earth. This second coming was not seen to depend on human actions. Jesus was no ordinary human, but God incarnate in human form. Thus, what Jesus did as Christ was not something that any mere human could aspire to do. There were many interpretations of this eschatological teaching of the Kingdom. One school taught that we must have faith in Christ, throw ourselves upon his mercy and hope for the best. Another taught that paradise would come when all humans accepted the teachings and became Christians, that is, followers of Christ. Yet another account saw Christ as a divine prophet who foretold the end of the depraved and evil earthly life. He said that the end is near and that the only way to prepare for it is to accept Him. Among early Christians, the latter two interpretations created a sense of urgency. Heeding the instruction of Jesus to go forth and preach, they worked hard to spread *The Word* as fast as possible.

With the conversion of Rome to Christianity, the Catholic church emerged as the dominant religious institution in Europe and reigned supreme throughout the Middle Ages. The orthodox teaching was that Christ would, "in the fullness of time," return to establish the earthly paradise. Another commonly accepted belief was that, while waiting, those who had faith, were baptized, and obeyed the teachings of the Church, would go to Heaven when they died.

Given these beliefs, there was little incentive to remake the world as given by God. The feudal patterns of life that developed in the Middle Ages, and the forms of political organization that went with them, were mirror images of the hierarchical order of the church. Kings and queens were expected to bow to the demands of the Vatican in religious matters. With the emergence of the modern worldview, however, Church authority in secular matters was questioned by Modernism. Church authority was further challenged by the schism of the Protestant Reformation. Especially in the early stages of this transition, only the orthodox, that is Roman Catholics, were allowed to own land in many areas. This had an interesting consequence in relation to technology. Protestants and adherents of other religious heterodoxies, prevented by discrimination from owning land, turned to commerce, manufacturing, and technological innovation. They became major contributors to the beginnings of the industrial revolution. Thus, excluded from an old order, they helped set the conditions for the new order that emerged with modern industrial society.

The emergence of the modern worldview, the rise of modern science, the weakening of church authority, the decline of feudalism, the increasing demand for skilled labor, the emergence of economies based on commerce and money: these and other forces undermined the old order and brought a new way of seeing the world. As the revolution in worldview and technology practices swept the West, grand visions of the future emerged. The eschatology of Christianity, as we saw in a previous chapter, was transmuted into Utopian visions of a future made secure and fine by human knowledge and power, gained through science and technology. The visions of both Bacon and Descartes assumed that we can learn the secrets of nature by means of science and mathematics, and having learned them, can make nature do our bidding. Since nature is a machine, a great clock made by a Divine Clockmaker who no longer intervenes, we can learn the principles that govern the clockwork and so make it run to satisfy our desires.

Since the churches had not totally lost their influence, religious reasons were often cited both in favor of pursuing this power over nature, and against such a pursuit. The schism in the church that gave rise to Protestantism also gave rise to a plethora of conflicting interpretations of the Bible. Some forms of Protestantism underwrote and embraced the new way to power as a fulfillment of human destiny, believing that God created the world for us to subdue and dominate. It is ours to use to satisfy our needs. They quoted Scripture to support their position. These interpretations ignored other Scriptures celebrating the glory of God's creation, urging us to be humble and respectful toward it. According to the latter, we can justify our use of nature only if we act as wise stewards. Here the word "steward" means one who cares for and looks after God's creation. The steward uses the land in trust from God, and undertakes to care for it as God wants, and not to alter it to suit human whims and desires. Eventually, modern industrial society's desacralization of nature undermined all such religious scruples and constraints. Even natural responses to the sufferings of other sentient beings were taken to be unscientific sentimentality without any rational basis. Schools and training institutions were caught up in the new religion of control over nature through technological progress.

With the ascent of the modern worldview, then, there emerged a conception of reality, of nature and humans that made it possible to think in terms of using concrete, technological means to make the world over in our own image. This conception was limited only by our own imaginations, without moral constraints or limitations, except where our actions might impinge adversely upon other human beings. This is a secular worldview. If progress is defined as increasing human power over the world through technology, and progress is realized when we have built a Utopian world of human design, then one might conclude that we have almost reached the limits of progress, for we have made great strides toward such a world. As we saw in the last chapter, this view of the self in the modern world shuts us out of the larger ecological world and conceals our own spiritual nature.

Much of the literature and art of the modern period reflects the sorrows and pains of the isolated, alienated, ego self, doomed in its limitations and mortality, with no way out of this predicament. This sense of alienation is a source of much existentialist philosophy. In addition, our compensatory pursuit of power over others and the world through technology has helped to create the serious crises we currently face. These crises are a loud echo of our original despair, the despair of being placeless without meaning. But perhaps because they are so threatening, the new crises have another significance, that many now recognize. They show us that we have been laboring under a culturally created worldview that is destructive, and needs to be replaced. This secular, mechanistic view of the world and its inhabitants has outlived its usefulness. We can now see that its limitations are a source of maladaptive practices that must be redesigned. Their redesign requires new values and paradigms.

II. Two Philosophies of Progress Applied to Agriculture

Let us now examine agriculture as representative of other technology practices in the West. We will use it to describe two different philosophies of progress and development. The first is the philosophy of *industrial agriculture*. It is a logical application of modern industrialism as we have described it. This philosophy measures progress in terms of farmer productivity, yield per acre, efficiency of distribution, commodity production, and market price. It ignores the actual costs of production in the form of hidden subsidies, loss of agricultural work and skills, degradation of the land, depopulation of the farm community, decline of the farm economy, and the negative effects of these factors on rural character and culture. This approach also ignores moral questions about animal factories and related issues of ecological responsibility.

The second philosophy, *ecological agriculture*, is based on natural patterns. Progress is measured by sustainability, continuity of the farm community and traditional values, long-term preservation and enhancement of soil fertility, economic integrity of farm communities, preservation of skills, and maintaining farm diversity. Agriculture is evaluated as a nutritional service as well as a biological process. Farming is both an art and a way of life. In ecoagriculture, participants choose low impact, appropriate technology practices and design new technology practices on the basis of ecocentric values. They take into account all values.

Industrial agriculture pushes a science-technology driven agricultural revolution. This reflects the narrow, short-term economic aims it uses to define progress and conservation. It also follows from its general philosophy of human domination of nature and the Earth. Ecoagriculture, in contrast, has an ecological perspective with a long-term outlook. Thus, crop diversity, natural minerals and fertilizers, and biological controls are favored over the dangerous, often persistent chemicals used in modern, technological-"scientific", petrochemical, factory farming. Ecoagriculture favors humane husbandry over animal factories. It measures progress in terms of flourishing farm communities, increasing quality of food, quality in personal character, and positive agrarian contributions to culture. It defines scientific progress in terms of increasing ecological understanding to enable farms to blend harmoniously with diverse natural communities.

Most of us know that we face extremely serious environmental problems, and that our survival in the long-term depends on ending the environmental destruction caused by industrial activity. We can find one source of these problems in the scientific-technological forms of production that drive modern industrial culture, and the compulsive pursuit of the new, expanding commodity production and consumption (technological and economic imperatives). In a world with declining margins of ecological safety, the environmental manifestations of these problems are acid rain, toxic wastes, the threat of nuclear annihilation, nuclear fallout and pollution from power plants, diseases and epidemics, habitat destruction, species extinction, ground and surface water pollution, air pollution, the greenhouse effect, loss of genetic richness, destruction of natural forests, erosion of topsoil, and depletion of the ozone layer.

The ideology of industrial philosophy does not see that these problems result from applying its basic values and methods to technology practices. It compounds the crises by attempting to solve them by the same measures and means that generated the problems in the first place. The results of this process can be seen in many areas, but almost nowhere more clearly than in agriculture. For example, petrochemicals used to control insect pests have become steadily more potent, and over the years have been applied with increasing frequency and in greater quantities, and yet the loss of crops to insects has remained constant, and in some cases has even risen. The result of such drastic measures is that food and land are polluted, with an associated deterioration of soils which contributes to further problems.

Since the introduction of industrial farming we have experienced a decline of rural communities and small farms, a degradation and erosion of topsoil, an accumulation of large amounts of farm debt, a near collapse of the rural economy, contamination of food, water, soil and air with biocides and carcinogens, a glut of some commodities and a lowering of nutritional values in our food. Increasing public subsidies and an increasingly vulnerable food supply are further consequences of this approach. The whole system of industrial agriculture is vulnerable to disruption, a condition that results directly from a philosophy of progress based on a non-ecological application of science and technology, one that ignores wisdom of place. Innovation, technical refinement, and quantitative economic values, are over-emphasized, while many of the traditional values central to survival are ignored.

The problems described above are associated with the rise of industrial culture's *ethos* that emphasizes mastery over nature, while promoting increasing levels of consumption of finite resources. A philosophy of "scientific management" (Taylorism), which is also part of this approach, has led to the disempowering of workers and deskilling of work (Cooley 1980), along with a declining influence of the middle class. Measuring progress by means of GNP (gross national product) tends to mask these negative factors. Calculations of the GNP include not only the obvious positive value of production, but also the economic exchanges required to counteract the negative effects of ecologically bad production.

The ethos described is easy to recognize, since the industrial paradigm of work, production, and efficiency has been applied to all sectors of society. In the process, the values of industrial philosophy have come to dominate politics and economic activity. There are even efforts in education to industrialize the mind and "factory-process" intellectual power. The search for ways to construct artificial "intelligence" and the extension of mechanical methods to reducing knowledge to information are part of this same process of applying monoculture to everything. It is a single-minded approach.

Industrial paradigms rest, as we have already pointed out, on the metaphor of the machine. They emphasize control and mastery, replaceable parts, artificial uniform time, mass production, mass education, and mass entertainment. The industrial mind pursues its specific goals by dividing production related activities into separate steps, and by constructing hierarchies of organizational control, ordered according to abstract principles that measure progress primarily in quantitative terms.

Our modern industrial ethos goes back to the philosophy of Descartes and other Moderns in its separation of mind from nature. The mind is not of nature; the body is only a machine; and the essence of mind and consciousness is calculative, productive thinking. One goal of such thinking is to discover principles and general laws that can be applied to the mastery of nature. No constraints need inhibit the application of the technological artifacts of scientific knowledge to nature, because it is devoid of intrinsic values. However, the religious beliefs that were the foundation of older, Northern European agricultural practices, had even more ancient roots than these philosophical ones. From these roots grew respect for the land and practices based on sustainable farming. In industrial culture this traditional wisdom is rejected as based on prescientific fancies and myths. It is replaced by an ideology of scientific-technological progress in which abstract, theoretical knowledge of general laws is favored. This ideology leads to the depopulation of the countryside, for it replaces old wisdom and practice with technique and machines.

The aim of science, in this philosophy, is to reduce everything to a comprehensive set of abstract, mechanical principles, stated as mathematical formulas. Applying such principles for purposes of analysis, calculation, division of labor, specialization, quantification and systematic methodologies is the work of a mindset blind to other forms of knowledge and values. The consequences of applying powerful technologies to personal competence are totally overlooked. To use a simple example, if humans become totally dependent on calculators, thereby losing their understanding of mathematical methods, they become disempowered and unskilled. When human skills are displaced by machines, work can become deskilled. The application of this logic to farming causes a loss of centuries of accumulated wisdom and ability based on sound agrarian traditions.

Good farming is an art, it is not merely the result of mechanically applying formulas and abstract knowledge. Wise farming practices are highly particularized with respect to the community and the land. However, modern theories fail to encompass all that humans have come to know *tacitly* through ancient traditions of farming practices built on place-specific wisdom. Ignorance can only be compensated for by embracing a larger art that relies on *tacit and intuitive* understanding, or a sensitivity to the land, plants, and animals. It also has large built-in margins of safety in the form of diversity, for example. Problems resulting from "scientific" farming are caused partly by a lack of sensitivity and intuitiveness. Another cause of problems is the lack of understanding of the whole context, a failure to employ a systems approach to understanding the ecological processes of specific places, including the land, culture, and character. It treats variables in an abstract mathematical way, but the lay of the land, yearly weather patterns, water cycles, rates of decay, the amount of humus in the soil, plant and animal variations, and the patterns of local culture comprise part of the total context to which sensitive farmers must respond. These factors cannot be adequately quantified or represented by means of equations and models. It is understandable that industrial farming misses the total picture, for it manipulates nature for the exclusive benefit of humans. *Anthropocentric* in nature, it is a result of three centuries of technological growth and optimism.

The integrity of rural culture is another important loss resulting from the industrialization of farming. Agricultural communities traditionally serve as vehicles through which accumulated values and sound farming practices are preserved and passed on from one generation to the next (Berry 1977). If recent trends continue, a small number of agribusiness factory farms will be controlled by an even smaller number of corporations. Many people think that this will result in a new form of corporate feudalism, with a tragic loss of rural culture. Certainly, "scientific" management has advantages for certain kinds of production, such as manufacturing steel and automobiles, and refining petroleum. But true wealth and long-term corporate success are found in personnel, work, service, products, and personal relationships. These support a sustainable culture. "Scientific" management depends on specialists; rather than being participatory, it strives for centralization and eschews local input; it attempts to exert market control, rather than cooperation; it creates lower skilled jobs, while increasing uniformity of production; and while it lowers direct production costs, it does not pay the high environmental and social ones.

Industrial agriculture employs mechanical systems as a means to control biological processes and all aspects of production, including workers, by fragmenting the production process into individual steps that can be measured and timed. It focuses on levels of productivity measured primarily as an output of units per acre and man-hour, thereby reducing all values to common monetary measures. Industrial agricultural practices, then, impose upon organic, biological, living processes, the values and market mechanisms of centralized control and mass production. According to the industrial paradigm, all productive processes can be "rationalized" or mechanized with a decreasing dependence on human labor, skill, and wisdom. However, recent experience has shown that large-scale farming is in serious trouble, and, in many cases, when total production costs are calculated, they often exceed the market value of the commodities produced.

Animal husbandry has been drastically affected by industrial farming. Selective breeding and genetic engineering have led to the development of docile hogs and cattle, that can be raised under controlled environmental conditions. Since economies of scale are essential to the industrial approach, large units are created. A hog factory might produce 350,000 hogs per year for market. Although a factory of this size may be inefficient and costly to operate, its inherent problems and costs can be ignored because tax shelters and incentives favor corporate, large-scale, industrial production. Under such conditions animals must be administered food supplements and antibiotics to keep them free of disease. Hogs, cattle, and chickens are also fed hormones and other chemicals to stimulate growth. But these practices create additional problems, such as antibiotic resistant strains of bacteria, and chemical residues in food, air, and water, that have increasingly negative impacts on human health. In view of these problems, the prospects of further genetic engineering of animals for economic gain, in the absence of ecological wisdom and moral sense, is fraught with risks and potential hazards. None of these hazards can be adequately assessed by industrial standards and conventional measures of progress. On the contrary, as we have seen, trying to deal with these problems in a "technical" way merely creates more problems. Thus, it should be clear that the short-term "efficiency" of this approach is no substitute for a sustainable, humane husbandry.

Industrial agriculture, which we have looked at in some detail, is part of a much larger industrial context. It is reported that about 90 percent of human cancers are probably caused by the environmental consequences of industrial activity. The natural forests of Western Europe and North America have virtually disappeared as a result of industrialism and its ecologically unsound forestry practices, that are based on the same methods as industrial agriculture. Fisheries, rangelands, wildlife, and watersheds, in addition to croplands, all exhibit increasing signs of damage caused to a large extent by industrial production and a consumer oriented society. It is apparent that the pressures resulting from conventional industrial practices on environmental integrity, human dignity, quality of work, distributive and procedural justice, and economic soundness and fairness, are beginning to facilitate a shift toward practices that will restore and sustain ecosystems and human health. Clearly industrial culture is up against the limits of its own paradigms and methods. It must be transformed into a new ecological culture or we will destroy ourselves and the ecological integrity of the Earth.

The quality and integrity of the natural and built environments must be included among the values by which to measure progress in our society. Destruction of the environment will ultimately lead to a declining culture. Quality of life depends upon healthy soil, water, air, and ecosystems and these can be maintained only through ecologically responsible agriculture, forestry, fishing, mining, and manufacturing. Industrial agribusiness cannot accomplish this. Its basic philosophy diminishes the quality and diversity of human communities and rural life, with their complex talents, skills, and self-sufficiency. Given all of its problems, we can see that the industrial approach must be changed. Ecoagriculture is a viable alternative by means of which to enter the Age of Ecology.

"Ecoagriculture" refers to farming based on ecologically sound practices. It is a generic term for a philosophy uniting and integrating the practices of organic farming, natural farming, sustainable agriculture, regenerative agriculture, permaculture, and agroecology. The principles of ecoagriculture are:

- that all things are interrelated,
- that practices must suit a place,
- that all costs and benefits must balance,
- that waste and by-products must be compatible with ecological processes,
- that nature knows best,
- that wise human action requires a balanced interdisciplinary, holistic, long-term approach.

A sound approach to farming requires recognizing that agriculture is both a biological and an ecological process. Given this, organic metaphors and field-process models are more appropriate and effective than the machine metaphors of industrial agriculture. Among other aims, ecoagriculture pursues mixed farming, smaller scale, and less specialized production. It plans for long-term sustainability and seeks to increase soil fertility and biodiversity.

Let us look briefly at each of the farming methods mentioned to see how diverse are the practices integrated by ecoagriculture. The natural farmer studies and imitates nature's processes for building soil, feeding the soil communities, and caring for water. Organic ecofarmers avoid the use of chemicals and fertilizers derived from petroleum, and seek to reduce pest problems by building up soil fertility, by planting strategies and similar biological techniques, such as using open pollinated crops. Sustainable agriculturalists practice cultivation that can be carried on indefinitely. They maintain healthy biotic communities by means of mixed planting strategies, and by employing perennials where possible. The regenerative approach to agriculture detoxifies and rebuilds soil health and fertility through natural, organic methods (such as composting), that increase biological activity and richness over time. Ecoagriculture philosophy moves beyond the linear, mechanical, industrial paradigm to ecologically based practices utilizing both older traditional farming techniques and contemporary ecological wisdom. The ideal ecofarmer is a community spirited but self-reliant, responsible steward who cares for the land, supports and respects rural tradition, and is receptive to new ideas.

It is undeniable that healthy agriculture is essential for a healthy populace and a sustainable culture. Health, technology use, and agricultural practices are interrelated. Knowing the ecology of each of these can assist us in pursuing *qualitative* progress, which eschews emphasis on technological power and increasing the GNP. Gross National Product (GNP) is a measure merely of production and consumption, not of *Greater National Quality* (GNQ). Sustainable and healthy nutrition is the result of sound, flexible practices based on an accumulation of experience and wisdom. Good farming practices reflect human dependence on the land, and respect for the diverse biological communities that exist with unique characteristics in specific places. Cultural diversity and biological diversity complement and support one another. But good farming practices do not exclude science and scientific knowledge. These can supplement the skills and knowledge of a craft that works with naturally developing patterns of the land. To ecofarmers the land represents more than a resource, object, or thing; it is a living ecological community to be cared for, respected, and understood. Together ecological philosophy and science can help to create this deeper understanding (ecological consciousness and sensibility) and new ecosophic farming technology practices. For the ecofarmer, nature has all of the answers; he or she learns from nature how to farm sustainably, not from abstract theories based on mechanistic models.

Having examined the philosophies and practices of both industrial and ecological agriculture, it is obvious that we cannot obtain a clear measure of progress unless we consider how the practices and values of our culture affect the environment and ourselves over long time periods— centuries. We need to look at the larger moral, aesthetic, cultural, and ecological dimensions of farm practices. In these areas industrial agriculture is clearly inferior to the best farming practices of the nineteenth century such as those currently used by the Old Order Amish (high farming), for example. The philosophy of ecoagriculture reintroduces some of these traditional values and practices and, in concert with appropriate technologies, blends the values of the older agrarian tradition with contemporary ecological understanding. Ecoagriculture revitalizes practices animated by a sense of community, practices characterized by a spirit of mutual aid. A rebirth of this spirit offers great potential for communities, and a secure future requires that we learn how to nurture this spirit.

It seems evident today that we can become either technologically sophisticated barbarian loners, or we can nurture persons, culture, and community life. Nothing is more basic to this end than the way in which people are fed—and housed. Hence, both farming *and* forestry need to be transformed by ecocentric values.

III. Need for an Ecological Philosophy

We have been looking in detail at agriculture to illustrate two different philosophies of progress and development. The reader can explore how the same considerations apply to forestry and other resource activities, since there are clear parallel developments and problems in the other productive sectors in our economy. Our conclusion is that it is critical to enlarge our conception of *progress* by placing science and technology subordinate to harmony with nature and the meaning and purpose of life. We must emphasize mature, whole persons in community rather than self-centered consumers and competitors. What value is automated, industrial production, if little opportunity exists for skilled, meaningful work? To chase thrills and ever higher levels of consumption, as an alternative, is to step onto a meaningless treadmill.

Choosing an ecological philosophy over an industrial one should not be taken as a condemnation of science. Ecological philosophy recognizes that science and technology policy and practices can be meaningfully redefined and assessed only within the larger cultural and environmental context of ecocentric values. Science can aid in this process of assessment. However, if we do not undertake a critical examination of the assumptions upon which conventional technology practices are based, "progress", defined as increasing technological power, will take on a force and life of its own. We should also emphasize here that science and philosophy as part of creative inquiry, do not belong exclusively to industrialism's narrow ideology of mechanism and its utilitarian values. A shift in paradigms is already underway in theoretical areas. Science and philosophy as open inquiry can help us to understand and assess the very ideological context in which they, as institutions, are embedded. As forms of open inquiry, science and philosophy are transideological. This is one important insight gained from the comparison of the two philosophies discussed here.

While individualist industrialism has given us much that is of value, its current level of power demands that we move away from anthropocentrism toward broader ecological, communal modes of thought, sensibility, perception, and action. We must reassess our current practices, for they are destroying our earthly home and scores of traditional community values we do not want to lose. When we examine the deeper assumptions about progress and development lying beneath the surface of our practices, we can see that genuine progress must embrace moral, spiritual, social, and ecosophic values. Such progress requires that we also embrace a larger, holistic philosophy based on creative, comparative inquiry, enlarged by ongoing spiritual disciplines. These disciplines must be appropriate to an Age of Ecosophy, both ecumenical and global, and yet applicable to the unique problems of each person, within the context of their particular place. Abstract theorizing can be used to support life, but by itself it can become a hollow, vain and even destructive pursuit.

In the next chapter we will consider the criteria that guide and define the design of appropriate technology practices. These criteria help to enlarge our idea of *technosophia*, which for us means not the wisdom of technique, but the wise design and application of technique in the creation of ecosophic technology practices.

Chapter 11

Ecosophic Technology Practices and the Art of Appropriate Design

I. Ecophilosophy and Conceptual Design

Ecophilosophy, as a branch of philosophy, is a creative activity, making use of comparative analysis as well as synthesis. Its purpose is to gain a wider and more comprehensive understanding and vision of human life and ultimate purposes. The aim of philosophy in general is wisdom — not just a large amount of knowledge or experience, but a reflective awareness of the human condition and human relationships with the Earth and nature. The aim of ecophilosophy is *ecosophy*, wise discipline of our own actions by living in harmony with nature so as not to damage the integrity of the Earth. In ancient Greece and China, traditional wisdom taught practices through which humans could attune themselves to nature and attain harmony. Humans were seen as ignorant and finite; nature as mysterious and infinitely powerful. It was believed that it is futile for humans to try to control the natural world, or even to drastically alter it. Modern industrialism teaches almost completely the reverse. But it is still folly to try to control nature, even though modern industrial philosophy accepts this control as a primary aim. It is obvious that our technological activities are having serious, detrimental impacts on the whole natural world.

Humans as cultural beings adapt to the world around them in many ways. As they mature, they become "enculturated", that is, adapted to the culture of which they are members, with its dominant worldview. This worldview clarifies their place in the culture, and gives them an understanding of how they are related to the natural world and to other human groups. When we look at philosophies, we can say they are adaptive if they are suitable, fit and appropriate to the situation of the humans involved. Adaptive philosophies facilitate living harmoniously. They are maladaptive if they prevent the culture from sustaining itself, or if they encourage conflicts with other groups, leading to wars that deplete the culture's resources. From our perspective we would also say they are maladaptive if they prevent human beings from realizing themselves in the ways we outlined earlier. We consider the criteria of adaptive success to be *flourishing* and *thriving*, not merely survival. In our culture, philosophy has become a self-conscious, critical, and creative activity that gives us the power to articulate the assumptions of our way of life, and evaluate these in relation to other philosophical possibilities, human potential, and the realities of nature. Philosophy, for us, is not limited to gaining a clear view of where we are *conceptually*, it also aims, through conceptual design, to develop practices better suited to our current situation as a culture and as humans.

Before we consider the philosophy of appropriate technology design in detail, let us clarify what we mean by philosophy as conceptual design. Concepts can be viewed as limits and boundaries to our experience and imagination; they can also help to give direction and form to creative action. They can be thought of as tools, and, like tools, can have a settled or conventional use, but they also have other possibilities. No rigid set of rules and principles governs conceptual distinctions. The philosophical description of the logic of concepts is an ongoing activity, since conceptual change is integral to evolving human thought and culture.

A conceptual system is more than a collection of individual symbols and words. Words and symbols belong in and get their meaning from a natural setting embedded in tradition and use, expressed in public language, within a form of life and culture. But the personal and interpersonal *depth* of words and symbols comes from their associations and from their allegoric, mythic, and metaphoric power. Specific concepts have their place within a given array of concepts in organizations of conceptual systems, ordered by means of models, dominant metaphors, and paradigms.

We can modify a concept within its context; we can change its relationship to its binding models; we can modify the models themselves. Concepts are always open-ended to a degree. We can realize greater freedom when we are able to disengage our thought from the hold of dominant models and paradigms. At a certain level of reflection the possibility of designing new models and paradigms emerges. Philosophy, in its most expansive form, is an activity that compares worldviews and is cross-cultural. This power of philosophy was clearly seen by Japanese philosopher Nishida Kitaro whose work is described as "[a] bridge between East and West precisely because he identifies himself with neither alleged perspective and sees more often than most that the work of philosophy is neither

Eastern nor Western, but takes as its material the overlapping insights of people anywhere in the world, and produces from that material a totality of thought transcending any particular cultural perspectives" (Carter 1989, 144). Through such comparative studies of worldviews philosophers learn the art of shifting paradigms and constructing thought experiments. They use different paradigm sets so as to distance themselves from their own identification with their inculcated culture-bound philosophy and personal philosophical assumptions. Philosophy practiced in this way is a transformative, creative activity.

For our purposes we have concentrated on critiquing the role played by the modern philosophy of Bacon and Descartes in influencing the development of technology practices in the West. The models and paradigms of machine and mechanism, derived from this philosophy, have been central to the process of industrialization, to the physics of Newton, to the market place, to modern science, engineering, the social sciences, and psychology. Translating the philosophy of the Machine Age into all aspects of Western culture stimulated innovation in all fields, but, as we indicated in previous chapters, we have finally reached the limits of this mechanistic philosophy. As early as the nineteenth century, there were signs in intellectual circles that this philosophy was beginning to break down, but the technology practices embedded in the dominant culture were slower to change. However, in recent years, technological development as a cultural activity has come under increasing criticism for a variety of reasons. The limits to technological development must now be the limits set by human freedom, dignity, and the ecological integrity of the Earth.

II. A Philosophy of Appropriate Technology

With the foregoing in mind let us now look more closely at the philosophy of appropriate technology. This philosophy had its origins in efforts to transfer "advanced" technology to developing countries. E.F. Schumacher (1973) and his associates in the United Kingdom started a firm they called the *Intermediate Technology Group*. Its purpose was to develop technologies that could be easily transferred to developing nations. After the Second World War, Western governments undertook projects to aid developing countries by transferring to them technology practices that were considered more advanced. These attempts at technology transfer often failed, for a variety of reasons (Goulet 1971, Norberg-Hodge 1991). Sometimes they turned out to be more beneficial to the "advanced" nations than to the countries they were intended to help. A large shoe factory, for example, brought in to replace small-scale cottage industries often employed fewer people (Schumacher 1973). Its products were often unsuitable for the local markets. It required raw materials and parts that had to be imported. The end result often was that a few had higher paying jobs, but many other people became unemployed as a result of the transfer. Or a technology might be introduced for which there existed no infrastructure for maintenance and repair. Or, certain medical technologies might be transferred that violated cultural taboos, hence would be resented, misused, or even rejected. Sometimes the effects of technology transfers were the opposite of those intended.

Reflecting on these problems of technology transfer, Schumacher and his associates concluded that the problems arose from the fact that the technologies were not designed to fit the specific cultural contexts. They saw that technology is not value-neutral, and it cannot be easily transferred to cultures with different histories, social structures, and values. A technology has to be designed to fit a specific cultural context. Initially, the main problem Schumacher and his associates were trying to solve in developing their idea of "intermediate technology" was that of advanced technological nations trying to get the developing countries to go from very simple to very complex, heavily capitalized technologies almost overnight. Hence, their use of the term "intermediate technology". The idea was to create technologies somewhere between a shovel and an earthmover for example, so that the developing countries could make a gradual transition to more productive technologies.

However, it was soon clear to Schumacher that the word "intermediate" sounds like a value judgement, and implies something less than the best. It also implies that technologies can be judged on some objective, absolute scale, when in fact technology practices are good or bad depending on the environmental context and on the aims and values of the people using them. Schumacher eventually adopted the term "appropriate technology", since this implies context-related judgements rather than cross-cultural bias and prejudice.

Although the concept of appropriate technology (AT) emerged in the context of designing technology practices for transfer to developing nations, it became evident to many people in the West that this philosophy could be applied in their own nations. Many of our most serious problems are a product of so-called advanced scientific-technological developments backed by large economic and institutional organizations. These development models stress bottom-line economics and technologically sweet values and ignore other important values. A number of law suits have been brought against large institutions for their participation in the development of technologies that displaced workers, eliminated small farmers, or produced lower quality consumer products. It became increasingly evident that all people need appropriate technology practices.

Just as we should comprehensively evaluate technology practices proposed for transfer to developing countries, so we should comprehensively evaluate technology practices for industrial nations. In other words, we should work actively to develop more appropriate technology practices ourselves. Having decided that, we need to agree on what we mean by appropriate.

The word "appropriate" is like the word "happiness". And as Aristotle said, although there is common agreement that happiness is good, there is not general agreement about what it is. Initially, we can say that if something is appropriate, it is apt, fit, suitable, just, proper, and right. An appropriate action is one especially suited and fit to its context. Take, for example, the use of tools. Using a tack hammer to upholster furniture is appropriate, whereas using a ten pound sledge is not. Also, a tool could be suitable to the job at hand, but it might be used inappropriately. Now consider technology practices. We have analyzed technology practices as having four dimensions: cultural, organizational, technical, and environmental, all of which must be harmonized. But what does this mean in relation to appropriateness?

Let us explore the contrast between appropriate and inappropriate practices. We can explain the difference between this value-laden pair of concepts with examples, to which context will be crucial. Suppose that the context for which a technology practice is being appraised is a monastic community dedicated to preserving certain forms of work with spiritual and religious purposes. This is true of the Zen monastery discussed in Chapter 1. In this context, the introduction of new technologies to speed up work would be rejected as inappropriate. The aim of the work in the monastery is not to get the job done as fast as possible. The point of the work is not to be more productive, so that other things can be done. The work itself is part of the spiritual discipline, hence its performance is not something to be hurried. Spiritual practice is woven throughout all of the monastery's activities, from washing dishes to sweeping the floor to doing formal zazen in the zendo.

Consider a different sort of example. Suppose that the main uses for electrical energy are low temperature applications, such as heating or cooling homes and businesses, cooking, and running small electric motors. Suppose it is suggested that we can generate this electricity by building very expensive, highly complex nuclear power reactors whose temperatures will equal those of the sun. These reactors will generate enormous amounts of waste heat and radioactive materials, create security problems, and require large amounts of costly borrowing to finance. Then we find, in contrast, that we could meet our low temperature energy needs in alternative ways, with small-scale, decentralized generation of electricity from small hydro, solar power, biogas conversion, co-generation, conservation, and passive use of solar energy. This alternative, compared to the nuclear power option, creates more employment, generates less debt, has few environmental hazards, and will serve our end purposes more efficiently. Given these circumstances, it is clear that the reactor option is inappropriate. It compromises a number of different values and suffers from serious practical problems that do not arise with the other more diversified, small-scale options. The diversified approach also gives people more chance to participate democratically in technology development. This type of participation is not possible with the nuclear power option, which involves secrecy, large bureaucracy, and huge government subsidies.

III. Some Criteria of Appropriateness

Technology practices, as we have seen, impact on everything we do, on society, and on the world around us. Therefore, it is most critical that they be appropriate. They must satisfy criteria of appropriateness and be evaluated and modified before they are deployed. This cannot be accomplished without the participation of a large number of skilled people and citizen representatives. Technology practices that allow wide citizen participation in their design and development are able to draw from the largest reservoir of knowledge and wisdom. The design of appropriate ecosophic technology practices, then, must be interdisciplinary and participatory. The criteria a practice must meet to realize these objectives are these:

- it must be ecologically sound;
- it must be equitable and sustainable;
- it must allow for decentralization, so that its activity can fit the specific characteristics of individual places and communities; that is, it must be human-scaled;
- it must solve genuine problems of human need, rather than those resulting from poor technology practices—this does not preclude practices that restore damaged economies and habitats;
- it must facilitate progress as human development, as we have defined it above, that is, not just as an increase in consumption or quantity of goods, but in terms of increasing the quality of life and possibilities for self-realization.

Let us examine these criteria in more detail.

It Must Be Ecologically Sound

Since we are discussing the creation of *appropriate and ecosophic* technology practices it follows that they must be ecologically sound. We could have called these technology practices just "appropriate", since the term "appropriate" can easily be construed to mean fit to the whole context: personal, interpersonal, communal, and natural. However, since this is the decade of ecology, and we hope that the nineties will mark a turn-around in our relations to the Earth, we need to stress ecosophy. We believe that all technology practices need to be reformed, redesigned, and made appropriate to the Age of Ecosophy. Since there is ignorance and widespread confusion about the meaning of ecologically sound, let us explain more fully what it means. To say a practice is ecologically sound is logically equivalent to saying it is *ecosophic*, that is, ecologically wise. If it is ecologically wise it will be harmonious with "ecos" in the fullest sense of that term. "Ecos" includes all relationships relevant to the practice in question. Thus a technology that is ecosophic will be *technosophic*, that is, it will exemplify wise use of "techné" (art, craft, skill) suited to a specific place. To realize ecosophy, a practice must be based on the wisdom of nature that shows us how to dwell wisely in a place. This wisdom is exemplified by the principles of ecology (as modified from Commoner 1972), which tell us:

- that nature knows best,
- that everything is interconnected,
- that every action has benefits and costs that must balance,
- that everything we do has impacts on ecological communities, however remote these might be.

To respect nature means realizing that it has the wisdom to take care of the evolutionary and ecological needs of species and communities, so long as we do not interfere. It means employing sustainable practices that do not take more from the Earth than it produces as interest on its biologically diverse "capital" or biomass. In natural selection ecoforestry, for example, this involves removing only those trees nature has selected for removal. To do this requires that we learn to read nature's indicators. Let us consider in greater depth, through other examples, what we mean by ecological soundness.

Many large corporations seem to think that their practices are ecologically sound if they can devise clever and even brilliant public relations ad campaigns to change public perceptions of the nature of their technology practices. It is public perception they strive to alter, not their actual practices. This has nothing to do with ecological wisdom; it is merely commercial cleverness. Forest industries, for example, in North America have conducted a massive ad campaign designed to convince the public that forestry is being practiced in a sustainable way; that the forest industry is concerned about the long-term future; that they have the expertise to manage our forests well; and that they are managing the forests in the public interest. The company executives and their consultants probably believe some of these claims, although it is difficult to see how they can believe them all, since numerous independent studies call every one of them into question.

As we have already noted, the position of the industry, and the forestry research establishment, and their government supporters, is that forestry is just like agriculture. The same basic methods of research that dominate industrial agriculture dominate industrial forestry. Since the Second World War, as we have pointed out, agricultural practices have relied on increasingly heavy uses of chemical fertilizers, insecticides, herbicides, fungicides, preservatives, and big machinery to replace older practices and to encourage large-scale production. The cost effectiveness of this approach depends on cheap oil and government subsidies. The price of food to consumers has been kept low only because many of the costs are hidden in the form of such things as taxes, soil loss, and destruction of rural communities.

This same situation exists in industrial forestry. The production of lumber and fiber from trees has been accomplished largely by *liquidating* centuries-old natural forests, rather than by sound forest stewardship whose primary responsibility is the preservation of natural forest ecosystems (ecoforestry). The accepted procedure of modern industrial forestry is to "harvest" all first-growth timber, burn the debris, scarify the soil, and then replace the biologically diverse forest ecosystems with large-scale monoculture plantations. Fire and herbicides "suppress" the natural succession of plants and trees. Creation of a tree plantation requires the use of insecticides and herbicides, the control of animals that damage young trees, and a host of other destructive practices. The full range of values of whole forests is not taken into account. And what is also ignored is that no human tree plantations have been sustainable: only nature has created sustainable forests. By cutting down and eliminating natural forests, the timber industry is destroying the productive biological capital and the genetic wealth of thousands of years of selection. The practice is akin to dismantling all of our factories and selling the parts on the international market for short-term gain. We should not wonder after we have done this, why we have lost our wealth generating capacity. The industry claims that their methods are necessary to assure forest regrowth so that they can meet sustainable objectives. They have "supported" these claims mainly by spuriously manipulating projections of future growth rates of wood fiber. They further assume that increased wood fiber production will result from new, as yet unproved methods of "intensive" management. Estimates of the rate of new growth have been based on the assumption that such "intensive management" will produce accelerated tree growth throughout most of the rotation cycle. This we now know is not true. Tree plantations are in trouble all over the world.

The value of the timber cut on public lands far exceeds the costs charged to timber companies. It has been patently obvious in this whole process, and the ensuing controversies about old-growth forests, that conventional industrial forestry is ignorant of the ecological effects of clearcutting all old-growth forests, and even mixed young-growth, naturally regenerated forests. As Chris Maser (1988) and others have pointed out, conventional industrial foresters manage primarily for above-the-ground objectives and pay no attention to below-the-ground ecological processes. They see forests not as ecological processes and communities, but as standing raw materials, primarily logs for saw and pulp mills, and short-term profit.

Any objective observer who takes the time to study both old-growth forests and tree plantations, and the overall effects of clearcutting, will conclude that clearcutting and tree plantations, except possibly on a very small scale, are not ecologically sound and produce fewer, and inferior products. Large numbers of people, including some foresters, have reached this conclusion, and yet clearcutting and plantation management continue unabated, for the aim of large transnational corporations is to maximize short-term profits to reinvest in other areas. It is clear that only massive public support for appropriate and ecosophic forestry practices (ecoforestry) will bring about a change from our current destructive practices to ecologically responsible ones. We can have both the forest products and the employment we *need*, and preserve the forest ecosystems and communities as well, by adopting natural selection methods of ecoforestry. To achieve this we must see the forest as a treasure to be maintained, taking products from it, while appreciating its diverse values and avoiding interference with nature's wise evolutionary and ecological processes. The following eight zone classifications for land would facilitate this move to wise practices: commercial, residential, ecoagricultural land, ecoforestry land, urban park land, recreational rural parks, wild lands, and ecological reserves.

To be ecologically sound a practice must be thermodynamically sound as well. It must be designed to minimize energy use, not only by recycling waste heat and other by-products, but also by cutting the energy requirements for accomplishing various tasks. The only way to apply this requirement across the board is to take different actions on several levels at once. So we will aim to conserve energy by designing and retrofitting our buildings to make use of on-site energy possibilities, such as solar, hydro, and wind, as well as by insulating and sealing. Our aim here is not to spell out each of these actions in detail, merely to suggest that there are many ways to work toward ecological soundness. They include, among other undertakings, stopping our disruption of ecological communities and processes, ending pollution of the hydrological and atmospheric processes, and redesigning technology practices so that they require fewer raw materials, and do not generate damaging waste products. *We must design and build for durability and minimum impact.*

It Must Be Equitable and Sustainable

To be equitable a technology practice must be accessible to public use and open to public comment. Too often new technology practices are designed and new products introduced, without those who will feel their greatest impacts being allowed a voice in their development. The practice of irradiating food and using new growth hormones and other substances to stimulate milk production are two examples among many of questionable practices over which the public has little control. Building new pulp mills, constructing new steel plants, opening new open-pit mines: these are all examples of projects that have in the past gone forward without public participation and discussion. An equitable process must allow for not only airing of complaints, but modifying plans so that the actions and products are not harmful to local communities, persons, or local, regional, and global processes. Note that local communities also include the nonhuman ecological communities.

A technology must not give advantages to one group in society at the expense of another. It must not give great power to a small minority. It must not promote great concentration and centralization of power and wealth. It must be sustainable, not only in its long-range ecological impacts, but also in its effects on traditional values, on the local economy, and on the way of life of the communities affected. A new industrial development that disrupts a local community by introducing major changes with negative impacts is unacceptable. Often, when a resource has been exhausted or the costs go too high, a plant is closed, causing economic devastation. It is possible in designing and planning new technology practices, to organize them so that not only do they have minimal negative impacts, but they produce significant gains for all parties involved. The current large-scale forest industry harvests for export of raw materials that are not processed in forest communities. There is then no value added to the raw material. In contrast, community based practices that are ecologically sound and equitable would, over the long haul, produce a continuous supply of raw material for local small-scale community manufacturing and processing. In contrast to current practices, this type of diversified, small-scale industry employs more people, on a sustainable basis.

It Must Facilitate Decentralization and Be of Human Scale

This objective will enable technology practices to fit the specific character-istics of individual places and communities. Both "scientific" agriculture and forestry operate on the assumption that understanding abstract "laws and principles" enables them to make generalizations about their activi-ties. Working from those generalizations, they produce designs for prac-tices and apply the designs universally, on a large-scale, with only slight modifications for location. This process ignores almost totally the actual unique and subtle differences between places. Farming and forestry are both arts, when practiced ecosophically to attend to *all* values. "Place", as we use the term, refers not only to the geographical and biological uniqueness of a location, but also to the human communities that are part of the place. As we saw in our discussion of technology transfer, ignoring the cultural and community context leads to serious problems. This holds true whether we are transferring a practice to another country, or to another location within our own country. A human-scaled practice can be understood and applied by ordinary people at the local level. Its lines of responsibility are clear, not obscure or remote. It is based on community processes, rather than complicated bureaucracy.

It Must Solve Genuine Problems of Human Needs

An appropriate practice is not designed to deal with problems resulting from poor technology practices, unless it aims to regenerate communi-ties—human and natural—that have been damaged by technological ac-tivities. Generally speaking, habitats damaged by human activity will repair themselves, given a long enough time. However, in some cases hu-man intervention might be necessary to restore natural conditions and to hasten the restoration process. Too much of our time is taken up in deal-ing not with genuine problems but with those that should not have been created in the first place. We are not only problem solving animals, we are problem causing animals. We ourselves are part of the problem.

The majority of the problems we now face are human-caused: acid rain, depletion of the ozone shield, soil erosion, pollution of air and wa-ter, extinction of species on a large-scale, deforestation, desertification, threat of nuclear annihilation, huge amounts of public debt, violence in the streets, problems of drug abuse and crime associated with all drugs (not just illegal ones), child abuse, family violence, depletion of raw mate-rials, littering, ocean pollution, war, injustice, human-caused cancer, AIDS—and the list goes on. It is difficult, in fact, to think of major prob-lems that are *not* human-caused. We fail to see that problems caused by our activities often are a result of those very activities. Consequently, we redouble our efforts to solve "new" problems, but use the same methods that caused the problems in the first place. The arms race is an example of such a vicious circle. An arms race is based on mistrust and conflict between nations, a political and social problem that can only be resolved through political and social means, not by threats and use of force. Once an arms race is under way, it is easy to justify ever expanding expenditures on armaments for "reasons of national security." As a result the arms race becomes a main factor in inflation and insecurity. It creates large public debt and distorts the economy. It undermines democratic institutions. Even when the conflict (in this decade the cold war) appears to be ending, it becomes very difficult to change the institutions and priorities.

The use of insecticides and other biocides in agriculture and tree farming is another example of measures taken to solve problems that are a result of faulty farming and forestry practices. The irony is that the more we resort to chemical "fixes", the more problems arise, and the more chemicals we believe we must use. The whole game has been exploited by hucksters. After having convinced farmers to farm in a way that depends on chemical fertilizers, they then convince them of the need for more chemicals to solve the problems that petrochemicals have caused. The result is a never ending cycle of dependency involving the banks, research institutions, government advisors, and industry. The long-range effects on farming and rural communities, on urban dwellers, on such things as ground water and soils, are discounted. When these effects can no longer be ignored, they are seen as new problems requiring other piecemeal solutions.

Instead of reconsidering the whole system of technology practices in agriculture (and elsewhere), we tinker with minor details of the system. The same considerations apply to every natural resource activity, including mining, forestry, and fishing. They apply to our personal lives as well. Many of our illnesses are a direct result of our lifestyles and diets. We spend huge amounts of money and other resources looking for cures for these illnesses, without doing much about the conditions and practices that generated them. We have already discussed the so-called drug abuse problem, a problem brought on partly by government policies and laws. Instead of looking at the conditions that generate drug "problems", the government has responded mainly by strengthening enforcement, disrupting supply, and threatening punishment to try to limit demand. These efforts have failed and will continue to fail because they involve a misunderstanding of the problem. It is assumed that everyone knows precisely what the problem is, but it is clear that this is not true. There is a need to examine the *underlying* causes so as to reframe the problems in more realistic ways. To do this we must examine our values, objectives, lifestyles, and basic practices.

The above are all examples of secondary problems that divert our energy away from problems of genuine human need, such as shelter, disease free food, clean air and water, social justice, meaningful community, and dignity. The large-scale, depersonalized, violent industrial technologies all disrupt and destroy the diversity and richness of nature and culture that enable us to address these needs. Hence, the need for a new philosophy of design based on ecocentric values and respect for diversity and pluralism.

It Must Facilitate Progress as Human Development

We use the term "progress" here as we defined it in Chapter 10. Progress is not just increased production and consumption of goods, it must improve the quality of life. Many previous sections of this book have dealt with the factors that promote human development and those that impede it. We have described human development as a process of realizing wholeness through spiritual disciplines and ecologically sound practices. We have looked at our current crisis as in part a product of a specific philosophy that promotes fragmentation of knowledge, work, community, and the person. We suggested that we need practices that are integrative and transformative. In connection with these practices we have reinterpreted Christian eschatology (since it is the dominant form of religion in the West) and critiqued the modern concept of progress. We have connected our reinterpretation with contemporary knowledge from ecophilosophy, transpersonal psychology, and cultural studies. We have taken from Christian philosophy an account that ties the stories of the fall and the teachings of Jesus into a triphasal conception of human development, from prepersonal (pre-egoic), to personal (egoic), to transpersonal (transegoic). Technology practices play a major role in enhancing our possibilities for development and progress and advancing our capacities for ecosophy. This being so, it is instructive here to look at the nature of *good work*, since technology practices are central to work, and good work promotes human development.

Most Western adults spend much of their time working. Work that is demeaning, morally corrupting, or physically debilitating goes against our search for self-realization and spiritual development. Work that is destructive of human community and of ecological communities weakens moral and spiritual values and is incompatible with ecosophy. Thus, saying that a technology practice should enhance the possibilities for human development and increase the quality of life, entails that it promote good work.

E. F. Schumacher (1979) identified the features of good work in terms of basic needs. These are:

- to satisfy basic physical needs,
- to realize individual excellence through skills and practice,
- to complete ourselves as social beings,
- to realize ultimate values and spiritual ends.

These four features help to illuminate the criteria for an appropriate, eco-sophic technology practice, that is, one that is technosophic. In Zen monasteries all these needs are met in daily life and work. We can see more clearly why the monk in the story in Chapter 1 did not rush to implement suggestions for making daily work more productive. The aim of daily life in the monastery is not production, but good work. Good work, for the monk, includes essential tasks and self-correction, perfection, spiritual realization, building and continuing the sense of community, and practicing the Buddhist way in every aspect of life.

To define work only in productive terms leaves out what is essential to our well-being and continuing development. Such narrowly defined, one-dimensional work soon loses meaning for us; it becomes a chore. To do good work is equivalent to leading a good life, a life of deepening and increasing richness and quality. Such depth is found in realizing a wider and deeper sense of identification and harmony with oneself, and with human and natural communities, not in amassing consumer goods. To act to complete ourselves as social beings is to act with an ever-widening appreciation for the contributions to our life made by others. It involves deepening and increasing our respect for all beings, not just our family, not just our tribe, not just our nation, not just human kind, but all beings.

Certainly a minimal requirement of good work is that it must enable us to act to satisfy our basic physical needs. What are these needs? In a noncontroversial sense we can say that our basic needs are modest. Humans need sufficient food and water, clean air, sunlight, activity, rest, physical contact and affection, shelter, clothes for protection from the elements, means to relieve themselves, and participation in communal activities. As a simple example, consider the low impact hiker who carries all necessities on his or her back. With only a 35 to 40 pound pack the hiker can spend a week in the wilderness and survive storms, heat and cold, and feed him/her self. Paring the physical necessities to a minimum presents a sharp contrast to the situation of the suburbanite with a four car garage and a large house filled with a variety of consumer items. Obviously, physical needs can be satisfied by very little, whereas "needs" that are influenced by cultural conditioning and unsatisfied cravings can grow indefinitely, always outrunning one's current power to purchase, control, and consume.

Here we must distinguish between *vital needs* and the "needs" acquired by artificially stimulated desires. Unsatisfied vital needs give rise to craving and physical suffering, but desire can arise from acquired hungers that have nothing to do with physical needs. This is partly because humans are social, moral, and spiritual beings, not just physical beings, but also because our society creates "needs" by offering us an endless supply of "new" consumer goods. Thus it is essential that we organize activities and technology practices by means of which we can satisfy our basic physical needs. Yet we have to accept the fact that we will continue to manufacture all sorts of items that people *want*, but do not vitally *need*. On the other hand, we now manufacture all sorts of things that we *should* do without, such as styrofoam cups and other kinds of plastic containers and wrappers. These are not required to satisfy vital needs, or natural desires, and are wasteful and harmful to the environment.

As we develop from infancy onward our lives are marked by two major themes: the acquisition of knowledge and skills, and the search for meaningful and nourishing human contact with others, such as playmates and parents, motivated by a desire to be accepted and loved. We can say, for the sake of simplicity, that beyond the physical needs we have mentioned, humans need to love and be loved; they need to acquire and share their knowledge; and they need to receive and give support. To be deprived of any of these is to have our development frustrated, our needs unmet. From an early age some young people have the good fortune of working closely with adults to acquire the skills and knowledge needed to support themselves and the community. Learning such skills satisfies their own physical and social needs, and serves the needs of their group as well. In traditional societies acquiring skills and knowledge and perfecting the capacities for using these skills was part of settled life patterns. In industrial society these patterns changed. The home learning of the older agrarian society broke down, as did the apprenticeship program, in which a young person lived with a master craftsperson to learn a craft. These traditions were replaced for the most part by the public schools, which in many aspects were modeled on industrial paradigms of organization. The mass manufacture of goods and services became a model for the mass school system through which large numbers of students are processed uniformly, age segregated, and viewed as potential contributors to production and consumption.

The public school system became the major arena in which a developing human being had to acquire skills and knowledge to prepare him or her for work. The trend in industrial nations has been to keep the young in school for longer and longer periods, thus prolonging the transition to adulthood. Often no clear connection exists between what is studied in school and available good work. Schools often give young people no clear idea of why they are studying what they study, and why they should learn the material they are required to learn. In a society in which technology practices are designed with appropriate, ecosophic criteria in mind, the educational process would have to be reformed so that meaningful learning experiences would prepare students earlier for appropriate good work.

When we join with other humans to accomplish some goal, whether this is climbing a mountain, planting a garden, or manufacturing some useful item, there is a dimension to the work that is social. This is the third need Schumacher sees good work fulfilling. Working with others to achieve worthwhile goals, we are not just engaged in a productive job but in a social undertaking, a communal act. Working with others in a spirit of cooperation, we are able to transcend our narrow egoistic preoccupations and concentrate our energies on self-transcending goals and values.

As long noted in both Eastern and Western philosophy, human beings are social not solitary beings. However, there are cultures that send individuals into the wilderness alone, on spirit and vision quests, to deepen their maturity and capacity for understanding who they are. After these journeys individuals rejoin the group and go through a ritual to reconnect them with the social order in a new, deeper, and more meaningful way. Monks and other religious pilgrims have also sought solitude to concentrate their energies on contemplation of the divine. Christ and Buddha spent long periods of time in the wilderness, fasting, meditating, and praying. Their missions, however, were carried out in human company. Both created a spiritual community of discipline and practice that was passed on to others transgenerationally.

Through good work we can realize ourselves as human beings, and join with others in activities that contribute to larger social and ecological values in our society and place. Our ecophilosophy considers anti-ecological acts to be immature, self-destructive, and antisocial. Such acts are often done by humans who have been damaged during their process of development (Miller 1990), and consequently have not learned proper actions and good work. We agree with Socrates that humans do destructive things out of ignorance of their true self-nature with its connections to all beings. Good work, with its learning processes, enables us to make these connections and thereby gain insight into our true self-nature.

Acting in community (Morgan 1984) with others to realize good work and positive values that contribute to our traditions and enhance our quality of life and that help others and respect nature, promotes our awareness of the self-transcending spiritual dimensions of human life. This is the fourth need Schumacher mentions that is satisfied by good work—to realize the ultimate values of human life, while walking a path that brings us closer to our spiritual destiny by connecting us with all creation. In brief, this is a need to recognize the way things are, given our nature as psycho-physical-spiritual beings. It involves the realization that the dark side of life, the shadow that we ourselves cast, is an extension of our own repressed and projected spiritual energies. We create adversity and conflict through our own patterns of living. To approach the natural world as if it is hostile to us, and as if we need to control it with force, is to fail to understand the ecology of the self, for we cannot control nature as something external to us. To recognize that nature is part of us and we are part of it, and that we are each part of something larger, is to enter the transcendent spiritual community of which all conscious beings are part, the community to which both Buddha and Christ showed the way. Our innate desire as humans is to realize ourselves, and what we believe is good, to complete ourselves. A unified, good practice is one that helps us to break through our self-and-other imposed forms of ignorance and fear, so that our hearts and minds are receptive to the larger dimensions of consciousness that open to spiritual communion with all beings.

IV. Appropriate Design

Having explained what we mean by good work and appropriate ecosophic technology practice, we can now discuss appropriate design. An appropriate design process necessarily combines art and science within its broad philosophy of ecosophic and technosophic practice. While the specialism of industrial society tends to divide art from science, the process of appropriate design seeks to rejoin and unify all aspects of human knowing and creating. Both intuitive and analytic modes of knowing are necessary to its activities. Meditation as part of self-mastery, and skills in the mediation of material mediums are also part of its process, for if all criteria are to be met the designer himself or herself must be rectified and corrected. As an artwork reflects the artist, a technology practice reflects its designers. We might be able to design something that is less than what we are, but we cannot produce something that is more than what we are. Nonetheless, the activity of design should be unifying and bring people together at a higher level of insight than that which generated the undertaking.

When an advanced technological society is in transition to ecosophy, practical problem solving and creative activity arise, for ecosophy is a holistic, interdisciplinary art informed by the unifying paradigms of ecological thought, sensibilities, and perception. A society organized around industrial paradigms and the economics of large-scale eventually stresses the limits of human community and ecological sustainability. This stress is currently forcing us to discard the technocratic paradigms and to shift to technologies of appropriate scale, whose design is possible only because there are designers who operate under new paradigms based on ecological patterns learned from nature. What is in process is a shift from the Cartesian-Baconian mastery of nature to the deep ecological aim of working *with* nature, now seen to contain intrinsic values, not merely those related directly to human use and exploitation. Appropriate design is informed by communal ecological principles that are an integral part of the education of designers. A formative educational experience based on these ecological insights and understandings infuses all techniques, skills, and knowledge, from conception to application, with ecosophic values.

In an ecosophic world, nature is seen to have values in which we and the gods participate. With appropriate design nature is resacralized for us, not by a division between the sacred and the profane, but by an encounter with the divine, or the sacred (ultimate values) *in* the profane, that is, in daily life. *The design activity itself becomes an archetypal example of the creative act that unifies our whole being and harmonizes it with the Earth.* The spontaneous creative act of design of appropriate practices fulfills human need, for it brings together the material, aesthetic, cognitive, moral, communal, spiritual, and the natural within a holistic harmonious activity. This activity yields practices that are themselves examples of good work; they perfect their practitioners. Technosophic design begins with a clearly understood problem context. This understanding requires accurate conceptualization, evaluation, and analysis of the problem. The design activity cannot proceed very far in practical terms without information and knowledge from a diversity of disciplines and specialties. It integrates imagination and knowledge through practices and values in which wisdom can be spontaneously manifested in actions. Rooted in self-correction, the design process aligns the designers with transdisciplinary values in the act of *whole practice design.*

This type of creative activity requires, in addition to a consideration of the problem, an understanding of our aims and rationale for seeking a solution. Perhaps the original "problem" was not a genuine one, but was perceived as such because of too narrow a frame of reference. Sometimes solutions require not new hardware or techniques, but a shift in outlook and a new practice. The aim of dominating the world is a problem, usually motivated by a desire for power over others as a way of validating oneself, or from a fear of being dominated. Philosophical and other forms of therapy are the most appropriate means of rectifying these types of problems in the interpersonal and intrapersonal domains. Satisfying *basic* human needs, on the other hand, calls for practical solutions involving cultivation and farming practices, as well as responsible ecoforestry, appropriate manufacturing, carefully regulated research, and equitable distribution of goods and services. When the aim is domination, the problems related to technology practice are not technical ones, since careful analysis of the intent to dominate will show that it is inconsistent with the ultimate values of community and self-realization.

Once the intent of the design and the designers has been rectified, and the problem is determined to be a genuine one, the rest of the design process flows through these stages: conceptual design, functional-material transfer (ecological and social inputs), engineering design, prototype construction, fine-tuning and modification, and finally, completed technology with organized techniques. Since technology contains skills and techniques that must be ordered and taught, we can add that a unifying myth (story) and ritual (procedure), as in the making of a samurai sword, should be part of the total design process. Truly ecosophic design processes reflect the actions of creation, for they utilize the tools of the technology as extensions of the users and are expressions of their freedom to engage in good work. From the full mythic perspective they become extensions of a nature that realizes itself through an encounter with the wholly "other" in the act of self-creation and transcendence.

The design process demands an encounter with nature itself through the human subject. Just as the Taoist wood carver "releases" the form inherent in the wood, so the appropriate technologist strives to "release" the forms and patterns inherent in nature, forms that resolve the problems of human need in ways that promote community and ecological integrity. To realize this type of design requires developing oneself in a way that transcends the urge toward mastery of nature. As we have seen, this urge to master is an extension of *anthropocentric ego* domination of what the Baconian-Cartesian technologist (or technocrat) considered a mere object, an it, or "other". Thus, the technological imperative of industrial society finally emerges as the technocratic urge toward domination of others and nature through theory, technique, and device. This technocratic turn ultimately undercuts its own expressed values, such as the dignity of the person and the democratic ethos, and consequently becomes self-destructive and threatens all of human life and all life on Earth. At this stage we must find creative ways to transcend the technological imperative. We must do this not by regressing to an earlier, more primitive stage of technology practice, but by preparing for the emergence of new, appropriate, ecosophic technology practices through the education of designers who are "pernetarian" followers of deep ecological platform principles. Pernetarians are *per*-sons who realize they are in *net*-works of plane-*tarian* relationships (Drengson 1989). They escape the limits and dead ends of the technocratic, industrial philosophy and open to the higher, deeper, wider consciousness of the transpersonal.

In the next chapter we will discuss the integrative study and education necessary for developing ecosophic technology practices, and issues related to mastery of self. The integrative approach described is one of the fundamental elements in this larger undertaking that will move us to technosophic practices.

Chapter 12

Integrated Studies in Technology Practice and Mastery of Appropriate Design

I. Introduction

To this point in our study, we have viewed human history from the perspective of technological development, defining "development" as increasing productivity and mastery over natural processes—the dominant view of progress and history in technological societies. We have seen that our society, from the beginning of the modern period through the twentieth century, has increasingly technologized human life and nature, extending the basic metaphors and models of control underlying modern philosophy. We have acted as if theoretical positions were scientific truths. As long as the activities following from these *presumptions* were reinforced by sufficiently powerful technology, it appeared that we were confirming and reconfirming the basic picture of reality upon which these activities were built. However, from the late nineteenth century on it has become increasingly evident that modern philosophy, along with its associated science and technology, is up against natural and human limits. The rapid deforestation of Eastern North America and the increasing rate of extinction of animal species demonstrated the limits of nineteenth century philosophy of technology. Only a few farseeing persons seemed to grasp the implications of increasing human power over nature, coupled with increasing numbers of human beings.

When we consider the impact of a single human person on the environment, magnify that impact by applying contemporary technology, then multiply that one human hundreds of millions of times, we begin to understand the dimensions of the environmental crisis of the late twentieth century. This is the crisis of a planet in trouble, a crisis that reaches to every part of the globe. It is a crisis in modern cultures, manifesting itself in the breakdown of civility and order, the disintegration of community and family, the glut of goods, and lowering of the quality of life. That one in four North Americans will have cancer, that most cancer is caused by environmental factors, that drinking water is polluted, that DDT is found in the fat of practically all mammals, that the ozone shield is thinning, that the greenhouse effect is altering climatic patterns: these facts are daunting even to skeptics. By this last decade of the twentieth century it is clear to almost everyone that our basic technological approach to life and its underlying philosophy are seriously flawed and in need of redesign.

Philosophies are not fixed, totally closed systems from which there is no way out. They are either tacit and implicit in a society, or made explicit through conscious philosophical activity. Our culture has been self-conscious of its philosophical foundations, and we have expended much intellectual effort searching for rational foundations for our lives and practices. However, we have been unable to provide these epistemic foundations by basing our approach on modern Western philosophy. In our discussion of this philosophy we have concentrated on its links to the technology practices that developed in the West in concert with science and industrialization. The breakdown of the old apprenticeship programs for training in the crafts, the undermining of family authority in teaching of the young, the disruption of indigenous and traditional agrarian cultures by the spread of urban industrialism—these and a host of other phenomena we mention as just some of the consequences of the spread of the modern industrial worldview and its associated priorities. This worldview does not see either nature or work as having a dimension of moral and spiritual commitment that would limit the pursuit of power-over and mastery of nature. In its philosophy, whatever we *can* do, we should attempt to do. There is no limit to technological power, and humans have the right to seek ultimate power over the natural world and even over human life, so as to advance their interests. "Interests" are values only for humans. No living beings, except humans, are sacred or deserving of respect. Each living being becomes a potential specimen, then a unit of inventory or a part in a production process, an economic commodity. The power of this modern thought lies partly in its capacity to divorce itself from the rest of nature, and to distance itself and its perceiving human consciousness from its natural context of concrete individuals and communities. The underside of this process is that it *fragments* the original unity of spontaneous experience. At its logical extreme, modern consciousness, formed by modern philosophy, does not ground intrinsic value *even* in humans. It is not even able to provide the rational foundation it claims we need for our human lives.

The allure of the modern outlook is that it asserts something with which we all agree: that all our learning and knowledge is grounded in experience. But what *is* experience? The word obviously means different things to different people. How is experience itself to be conceptualized? The way we conceptualize about our experience and the world around us is open-ended but not arbitrary. Our possibilities are far richer than we can ever describe at any given time. The power of modern languages, such as English, is based in part on an accumulation of linguistic material that both incorporates and transcends earlier cultures. In contrast, the power of the specialized languages of modern technological activities lies in their ability to ignore a host of factors and concentrate on just a few *calculable* ones. In this sense the presumptions of empiricism and rationalism incorporated in modernism are consistent with one another. Both, viewing experience of the world in a detached, objectified way, put certain limits on thought and perception. Modern culture, imbued with this philosophical outlook, technologizes both experience and nature. It creates artificial languages and models to replace the language of natural metaphors that flow spontaneously from the holistic consciousness of meditative silence. It creates an artificial environment that mirrors this technical, analytical, calculative process in its technological activity. It creates a system of training and education that leads not to community, wholeness, and wisdom, but to alienation, fragmentation, and folly.

II. Whole Technology Practices and Restructuring of Education

Throughout this book we have put technology into its larger natural context. We have seen how the meaning of the word "technology", when used by itself, is unclear. We are led to think that it consists only of devices, only of hardware, or only of technical knowledge. And this leads us to ask questions such as, "Is technology value-free?" Since, in our analysis, we are exploring the *ecology* of "technology", we have emphasized the word "practice". "Practice" also means different things to different people. It commonly conjures up the idea of repetition with the aim of improvement. When we join the words technology and practice to form the term, *technology practice*, we immediately broaden the meaning of practice by including the larger context of technological activity and natural processes. By so doing we include the environmental and social dimensions.

The concept of *technology practice* leads us quite naturally to consider evaluative criteria, ultimate aims, and sacred values. When we do this we can see that the dimensions of whole practices include:

- technical knowledge and skills,
- organizational know-how and its structures,
- cultural values and aims of productive activity,
- environmental impact and nature's contributions to the whole practice.

We have pointed out that attending to cultural and organizational structures immediately helps us to see the role that individuals play in technology practice, and how participation in the practice affects their sensibilities and cognitive development. We then must consider how these practices affect natural and human communities. In considering all of these interrelationships we *ecologize* the concept of technology practice, especially when we assess or contemplate the design of new practices. Since we do not understand the world when we see it only in fragments, we must unify ourselves to avoid fragmented vision. We are part of nature and not isolated individuals or a species apart from it. Our wholeness requires reconciliation with nature. The history and development of technology practices shows how whole systems develop and form interrelationships. Practices that do not exhibit ecosophic harmony ultimately damage workers, consumers, cultures, and nature because their violence as power-over is given force.

Given the above considerations, we now will consider how we might restructure our educational activities so as to minimize violence and fragmentation of self, community, and nature. We need to find educational ways to heal and make ourselves whole again, to reinvigorate responsibility, and re-enliven the sense of the sacred in our practices. We have suggested that one way to do this is to practice philosophy as a comparative, creative activity that aims at ecosophy. We need an appropriate philosophical activity that will help us to understand our situation comprehensively, so as to have a vision of the whole. Meaningfulness is not found through separation and atomization, it lies in appreciation for the *integrity* of natural wholeness and ecological balance. It lies in respect for all beings, that gives rise to the power of unconditional love.

Both the meaning of our lives and our own deeper identity are inextricably bound up with the fate of all those beings who suffer from our exercise of power. Wisdom must be in our practices, not a distant goal we might achieve in the future. On our present course, we will soon destroy the ecosphere of which we are a part. Wisdom is not a body of facts or technical power; it is the capacity to act with respect for the intrinsic worth of all beings. Wisdom is active, compassionate listening from the heart.

Public education in the West became increasingly fragmented as it developed hand in hand with modern science, technology, and industry. Just as the production process was made more powerful through abstraction and specialization, so education became increasingly focused on the abstract and specialized, and aimed to produce workers and professionals to serve the industrial state. But the aim in education must not be just to train specialists, those who know more and more about less and less, but whole human beings. The specialized expert suffers from tunnel vision, just as does the corporate executive whose decisions are guided by only a few economic values, instead of the *whole range of values* open to us as complete humans. To educate is to prepare for life as a whole, and life as a whole is an ongoing process of learning.

The underlying rationale for specialization is that the world is too large a place for one person to grasp and study on his or her own. Thus, we divide up the tasks. However, this only serves wisdom if we have a way of reuniting our activities; if we have a way of bringing our knowledge together in a comprehensive and comprehensible vision of ourselves, our community, our culture, other cultures, and nature. Unfortunately, thinking within the industrial paradigm has become so compartmentalized, and institutionalization of our thought processes and methods has become so profound, that we find it almost impossible to act wisely on the basis of the information and knowledge available to us. Lacking a comprehensive vision of the whole of life, our personal integrity is compromised. Self-ignorance and self-deception pervade our culture. As a result, even though it is obvious that we must stop destroying the ecological processes that forests, for example, represent, must cease clearcutting and so-called scientific forestry and move to alternative, ecosophic practices, we do not do this. Denial looms large. It is too painful to reconsider our values. We continue to destroy the forests with ever accelerating intensity to support "the economy". We follow the same process in each area of human technological activity as it impacts upon human dignity and nature. Yet, we must first consider our values and ultimate aims, then when these are ecosophically clear, we can design our economic activities appropriately. Then we have a chance to realize sustainability.

In earlier chapters, we offered many ways of seeing technology practices; we sketched the dimensions that must enter into our philosophy, if we are to understand these practices and develop new, more appropriate, technosophic ones. Our educational practices must reflect the shift in paradigms described here. In a previous book, *Beyond Environmental Crisis*, I developed a detailed account of philosophy as a practice that facilitates deep shifts in perspective and paradigm (Drengson 1989). There I described and illustrated how an activity and practice can become a Way in the Eastern sense. I have cited Aikido as an example of a practice that is consonant with the Way of nature, therefore wise and compassionate.

We need to create a philosophical practice that is like Aikido in leading to deeper self-knowledge and empowering us to design new technology practices harmonious with the Age of Ecosophy. Our educational activities and practices must facilitate the shift to appropriate, ecosophic technology practices. So as to promote this deeper, more comprehensive understanding of technology in terms of practice, let us consider the following proposal for an integrated approach to technology studies. The aim of such a study is the mastery of the technosophic design and application of ecologically wise technology practices.

Our study of technology needs a comprehensive approach, if we are to genuinely alter our current destructive course. We have a responsibility to change our educational and design practices in order to adopt an integrated approach to technology practices that will yield harmonious relationships to one another, to other cultures, and to nature. The proposal offered here is for college education, but a program of integrated studies of technology practices should be in place at all levels of education, from grade school through graduate school. Here, then, is our proposal.

III. A Proposal for Integrated Studies in Technology Practice

The aim of Integrated Technology Studies is to further our comprehensive understanding of technology as a whole practice in relation to its human and natural context and impacts.

A. Rationale for a Program

Human technology is the single most powerful force for change in the twentieth century. It is by means of technology practices that we reorganize and reshape the world around us. Our technology practices affect everything we do, everywhere we go, and even what we become. They shape our expectations, our definition of progress and the way we see the world. They influence our literature and art, and work to shape our destiny. They are often alleged to be value-neutral, because they have been studied in fragmented ways rather than as a whole. We can no longer afford to do this, for we live in a dynamic technological environment. Thus, we need a comprehensive understanding of technology practices which includes their total human and natural contexts. We must understand the relationship between our technology practices with their associated values, and the environmental crisis. Recognizing the power of technology and our responsibility to understand, build, and use it wisely, leads us to recognize how urgent it is to approach its study with comprehensive interdisciplinary inquiry and communication. We need to understand technological development and practice historically, environmentally, culturally, technically, and ecologically. Because of the breadth of issues, different sub-area focuses will be included in integrated technology studies.

B. *The Program Must be Campus-wide and Interdisciplinary*

The impacts of technology in modern society are pervasive. It is difficult to anticipate the consequences of new technology practices in part because we lack comprehensive understanding. This understanding can be gained only by unifying our knowledge of the historical, technical, cultural, cross-cultural, and practical aspects of this phenomenon. Our inquiry must synthesize, integrate, and communicate knowledge drawn from all sources of knowing: technical and scientific, logical and conceptual, affective and imaginative. To do this we must bring together all subjects, disciplines, and arts available on campus, as well as some from off campus. The program assumes that technology practices (like medical practice) include four major dimensions: cultural, organizational, technical, and environmental.

C. *The Program Must Have a Strong Environmental Studies Component*

Environmental Studies is one university program comprehensive enough to integrate all aspects of technology studies. Contemporary environmental problems and the impacts of modern technology on the ecosphere make it imperative that technology design and assessment be integrated with environmental and ecological criteria at the conceptual level, before being developed and applied. The management of technology practices requires strong ecocentric value components if new policies and practices are to avoid costly and environmentally damaging mistakes.

AN INITIAL CONCEPTUALIZATION FOR A PROGRAM   The emphasis in graduate work in technology studies will be on research. As with other programs, *Integrated Technology Studies* initially will draw from courses and resources now available on most university campuses, but, in time, also from newly established programs in related fields of study. Technology studies should be available at the masters and doctoral level, as well as for undergraduates. Undergraduate programs should be structured to provide both a discipline major and a B.A. or B.S. in *Integrated Technology Studies* as part of a double major.

There will be some specified core courses required of all students electing to do an advanced or an undergraduate degree. Other requirements will be *Environmental Studies* core courses, where they exist. Where they do not, substitutes covering contemporary environmental problems should be sought. The rest of the program will be determined by the student's area of concentration. Graduate students should be able to design their own programs in consultation with their advisory committees.

There will be three major areas of concentration:

- Study and assessment of technological and natural processes, implications, and forecasts;

- Current and historical impacts of technology practices on the human and nonhuman contexts;

- Innovative problem solving and design of new technology practices, based on integrated, whole system approaches.

All three areas allow for a wide range of research projects, and are open-ended enough to encourage radical, innovative thinking and experimentation. For example, assessment and study of technological alternatives in waste management would fit into the first area; information technology and issues of privacy and rights into the second; and design of theory and practice of renewable energy technology practices into the third (see also the following section on six areas of emphasis).

Some special interdisciplinary seminars and courses should be offered, starting with first year lower level survey courses with fixed content, and upper level seminars whose precise content would vary from section to section. Typical seminar titles might be: Renewable Energy Systems; Information, its Management and Communication; Historical Development and Transfer of Technology Practices; Technology, Leisure and Culture. Additional seminars for both faculty and graduate students in such programs could focus on timely topics and issues, especially of local and regional importance. Students and faculty could organize conferences and publish the papers; campus-regional newsletters could be published and distributed once each term. There should be titled chairs for distinguished professors in *Integrated Technology Studies*.

At the end of their first four years these programs should be reviewed and evaluated. Plans for future development will be based on the results of these evaluations.

FURTHER EXTENSIONS OF INTEGRATED TECHNOLOGY STUDY IN RESEARCH Institutes for *Integrated Technology Studies* should be founded. Some functions of the Institutes will be to publish a variety of journals and other materials on the nature of technology practices and technology studies. They will produce papers and monographs on applications of Technology Studies and the design of practices having unique requirements to meet the special problems of the land, the wilderness, forests, and communities. Some examples might be: projects in sustainable forestry at the community level; new forms of sustainable, holistic, resource management of mineral processes; experiments in new forms of recreation, leisure, and entertainment that are environmentally informing and low impact. The institutes will provide consultants for special projects.

The institutes will have close ties with centers for sustainable development, community planning institutes and other similar organizations. They will form networks with other workers and researchers. They will encourage the study of whole system design, and foster the participatory study and practice of design philosophies calling for rigorous new standards of quality. These standards should be reflective of present and future concerns, such as ecological values, cultural identity, native cultures, and technology transfers to other countries. They will strive to bring together working groups from government, business, education and the community. Both the institutes and the *Integrated Technology Studies* programs will encourage wider citizen participation; for example, through citizen study groups, workshops, and citizen advisory councils. The institutes will work cooperatively on environmental projects with local and regional communities. This type of joint action will help tap the wealth of creative potential available in their regions for innovative design of environmentally sound technology practices in forestry, agriculture, mining, renewable energy, shelter, solid waste management, and other areas of concern.

Environmental Studies departments could have special jurisdiction over the institutes, but the overall administration of the institutes and the integrated technology studies programs would be better overseen by a university-wide committee made up of faculty, students and administration.

AREAS OF EMPHASIS   As mentioned, all undergraduate majors and graduate students should be required to take certain core courses. These courses will provide a broad understanding of the technical, historical, valuational, philosophical, ecological, environmental, social, and cultural aspects of technology practices and the many issues and problems associated with technological development.

In addition to the core courses, students will fill out their course requirements, depending on their particular interests, by choosing from one of six areas of concentration, called *Areas of Emphasis*. These six areas are:

- information and communication technologies;
- alternative, appropriate-soft technologies (e.g.renewable energy);
- history, development, and transfer of technologies;

- technology, literature, and art (for example, leisure and culture);
- design of technology practices (emphasis on process and activity relevant to multidisciplinary design and development);
- contract option (student designed program).

The program will stress throughout that integrated technology studies encompasses the organizational, cultural, technical, and environmental dimensions of technology practices as these dynamically interact to impact on and change the world. Environmental problems will not be solved unless we create and master a process of technological design, development and application based on ecosophic (ecologically wise) criteria.

SOME FINAL CONSIDERATIONS   It is now widely recognized that progress toward peace, environmental harmony, and social justice depends on the development and harnessing of appropriate technology practices through interdisciplinary cooperation. We face a multitude of urgent problems. Just one area of grave concern is how current technology practices are adversely affecting the weather and atmosphere. That they are having major effects is undeniable. Our only option is to adopt alternative, ecologically sound practices. Countless issues in modern society—privacy and access to information in an electronic information technology era, access to technology and power, the full implications of biogenetic engineering—need to be addressed in a comprehensive and comprehensible way. Programs in integrated technology studies, such as the one outlined, offered through high schools, colleges, universities, and graduate schools, will help to provide the knowledgeable and skilled people we need to begin to turn our situation around.

Scholars and researchers must lead the way in seeking an understanding of how technology practices as a whole function, and how they can be improved, consistent with rigorous environmental, economic, and social criteria. The key to long-range, sustainable cultures and economies lies in developing new technology practices appropriate to the values and limitations of our planetary, cultural, bioregional, and personal contexts. Universities and colleges must provide more leadership in the creation and study of innovative approaches to technology practices. They must offer their students the opportunity to pursue a comprehensive, integrative understanding of human technology practices as a whole, within the total ecospheric context. Besides providing the knowledgeable citizens we need, such programs will fill a central research need in environmental issues at the undergraduate and graduate levels.

IV. Importance of Self-mastery

As noted earlier, the aim of our new approach to technology practices is to shift our current values away from trying to control and gain mastery over nature. Our aim must be not to master nature or other people, but to develop self-mastery and self-discipline, to master arts by which we actualize ourselves, improve our communities and relationships, and realize harmony with nature. These values must determine our economic practices. Of course, we must continue to work toward peace and nuclear disarmament, we must work for social justice, we must work to solve problems of human overpopulation and human need, we must work to eliminate environmental degradation. But we must give priority to the mastery of design processes that create appropriate, ecosophic technology practices. We must focus our efforts on education for the development and proper use of these practices, as we have described them here. Such education should build both character and community.

The great political movements of this century aim to realize humane and ecosophic relationships through social justice, world peace, environmental harmony, and enabling appropriate technology practices. Understood holistically these are interrelated aims and each is part of our search to actualize ourselves as whole persons, living in whole communities, relating to others in mutual respect, in tune with the myriad beings of the natural world. The concept of holistic mastery, then, shifts its sense away from the dominant, hierarchical models of industrial society, with their emphasis on power-over and top-down management and control, toward decentralized, participatory, democratic but diverse cultural activities and relationships. Above all ecosophic values must guide our activities.

As a total educational process, culture should facilitate the practice of spiritual discipline by which to improve and correct ourselves. To achieve deeper understanding, an enlarging generosity, a deeper sensitivity to other beings, a wider, ecocentric vision of ultimate values, and the sense to live wisely by these: this should be an overriding aim of education. The quality and value of a technology practice reflects the quality and values of the persons who create and apply it. Instead of spending resources on technicians and experts, and complicated and costly machines, we should concentrate on developing the quality of our persons, on improving our relationships to all beings. A self is not an isolated atom, but also a community of relationships held together by an enlarging and deepening intelligent sensibility. The quality of these relationships must help define the quality of our lives.

We reach maturity as an industrial technological society when we gain the capacity and freedom to master the technological process *itself*. When we have understood appropriate and ultimate values, then technological development will serve nature. A mature society develops new practices not by compulsion, but by free choice based on a comprehensive understanding of the total context, oriented by a concern for ecosophic values. This mature mastery of the technological process gives rise to a new kind of creative freedom which can design and produce ecosophic technology practices. We have no need to exert power over others and nature, if we are masters of our own lives. Then we can create respectful relationships and activities that help us grow and deepen our appreciation, love, understanding, knowledge, and wisdom.

V. Two Approaches to Learning

We have seen that specialization and compartmentalization of knowledge have, in industrial society, tended to separate humans from their technological processes. This in turn results in worker deskilling and alienation. The machinist becomes a machine tender, and then just "labor." We do not claim that specialized knowledge is worthless, or that we should forego its pursuit. Some division of labor is necessary to advance our knowledge of the world and society. However, without comprehensive vision and a clear sense of ecosophic values, specialized knowledge becomes *dangerous*. We must find ways to reunite ourselves and to reconnect with the processes of nature and of our complex society. One of the important ways to regain this comprehensive understanding and holistic vision of life is to reintegrate our educational processes. An ecosophic learning process involves not just analysis, breaking a subject down into more simple units of comprehension to facilitate learning, but also processes of synthesis moving to wholeness. We need new stories and myths that encompass and integrate our accumulated knowledge, that make it accessible in daily life in practical ways. Our lives then are drawn toward inclusive, comprehensive stories that facilitate wisdom. Here we imply two complementary approaches to learning.

As the final topic in this chapter, let us examine these two approaches to learning which we will call the *piecemeal* and the *holistic*. These ways of learning can reinforce each other in an integrated process that leads to mastery. In our culture the analytic, more fragmented approach has become dominant, and is reinforced by specialism. In order to facilitate teaching (learning) of both complex *practical* activities—such as handball, carpentry, and skiing—and *theoretical* subjects such as physics, mathematics, and philosophy—to mention just a few—it is useful to break the activity or subject into segments of some sense.

Learning any *practical* activity can be facilitated by dividing the activity into parts, stages, and phases. In skiing, for example, one practices edging, sideslipping, kick turns and weighting-unweighting. There are many theories about the best way to accomplish each of these techniques. However, theories and skills separately, do not make a master skier. Normally, even while one is being instructed in the separate techniques, one is also learning the art as a whole. The art as a whole is implied by or contains the individual techniques, for a technique *is* a technique by virtue of the fact that it is part of the whole art. Once you put on skis they become extensions of yourself, and it becomes impossible to practice just one technique such as sideslipping without engaging in others. The different skills and techniques blend into one another as part of this one whole process or activity.

When we consider the learning of *theoretical* subjects, we recognize that the world is too vast and complex to submit to ready description. In order to understand it we must divide it into comprehensible segments. The academic disciplines illustrate such a division. In a study of water, for example, some focus on water born plants, some on the use of water for power, others on water as a life habitat—the possible divisions are many. Clearly we can break the study into smaller and smaller components, and a person could spend a lifetime studying one small area. To be specific, all sorts of skills, techniques, technical terminology, and models could be developed to study an elephant's toenail. Each part of the elephant could be similarly examined. When they are brought together and unified these studies fit together to produce a body of knowledge about elephants. And yet, without looking at the elephant as a whole, taking into account its historical development, its ecological context, and its many relationships, one would know a lot of elephant *facts*, but one would not know elephants. There are many ways to analyze water, many ways to approach knowing water, but ultimately we need to aim at a holistic understanding, one that relates water to its environment and considers all its functions and relationships. A division of labor can become a method of teaching and then solidify into a way of seeing the world as a collection of fragmented, externally related parts.

In contrast to learning an art in the *piecemeal*, divided way, one can learn it *holistically*. This approach can be especially successful with children, although adults often find it more difficult. Children often become excellent skiers without any formal lessons, or instructed practice in specific, separate techniques. They put on skis and just start learning to ski. Usually they just follow other more advanced skiers around on the slopes. They imitate what the advanced skiers do, while skiing for fun. For them it is just play. Swimming, playing the violin, and learning martial arts are other examples of this holistic approach. Zen archery, according to Herrigel's (1953) description of his own experience, is taught in this way. This unified, experiential approach can be frustrating for an adult who is used to having questions answered, techniques described, and speculations explored. Adults seem to need such verbal interaction. Children, however, learn even language in this holistic, imitative way. But later on, as adults, we learn a second language usually by means of rules, grammar, vocabulary, and mastery of specific skills.

In the intuitive, imitative approach to learning (Suzuki violin or Zen archery), we have the purest form of the holistic way of learning; it stands in strong contrast with the analytic, piecemeal approach. As noted above, both the piecemeal and the holistic approaches usually proceed with the whole art as a background and a reference point. The problem with specialism is that it can work to prevent a grasp of the discipline as a whole art; it can frustrate and block its *mastery*.

Both the piecemeal and holistic approaches to learning have their advantages and drawbacks. For example, learning an art by means of instruction in separate techniques can interfere with a sense of the whole art's "flow". On the other hand, the imitative, holistic approach can lead to technical imprecision in details. Both the piecemeal and the holistic approaches can be barriers to mastery at a deep level, unless they are realized to be complementary. Mastery is not the same thing as expertise.

One of the things that differentiates a *master* from an *expert* is that a master not only is fluent and creative *within* the discipline or art, but also understands the larger context of the practice. Such an understanding provides a basis for approaching life as a whole. Arts like archery and wilderness travel, understood as whole practices, display the unity of meaning that reflects the sacred. The self-mastery required by such an art is also the discipline needed for living wisely. Mastering an art leads to a more balanced, confident, and mature approach to life in general. The art's spiritual dimensions lead us beyond egotistical striving. That most arts, pursued far enough, can reveal this spiritual dimension is a well known rationale for their practice in the East, where in Japan they then are referred to as "do" as in the Chinese Tao or the Way. The art of poetry, for example, can be not only a way of expressing a variety of ideas and emotions; it can also be a Way which anchors and harmonizes one in and with the world, a way to relate creatively and freely. The mastery of an art or a discipline as a "do" or "tao" develops the whole human self and leads us out of the fragmented, piecemeal view of life to wholesomeness. The design of technology practices should be undertaken as such a whole art, as a tao.

Mastery is the personified embodiment of an art which has universal meaning. The paradigms and ideals, the standards of excellence of an art, are high marks set by other masters. Although the methods of masters are worthy of emulation, if an art or discipline is to have an authentic embodiment, each of us has to practice it in our own personal way. We go beyond imitation of another's "perfect form" to develop our own unique style. Mastery of an art as tao is a way of unifying us with a larger tradition. It gives our particular acts significance, depth, meaning, and value. They are part of an ongoing and evolving tradition. Blending the analytic and holistic in mastery merge tradition with the cutting edge of creative activity.

In our pursuit of excellence we must design new technology practices with the above considerations in mind. Our new practices will better serve our personal goals, our community responsibilities, and our ecosophic aspirations, if we can employ a balanced approach to future development and master the art of appropriate design. We can do this if we can approach the design of ecosophic technology practices as a holistic art in the Eastern sense of tao. In the Epilogue we will explain this further, and show how technology practice as a "Way" gives larger significance to our individual activities.

We have just offered some suggestions for future work to further the long range aims of this project in philosophy of technology. The educational program recommended is just a beginning. As of now, a significant number of major universities in North America do not even have a well funded undergraduate program in environmental education, let alone a program in integrated technology studies. Despite considerable efforts to make environmental studies a central part of curriculum, there has been only modest success.

Universities set an example that the rest of the education system follows. In recent decades they have lost some of their original sense of direction and have become increasingly fragmented by professionalism and specialization. Funding which has spurred development in many applied areas has been increasingly linked with status quo business concerns. Research has always had some funding directed priorities. It would not take a great effort or cost much to get researchers to work on interdisciplinary education and research programs which would spur the development of technology practices which meet the criteria and conditions that have been spelled out in this book. The needed changes require better understanding of how to focus funding and energy for this work.

The published work of C. A. Bowers (1993) and David Orr (1992) provide some of the necessary foundation for ecocentric programs in environmental education and development of ecological literacy. Bower's work is especially important to understanding the process of learning in education colleges and in the public school system and how these could be shifted to new ecocentric paradigms. Orr's work helps to explain what ecocentric education requires in terms of its ecological dimensions.

More needs to be done to connect the approach to technology set forth here to the larger circle of studies already done on the different dimensions of technology practices in addition to the ones just mentioned. Let us hope that other energetic scholars from the relevant areas of cultural studies, policy and administration, economics, social sciences, natural sciences, and other technical fields will make this needed effort.

Epilogue
Technology Practices, the Age of
Ecosophy, and Reflections on the Way

I. Eight Cities in the Wilderness

For many years I have had a recurring vision I call the *eight cities in the wilderness*. The city is often seen in contrast to wilderness. Throughout history the idea of the wilderness—as represented by the wild forests, deserts, mountains, oceans—was seen as an unsettled place free of the hand of humans. Some monastic communities based themselves in the wilderness or desert. Many major religious figures withdrew into the wilderness to meditate, pray, and search for Divine vision. How we conceive of wilderness and cities is a function of our view of nature, human nature, and the cosmos. These larger views are part of our story. My lucid vision is of an evolutionary array of cities, each representing specific ideals, values, and ways of life. What I see before the first city are primal human communities, living in ecological balance with nature, whose members see themselves as person-beings within myriad communities of natural beings. These pre-urban communities do not set themselves apart from nature: the animals are human ancestors and companions, the forest is a friend and protector, the desert provides for their needs. Their Edenic consciousness resides in their unity with nature, even though awareness of humans as a unique species is emerging.

In my vision I travel through wilderness, deserts, forests, grasslands, jungles, and mountains. As I travel I come upon cities from time to time. They do not always appear in the same order from one vision to the next. I describe them here in an order related to the history of Western culture and our ideas of progress. Keep in mind that for Western urban humans the wild—such as forests—was often seen as the wholly other. It was often a symbol for the dark subconscious, the shadow of civilization (Harrison 1992).

The first city I come to is the *city of the tribe*. This is the mythic city that emerges after the destruction of the Tower of Babel. In it the human story ideal is the hero, for example, the wandering pagan who returns home with knowledge from other cultures and beings. Humans in this city still see animals as companions, and there are many human-animal beings in their mythology, forms that persist in oral story traditions as the city evolves.

The next city is the *city of humans*. It is the ideal city of the ancient Greeks represented by Athens. The hero or heroine is the philosopher ruler, who is a wise leader. This city is one of polity and discussion. It is a city of assembly and games. The old spirits of nature are still present in myths, but other deities, associated with cultivation of the land, also are present. The major form of adventure is the journey of discovery. The tribal unit has broken down, the equality between men and women is breaking down, and a hierarchical mode of thinking and power emerges as the city ages. The principal preoccupations of the City of Humans are organization, trade, political power, and artisan greatness. In the West a major city of this type was Rome.

But Rome, as the city of humans (and agrarian pagan deities) goes through changes and new ideals emerge, through cross-fertilization between Greek philosophy and Old and New Testament teachings. The *city of God* is born. In the city of God the ideal human is the saint. The paradise is called the Kingdom of Heaven. The most authentic adventure is the pilgrimage, as a journey for salvation. Earthly life is a stage upon which the human drama is played out in preparation for a Heaven set apart from nature. The ultimate aim of human history is determined by God. This is the city of theocracy.

The city of God sets the stage for the emergence of the feudal city of Medieval times, called the *city of chivalry*. In this city the ideal humans are represented by the knight and the lady. Honor, courage, loyalty, and romance are high values. The principal journey is pursuing the holy grail, fighting dragons, and adventuring in strange lands among alien people. The knight must go through many contests and trials to be worthy of the lady (purity) and to become a transformed human. A preoccupation of this city is with the esoteric symbolism of enchantment. During its time the spirits of nature mythology and the idea of the Shaman re-emerge. The Shaman, who is one of the ideals of the pre-urban communal tribe, takes on the form of the sorcerer or magician. Nature is an enchanted place, filled with all sorts of fantastic beings. Recently, this view of nature has resurfaced in books like *The Lord of the Rings*.

The city of chivalry recedes into the background as the *city of earthly progress* emerges. It is the renaissance city in which Greek ideals are reborn within a new conception of progress, distilled from Christian eschatology but now applied to science and technology. The ideal human of this city is the scientist-thinker, the well-rounded individual whose power comes from cultivation of both intellect and imagination. Leonardo Da Vinci represents the embodiment of this ideal. In this city Modernism as a philosophy is born; the world is seen as an empire of knowledge, and knowledge is the key to power. In this city production is organized through the factory; exchange is ordered through the use of money. This is a city of commerce, which breaks with its feudal past.

The city of earthly progress fades into the background as the *city of technocracy* emerges. In this city the ideal human is the expert, the highly sophisticated technician, who serves as consultant and advisor. The industrial complex becomes the primary mode of production and its mechanistic models become the form of organization imposed on the society as a whole. The greatest adventure is in the use of technological devices— railroads, cars, buses, steamships, planes, rockets, cyclotrons, and many others. The corporation orders business and government. The influence of older institutions on the direction of policy weakens, allowing productive efficiency and monetary considerations to play a dominant role in shaping major policies, and in measuring progress. In this city nature is seen as a storehouse of raw materials. The major aim of human life is to technologize the world, except for remnants of wilderness, relic forests, and marshes, set aside as genetic reserves, of historical interest, or for recreation. Even the human person is technologized. A dominant form of literature is science fiction which merges humans and androids, hybrids of human and machine. Human-machine hybrids are made with "superior" manufactured parts. Nature has no spirits or secret powers. It is treated as an artifact. It is only an object upon which to ply our skills. The ideal environment is the technosphere.

In the city of technocracy mechanized technological structures are in power. However, by "taking over" all spheres of nature and human life, they expose their own Achilles' heel. A technological structure fails to understand humans as *of* nature. Thus, it has lost the life of the spirit and meaning. It crosses all the older sacred limits and trespasses into domains where it distorts and disfigures the spirit of life itself. In so doing, it brings down upon itself a host of natural disasters and dislocations. It perceives these as problems to be solved by technical means. Among these are rising crime, environmental disasters, cancer, and other epidemic diseases. All of these are attacked by "wars-on" approaches, using all the legal, technical, technological, and other forms of "power-over" organization possible. But these only make the problems worse and furthermore produce secondary problems. Some within the city of technocracy see the authentic problem to be a loss of connection with and respect for nature and its wisdom. There is a need for spiritual disciplines.

Next I see the *city of planetary consciousness*, the city of the planetary person. In this city, the ideal person is a master-generalist, who has transcended the egoic stage that sought to control others and nature. Planetary persons live in the transpersonal stage, a form of maturity that spontaneously places appropriate limits on technological activity. They see technology practice as a way to transcend the games of power of the late technocratic city. They are globally aware while being devoted to and firmly rooted in the uniqueness of place. It is in the city of planetary consciousness that an ecological conscience emerges. This awareness creates a new ecophilosophy of wise practices. Just as the city of technocracy was the city of the industrial complex, the city of planetary consciousness is the city of human scale. It is a decentralized, democratized city that has put wildness back into its yards, gardens, and parks. It is the city of the ecosteward who lives in the Age of Ecology. It is an emerging city which cultivates integrative systems of relationships and processes; it is a city of mastery of self and of whole arts based on respect for nature. As a transition city in this vision it leads to the city of being.

The *city of being* dwells in the Age of Ecosophy. It is the city of the deep future. In this city the ideal is the sage, who masters spiritual disciplines that bring together all earlier teachings. In the city of being a continuously evolving consciousness deepens in nature spirituality. It is a city organized through communal networks of both human and natural communities. It is a city of *satchitananda*, that is, a city in which unalloyed being, bliss, and wisdom are realized. Here all dominance, control over others, and hierarchy of authoritarian domination have been eliminated from living practice. Appropriate, ecosophic technology practices replace the transition forms of ecologically designed production created by the city of planetary consciousness.

In this vision of the eight cities and the wilderness, there are some in each city who keep alive the practice of the Way. To practice the Way achieves harmony within and harmony with nature. The Way is marked by wisdom and compassion. The Way represents full completion and the realization of unity of self in the larger ecological Self. To follow the Way is to cultivate practices that unify our total being and give us access to a deeper wisdom. In each city, and even in the pre-urban tribal community, there are persons who pursue and realize the Way. Their example inspires others in each city to transcend and change its structures. In the last city, the city of being, there are no more limits or dichotomies, no divisions between humans and nature. The wilderness and our own wild nature are no longer fenced, whether conceptually, legally, or technologically. The city of planetary consciousness is a city of restoration, or rebirth of the spirits of nature in human consciousness, but in the city of being the spirits of nature, the gods, humans, and the Earth dwell together in harmony.

The city of being represents the transcendence of urban form, for in this city the mass mind wanes and the pre-urban ecological community reemerges through the post-urban ecosophic mind. The city of being is the city of the future primal person, whereas the city of planetary consciousness is the city of the neonaturalist. The city of planetary consciousness practices organic gardening and farming, but the city of being practices natural gardening and natural farming in which very little is done. The city of planetary consciousness practices sustainable development, but the city of being develops sustainability.

I see this vision of eight cities and the wilderness as a story of the human journey out of the intimate union with nature to self-conscious awareness, to species-consciousness and separation, and then on to unity with nature, but now with transpersonal conscious wisdom. The ideal of the ecological steward is the human who guides but does not control, but when nature is restored and we have matured fully, the ecosteward is transcended by the sage of being. The sage lets nature flourish and guide, and has his-her spiritual needs satisfied by being, not by having.

In my description of the vision I have not so far spelled out the changing conceptions of technology practice that are part of the evolutionary processes the cities represent. Let us now bring this dimension into sharper focus in relation to *ecosophy and the Way.*

II. Ecosophy and the Way

Humans have been called the toolmaking animals. If by toolmaking we mean not just fashioning a "tool" now and then, which many other animals do, but the systematic fabrication and improvement of implements used methodically to accomplish a variety of ends, not all related to vital physical needs, then we could say that humans are distinctive in being the technology creating species. In this sense, the technological process is a culture-laden one which passes from one generation to the next through cultural symbols and rituals.

Humans are thus culture-creating beings who express themselves through technology. They create technology practices as part of larger cultural activities, not only to accomplish tasks that have obvious, immediate, practical survival aims, but to complement, celebrate, and extend their lives *as cultured beings.* Even in so-called technologically simple, or primitive, hunting-gathering cultures, technology practices are interwoven with deep and sophisticated religious, aesthetic, moral, philosophical, and mythic elements. Only in advanced technological societies dominated by the philosophy of Modernism, do we find cultures in which there is an effort to make technology (and science) value-free. Its designers and users defend its value-free status with remarks such as: "Guns don't kill people, people kill people;" "Nuclear power is neither good nor bad, it's the use we make of it that determines whether it's good or bad;" "Science is a value-free activity. The scientist merely tells us how things are; merely reports the facts; doesn't tell us how we ought to act." These and similar statements are made to convince us that modern technology, with science as one of its major driving forces, has no value dimensions. And yet these claims are usually followed by statements that reveal a bias in favor of the activities or technologies in question, extolling their values and all the good they will bring.

In our fundamental description of technology as a *practice* we lay bare its value-laden dimensions. All science and technology is conducted according to specific values and within a range of assumptions constituting a worldview, which is not itself science but philosophy. Secular, technological society attempts to hide this context, to give the impression that its worldview is not a philosophy, but a system of objective truths based on science. However, this is not true as it becomes clear when we attempt to transfer technological practices to other cultures. Then we see that modern Western technology and science *are* value-laden expressions of our culture. We undertake this transfer by claiming that these forms of adaptation are superior to those of other cultures. We claim that our technologies will improve their way of life; that they represent progress; that they promote "development". We have replaced our earlier missionary zeal, driven by religious and hidden imperial motives, with the zeal of Modernism, offering its technology practices as saviors. (In connection with this process see Norberg-Hodge 1991 and Quinn 1993.) In the city of the technocrat, technological development becomes a religion, and its kingdom of heaven is technotopia.

In modern secular society the spiritual dimensions are separated from the main activities of daily life. Commerce supposedly adheres to a basic Judeo-Christian ethic based on fair, honest dealing and keeping contractual agreements. But science and technology are alleged to be in themselves value-free. The technocrat considers technologies good if they work when applied. The design of technology (and science) is thought to be freed of moral and spiritual restraints, since its aim is only knowledge and practical skill. Whether the technology is used and how is up to those who make policy and practical decisions. The economics of a working technology determines whether it gets widely used. In these and other ways, technological society fragments and divides its decision making processes. It divides and fragments responsibility. It is not individuals who act but corporations, committees, and government agencies. When a complex, modern jet aircraft is built, for example, no one person or small group of people, can say, "I did it," or "We did it;" no one in particular can come forward to take credit for this artifact. Modern tech-

nological products are a result of divided or fragmented moral account-
ability.

In the ancient tradition of the teachings of the *Way* ("Do" or "Tao"),
basic commitments are related to personal responsibility. The "Way" is a
spiritual path that an aspirant takes up by conscious decision. To follow
the Way is to be involved in ongoing self-purification, self-transcendence,
and Self-realization. Self-realization comes through self-transcendence,
becoming aware that the small self (ego) is part of a large Self (the full
ecological, transpersonal Self) that illuminates all beings. Buddha, Christ,
and Lao Tzu were embodiments of the Way. All three emphasized that
the Way requires making a commitment to certain moral precepts, which
are the same in all three teachings: One should lead a life of nonviolence;
one should lead a life of compassion and love for all beings; one should
lead a life that is respectful of all existence, taking only what one needs
to flourish. Although *compassion, frugality,* and *nonviolence* are the three
cardinal virtues of the Way, other guides to moral and spiritual life flow
from these basic precepts. To be compassionate implies having humility
and respect for the self-integrity of all other beings; it implies helping
others but not meddling in their lives. Nonviolence implies not killing
and physically harming other beings, and not interfering with their destiny. One does not place oneself over them so that they work only for
one's own benefit. Nonviolence applies not just to actions but also to our
language, and the feelings and attitudes we express toward others. Frugality means living in a thoughtful, considerate way, mindful of how our
consumption affects others; we respect the natural world and the products of other beings' labor. Truthfulness, honesty, and other virtues follow
when one accepts the cardinal values.

The principles that follow from these three treasures as spiritual rules
are guides to those on the path, that is the Way. As one advances on the
Way there comes a time when rules recede. One is then guided from
deeper sensibilities representing an extended sense of identification with
all other beings (Naess 1991). All virtues of the Way are unified through
ecosophy, or ecological wisdom and harmony. For the sage of being the
imperative is "Realize ecosophy!" This is a voice beyond the environmental crisis.

A most significant development in Modernism is technological society's separation of church and state. The historical reasons for this in the
West are well known. The church became a powerful bureaucracy that
lost touch with the Way of our greatest spiritual teachers. It became embroiled in partisan politics; in wars; in influence peddling; in selling sacra-
ments; in inquisition; in blind opposition to genuine advances in
learning. It became hamstrung by its own ever multiplying system of arbitrary and confusing rules and regulations. It lost its vision and its sense

of direction. It lost touch with both the demands of earthly life and the unconditional freedom of the Kingdom of Heaven. The Kingdom that is found through the heart, that lies "ready at hand", and is "shown to us through love (agape)" was no longer in its practice. It lost touch with the love that Jesus taught is consonant with the Way of light and truth. In its haste to ban "eros", the church also lost "agape", not realizing that the same divine energies power both, forgetting that human spiritual life must unify our psycho-physical being in this earthly life here and now. This love of the Way, which it lost, is the love that transforms the personal (Jesus) to the transpersonal (Christ).

Modern Western society rejected the church as the dominant authority because it became an oppressive power that had lost contact with the sacred. In its place there emerged a secular society. As a result, two of the most powerful activities of modern life, technology, and science, developed within a spiritual and moral vacuum without reference to the Way. Work became separated from spiritual and moral cultivation and practice. It became just a job, an undertaking to earn money, not a calling, not a commitment, not service to others, and not a means to perfect oneself in devotion to the Way.

Perhaps this turn of events was historically necessary, but it is now both historically and environmentally necessary to end this division and to reanimate our daily lives with new forms of ecosophic spiritual practice. The practices we need are not those lost in the structures of the past, but those that revivify and re-vision our traditions with fresh understanding and new methods. We need now to recognize that spiritual *discipline* is not and should not be spiritual *imprisonment*, that the practice of a spiritual discipline should be an empowering center for daily life and work. But this will happen only if we free spiritual disciplines of the jargon that plunges us into sectarian debates and historical controversy. In this book, we have illustrated how this redefinition might be done by showing how the dominant soteriological story of Christianity, incorporating the Old Testament story of Adam and Eve and the New Testament story of Jesus revealing the Christ, can be reinterpreted with the aid of our current understanding of transpersonal psychology, Eastern traditions of the Way, and ecosophy.

Ecosophy cuts across all cultures and levels of development and forms part of a new transpersonal ecological consciousness that is universal and ecumenical. Cross-cultural, comparative ecophilosophy as a practice is broad enough to enable us to arrive at this planetary harmony between *diverse* cultures. The practice of ecophilosophy is appropriate to our age of global technology and ecological limitations. We find it as a common ground that joins us together to prevent violence, further social justice, and stop the destruction of ecological communities. We will work to restore the integrity of the Earth. Appropriate ecosophic technology practices play a key role in all of these endeavors.

We must reclaim technology practices from special interests and the elite. We must make them part of a larger educational and spiritual undertaking that addresses vital human needs and nurtures whole persons. These integrated ecosophic persons, working with others, will create new forms of community and culture that foster harmony with nature as a whole. Our daily practices must themselves be instances of healing the planet, communities, and ourselves. The practice of the Way completes itself in each of its acts, for each of its acts, fully understood, *is* the Way. In order to penetrate and realize the transhistorical dimension of the sacred, which is found only in the whole present, we must transcend linear historical time. In our daily lives, in each act, in work, in play, in family life, in recreation, and in social life, our practice of technology must be self-transcending and ecosophic. In actualizing this wisdom in our daily lives, our practices become whole, and then the present threat of the death of nature and the destruction of the ecosphere will become a nightmare from the past, and then just a dream.

We (meaning industrial nations, and especially Canada and the United States) must now build cities of planetary consciousness appropriate to the Age of Ecology. By following the Way we will lessen the suffering that humans cause to other beings. These beings will then no longer mourn our presence on Earth as representing their bondage and destruction. They will join with us in a planetary symphony in which all have a part and through which all join in the great harmony that celebrates and praises the Way. As we follow the Way more fully we will see the birth of many new ecosophic communities, many new Edens, each in communion with all other beings, each based on place specific wisdom. The spirits of nature will reappear and help us once more. Humans will no longer be the problem-making species. We will no longer feel alienated and alone, but will once more be part of the ongoing cosmic harmony. We will then have reached the Age of Ecosophy and will be building cities of being. If our practices are authentic and harmonious with the Way, this vision will be a reality. We have roughly described the eight city vision, leaving out the details because we must draw this journey to a close.

III. History and Destiny

We end by returning to our earlier discussions of history and destiny. We described traditional Western religious teachings as based on a type of story associated with written texts. Texts are artifacts made by the technology practice of writing and reading. Historical consciousness arises through literacy and out of separations made possible by changes in knowledge and technology. Christianity is a religion of historical consciousness.

As already noted, the story of Adam and Eve links the emergence of self-reflexive and species consciousness to gaining knowledge of good and evil. This knowledge comes from eating the fruit of a tree. The tree in ancient oral cultures is a multidimensional symbol. It represents the organization of knowledge as a whole. The tree grows in the Garden of Eden, which humans leave to become agriculturalists. However, the tree in Western civilization represents classification systems which predate and include literacy, but also represents shadows, wildness, and growth. Trees give life, but they can also conceal danger. The older tree of knowledge is to be replaced in Christian teachings by *The Word* which comes from The Holy Book. The tree is also replaced by the plants of agricultural civilization. Throughout the Bible the teachings use the lessons of good shepherds and good farmers to explain what the Word means, what the Way is. *The Word* gives eternal life, just as the tree gives life to other beings. But the old tree represents the ancient Earth based wisdom and so must be transcended by the new spiritual tree of life, that is, The Word as doctrine. Doctrine and text are central to historical Christianity. Out of texts religious doctrine and theology arise.

Although every religion of civilization has doctrinal elements, it also has other elements that include religious experiences, personalities, ceremonies, and practices. In oral traditions religion is sparse and lives in practice and ceremony, not in texts, since there are none. Life is here and now. The past exists only in memory. The future is real only insofar as we can see it in visionary experience. Other spiritual beings are all around us, for in the textless society the world of sense is ever present. Language is spoken, and the words disappear as they are said; it is an ongoing process, not an artifact. Written words *are* of the past. They are artifacts which exist in the present, and do not disappear, hence, they can be examined and analyzed. But this is not true for the oral story telling traditions. All story telling is in part memory, but also in part creative act and performance. Stories are not repeated mindlessly verbatim, but organized through patterns, cycles, themes, and the like. No one person organizes or knows them all. Text based religious doctrine takes away immediacy and spontaneity, and there is gradually a general loss of the ability to tell stories. There is centralized authority over life stories.

This whole process we have been describing has parallels in technological development with respect to the emergence of vernacular technologies, that is, technologies specific and appropriate to particular places. In some cultures technology, story telling, and art are all coherent interrelated processes in which everyone participates, the whole ecological community, including the plants, animals, guardian spirits, ancestors, and so on. In this way harmony is realized. Technology practices emerge in the same way.

It is recognized in primal Shamanic cultures that one has to be in harmony with the spirits and beings of nature. This is achieved by a variety of practices. Ritual purification, ceremony, festivals, communal sweat baths, and vision quests are all ways of unifying the group and harmonizing with nature. The self, as individual person, is deeply respected for its deep sources of wisdom which come from its past, from its contacts to the spirit world, and from its contacts with other beings. Primal cultures did not break with the natural world as Western historical consciousness did.

The story of Adam and Eve tells of leaving the Garden of Eden (harmony with nature in primal culture), to enter the world of history (the time of trial and disharmony with nature). Their descendants must toil and live in the world with no hope of blessedness, unless they find grace. Christ brings *The Word* that frees the soul of damnation (salvation from history). He will in the fullness of time return to bring an eternal paradise, the Kingdom of Heaven on Earth.

So Western agricultural humans separated from the rest of nature and primal cultures at the dawn of history. And what *is* history but this period of great change and struggle in linear time? In Western history humans assert themselves because they believe they are in the image of the Creator and that their destiny is to have dominion over the world. Humans above all others are favored by God. However, we have fallen from God's grace because our ancestors sinned, and each of us sins too so far as we assert ourselves over God's Word. The original act of civilization involves being alienated and cut off from the source, from the divine ground of being in which all beings participate. Historical consciousness is thus alienated and out of harmony with the creative source of its own life. Primal cultures rarely lose their ability to enter the transhistorical, whereas historical societies often do.

For the historical, doctrinal religion, accepting God's Word liberates us from the fear of damnation. (What is Hell but the eternal replaying of the torments of history?) We are free to make ourselves, improve ourselves, become in the likeness of God through Christ, the Savior. It is the Word we must accept. However, the texts are not self-interpreting, at least not through most of Christian history. They are read, understood, and explained to the laity by an organization of professionals. In primal cultures there are no professionals. People are always changing roles and identities. Who they were in the past is no longer of any consequence. History is a worship of the past as fixed identities (biographies).

History is also the time of great change. Its guiding light through most of western Civilization is the Christian Bible and the Doctrines revealed therein about sacred time. These doctrines are hidden (esoteric) in the text, just as Jesus' parables hide the inner truth of *The Word*. To grasp the truth is to be set free of the torments of history to realize Heavenly bliss. The past holds our sins, the present our key to salvation, and the future our possible bliss. The present is tenuous and we must act now or risk eternal damnation. The historical ego self feels that time is running out. There is an urgency to act or be damned for the sins of the past. This historical consciousness is born out of the technological revolutions that began to emerge with literacy rooted in agriculture. With literacy in the West comes a different type of thought, a different type of logic and mind, and possibilities for new forms of culture and enculturation (Ong 1982).

Technological development changes our sense of time. In the prehistorical period people dwell in the timeless, and change is almost imperceptible. During the historical period change accelerates more and more and the timeless slips away from us. In the posthistorical phase time will alter once more to a sense of slow natural patterns and stability.

Through our own historical dynamics the secularization of culture in the modern period goes hand and hand with the emergence of a culture whose priority is making the world over in the image of what it conceives to be paradise. This is the Cosmopolis that Toulmin (1990) writes perceptively about.

We divide the earthly life into three great periods: prehistory, history and posthistory. There are many secular thinkers (for example, Bell 1979, Boulding 1965, and Seidenberg 1950) who think that history is a time of transition: It represents the emergence of technological innovation and change as a focus crystallizing in the science driven technologies of today. The pace of change picks up throughout history along side of technological innovation. The modern state is associated with the emergence of mass society and mass technology which leads to massive disruption and global change. The culmination of this whole historical process thus seems at hand, for the simple reason that all of the growth curves are geometric, (waste generation, soil erosion, deforestation, energy use, and others), but the Earth's ecosystems have finite limits. We have reached and are passing these limits. This, then, must be the great turning point (Capra 1982), *the place where historical progress as growth is transformed into something else.* We have reached the limits of the large and centralized, it is now the time of the almost insignificant and place specific. The next era of posthistory ushers in technological cultures based on bioregional identifications and boundaries (Sale 1985), related through community networks; vernacular technology practices emerging from grass roots communities that have reinhabited their places; diverse cultures that are based on ecocentric values and nonviolence; decentralized solar energy use; global pluralism, and universal civility.

The prehistorical is the context of primal culture; the historical of the time bound, self-oriented cultures; the posthistorical of the neo primal transpersonal cultures. Through deep, place specific knowledge and accumulation of wise practices over time, there will evolve technology practices which are highly sophisticated but also extremely simple, like those of aboriginal peoples. In the posthistorical period the cultures which have gone into history will rejoin the Earth's other cultures and beings and become harmonious contributors to order and beauty.

To move into historical consciousness is to move into the dramas of the self, as this is reflected in the novels, operas, and plays of the modern West. The cultivation of the inner speech of introversion in many ways replaces the communal dialogue of traditional culture. This interiorization is conditioned by literacy. In the West literature gives rise to elitism as those with power attempt to enforce their uses of language as the only proper ones; they would write and live the stories that others envy. The self-seeking of historical civilizations is sometimes crystallized in the ego of a ruler, as is told in many of the stories of feudal China, Japan, and Europe. Such ruler's self-preoccupations become destructive to the good of the community. People imitate the rulers and the upper classes, especially in modern democracy.

The individual who goes through self conscious development in history, then, thinks life turns entirely around what they themselves do. They must make their name in history! But the wise person of posthistory realizes that this is vanity. History is not eternal, and written records are only a little less ephemeral than spoken performances. History in a deep sense only exists because of books and records. To realize this is to arrive at the threshold of a new awareness, a transhistorical consciousness, for one realizes that all the other human selves caught up in history are also thinking they are alone and entirely unique. They also feel this need to *mean* something, to be *somebody*. Understanding this can give rise to compassion and concern. With compassion comes deep and wide identification with all other conscious beings and realization of the ecological Self, which lives here and now timelessly with no sense of urgency; this is transpersonal consciousness. Let us look at the example of Jesus in this connection.

Jesus is the historical person who was born and lived in a certain period. He has a history. Jesus comes out of the Holy Spirit (the prepersonal and prehistoric) into the world of the flesh (the personal world of history). Through his acts (with a sense of urgency), he makes his place in history. He is crucified on a cross, the vertical axis of which represents the timeless, transhistorical, and the horizontal axis the linear time of history to which his hands, the makers and users of technology, are bound. The historical person (Jesus) dies on the cross and Christ (transpersonal consciousness) is born. His power requires no technology for it is the power of love (which is God). The realization of the Kingdom is within the heart. The Way taught (shown) by Christ is the Way of love, that is, timeless compassion, not the urgent, erotic passions of the historical ego.

The historical civilization of India also gives us this same basic story with Sidhartha becoming Buddha. As Eliade (1974) and others have observed, once humans enter historical awareness they devote considerable effort to trying to escape it. This escape is possible in a number of ways, for example, by imagining a future paradise where we are immortal and the personal, historical self just goes on in a painless, blissful state forever. The other way is to realize the timelessness of the transhistorical, transpersonal, ecological Self here and now by means of which the ego is transcended. Buddhism, insofar as it emphasizes practices, keeps focused on transformational processes here and now. Christianity, insofar as it is a religion of doctrine, emphasizes the future condition as described by abstract, "timeless," nonexpiring doctrine. Christian practice of compassion, however, is akin to Buddhist practice of "blessings to all beings."

The great changes of technological society now bring us to the end of Western history as a story of technological power over nature and others. To build new cultural ways requires seeing through these stories that have powered the energies of our civilization in the modern period. It is clear that these stories of monocultural centralization are just one version of the sacred tradition represented in secular form. They have taken us as far as they can. Every such story has limitations and when applied overzealously it becomes maladaptive. When humans hear only their own story, the rest of creation trembles. When they hear the stories of all beings, all creation rejoices.

To enter the visionary is to enter the transhistorical and transpersonal. As twentieth-century Western intellectuals, our visionary capacities are rusty and our skills of narration in need of perfecting. We hope that the reader's own imagination and narrative sensibilities have been stimulated by this journey and that our technology is now seen in greater relief.

All around us are opportunities for richness, diversity, and great quality. Each of us can live in ways which are artful, creative with beautiful actions that celebrate this mysterious Earth with its endless possibilities for realizing joy with other humans and other beings. Let our work become sacred play through ecologically wise and harmonious technology practices in communion with each other and the rest of nature.

Bibliography

Abbey, E. 1975. *The Monkey Wrench Gang*. New York: J. B. Lippincott.

Albrecht, William. 1975. *The Albrecht Papers*, vol. 2: *Soil Fertility and Animal Health*. Kansas City: Acres USA.

Alexander, Christopher, 1979. *The Timeless Way of Building*. New York: Oxford.

Barbour, Ian. 1980. *Technology, Environment, and Human Values*. Englewood Cliffs, N.J.: Prentice-Hall.

Barrett, William. 1978. *The Illusion of Technique: A Search for Meaning in a Technological Society*. New York: Anchor.

Bell, Daniel. 1979. "Communications Technology: For Better or For Worse." *Harvard Business Review*, May/June: 23–33.

————. 1976. *The Cultural Contradictions of Capitalism*. New York: Basic.

Berger, John. 1985. *Restoring the Earth*. New York: Knopf.

Berman, M. 1981. *The Reenchantment of the World*. Ithaca: Cornell University.

Berry, Thomas. 1988. *Dream of the Earth*. San Francisco: Sierra Books.

Berry, Wendell. 1977. *The Unsettling of America: Culture of Agriculture*. New York: Avon.

Blackburn, T. and K. Anderson. 1993. *Before the Wilderness: Environmental Management by Native Californians*. Menlo Park, Ca.: Ballena Press.

Bly, Robert. 1988. *A Little Book on the Human Shadow*. (Edited by W. Booth). New York: Harper & Row.

————. 1990. *Iron John*. Reading, Mass.: Addison Wesley.

Bookchin, Murray. 1982. *The Ecology of Freedom: The Emergence and Disso-lution of Hierarchy.* Palo Alto, Ca.: Cheshire Books.

Boone, A. J. 1970. *The Language of Silence.* New York: Harper & Row.

Boulding, Kenneth. 1965. *The Meaning of the 20th Century.* New York: Harper & Row.

———. 1989. *The Three Faces of Power.* Newbury Park, Calif.: Sage Publications.

Bowers, C. A. 1988. *The Cultural Dimensions of Educational Computing: Understanding the Non-Neutrality of Technology.* New York: Teachers College Press.

Boyd, D. 1974. *Rolling Thunder.* New York: Delta.

Bramwell, Anna. 1989. *Ecology in the 20th Century.* New Haven, Conn.: Yale University Press.

Brower, Kenneth. 1978. *The Starship and the Canoe.* New York: Bantam.

Brown, L., et al. 1993. *State of the World.* New York: Norton.

Bruntland, G. 1988. *Our Common Future.* London and New York: Oxford University Press.

Buber, Martin. 1960. *Paths In Utopia.* Boston, Mass.: Beacon.

Burke, James. 1978. *Connections.* London: Macmillan.

Cairns, J., ed. 1989. *The Recovery Process in Damaged Ecosystems.* Ann Arbor, Mich.: Ann Arbor Service Publications.

Callenbach, Ernest. 1972. *Ecotopia.* Berkeley, Calif.: Banyen Tree.

Cameron, Julie. *The Artist's Way: A Spiritual Guide to Higher Creativity.* New York: Putnam.

Camp, Orville. 1984. *Forest Farmer's Handbook: A Guide to Natural Selec-tion Forest Management.* Ashland: Sky River Press.

Campbell, Joseph. 1973. *The Masks of God: Creative Mythology.* New York: Penguin.

Capra, Fritzjof. 1982. *The Turning Point: Science, Society and the Rising Cul-ture.* New York: Simon & Schuster.

Carr, David. 1986. *Time, Narrative & History.* Bloomington: Indian University Press.

Carr, Terry, ed. 1980. Dream's Edge: *Science Fiction Stories About the Future of Planet Earth.* San Francisco: Sierra Club Books.

Carson, Rachel. 1962. *Silent Spring*. Boston, Mass.: Houghton-Mifflin.

Carter, Robert. 1989. *The Nothingness Beyond God*. New York: Paragon.

Carter, V. and T. Dale. 1974. *Civilization and Soil*. Norman: University of Oklahoma Press.

Castaneda, Carlos. 1973. *A Separate Reality*. New York: Pocket Books.

Chandler, Alfred Jr. 1980. *Scale and Scope: The Dynamics of Industrial Capitalism*. Cambridge: Harvard University Press.

Chomsky, Norm. 1988. *Manufacturing Consent*. New York: Random House.

Clarke, Arthur. 1956. *The City and the Stars*. New York: Signet.

———. 1968. *2001: A Space Odyssey*. New York: Signet.

Cleary, Thomas, ed. 1989. *Zen Essence: The Science of Freedom*. Boston, Mass.: Shambhala.

Coates, Gary. 1981. *Resettling America: Energy, Ecology, and Community*. Andover, N.H.: Brick House.

Cohen, Mark, N. 1989. *Health and the Rise of Civilization*. New Haven, Conn.: Yale University.

Commoner, Barry. 1972. *The Closing Circle*. New York: Bantam Books.

———. 1976. *The Poverty of Power*. New York: Knopf.

———. 1992. *Making Peace With the Planet*. New York: The New Press.

Congdon, R. J., ed. 1977. *Introduction to Appropriate Technology*. Emmaus, Penn.: Rodale.

Cooley, Michael. 1980. *Architect or Bee?* Slough, England: Hand and Brain Publications.

Daly, H. and J. Cobb. 1989. *For the Common Good: Redirecting the Economy Toward Community, the Environment and a Sustainable Future*. Boston, Mass.: Beacon.

Danto, A. C. 1985. *Narration & Knowledge*. New York: Columbia University Press.

Devall, Bill. 1993. *Living Richly in an Age of Limits*. Salt Lake City, Utah: Gibb Smith.

———. ed. 1993. *Clearcut: The Tragedy of Industrial Forestry*. San Francisco: Earth Island Press.

Devall, Bill & George Sessions. 1985. *Deep Ecology: Living as if Nature Mattered.* Salt Lake City, Utah: Peregrine Smith.

Diamond, Stanley. 1981. *In Search of the Primitive.* London: Transaction Books.

Dogen. 1985. *Shobogenzo.* Trans. T. Cleary. Honolulu: University of Hawaii Press.

Domini, A. L. and P. D. Kinder. 1984. *Ethical Investing.* Reading, Penn.: Addison-Wesley.

Drengson, Alan R. 1989. *Beyond Environmental Crisis: From Technocrat to Planetary Person.* New York: Peter Lang.

————. 1993. *Doc Forest and Blue Mountain Ecostery.* Victoria, B.C.: Ecostery House.

Duer, H. P. 1985. *Dreamtime: Concerning the Boundary Between Wilderness and Civilization.* Oxford: Blackwell.

Duncan, David. 1983. *The River Why.* New York: Bantam.

Dunn, P. D. 1978. *Appropriate Technology.* New York: Schocken.

Eckersley, Robyn. 1992. *Environmentalism and Political Theory: Toward an Ecocentric Approach.* Albany: SUNY.

Ehrlich, P. and A. Extinction. 1981. *The Causes and Consequences of the Disappearance of Species.* New York: Random House.

Eliade, M. 1974. *The Myth of the Eternal Return: Or, Cosmos and History.* Princeton, N.J.: Princeton University.

Eiseley, Loren. 1960. *The Firmament of Time.* New York: Atheneum.

————. 1970. *The Divisible Pyramid.* New York: Scribners.

Eikins, Paul, ed. 1986. *The Living Economy: A New Economy in the Making.* London: Routledge.

Ellul, Jacques. 1964. *The Technological Society.* New York: Random House.

Ervin, K. 1989. *Fragile Majesty: The Battle for North America's Last Great Forest.* Seattle, Wash.: Mountaineers.

Fandozzi, E. 1979. "Art and Technology" in *Research in Philosophy and Technology*, Vol. 2.

Faulkner, Edward H. 1943. *The Plowman's Folly.* Norman: University of Oklahoma.

Ferré, Frederick. 1988. *Philosophy of Technology.* Englewood Cliffs, N.J.: Prentice-Hall.

Fields, Rick. 1991. *The Code of the Warrior.* New York: Harper Perennial Books.

Foreman, Dave. 1988. *Ecodefense.* Tucson, Ariz.: Ned Ludd Books.

Forester, Jay W. 1973. *World Dynamics.* Cambridge: M.I.T. Press.

Fox, Matthew. 1988. *The Coming of the Cosmic Christ.* San Francisco: Harper & Row.

Fox, Warwick. 1990. *Toward A Transpersonal Ecology: Developing New Foundations for Environmentalism.* Boston, Mass.: Shambhala.

Frankl, V. 1959. *Man's Search for Meaning.* Boston, Mass.: Beacon.

Fromm, Eric. 1978. *The Revolution in Hope: Toward a Humanized Technology.* New York: Bantam.

Fukuoka, M. 1978. *One Straw Revolution.* Emmaus, Penn.: Rodale.

Galbraith, John K. 1967. *The New Industrial State.* New York: Signet.

Gleick, James. 1987. *Chaos: Making a New Science.* New York: Penguin.

Goering, Peter, Helena Norberg-Hodge & John Page. 1993. *From The Ground Up: Rethinking Industrial Agriculture.* London: Zed Books.

Goldsmith, E. 1993. *The Way: An Ecological Worldview.* Boston, Mass.: Shambhala.

Gore, A. 1992. *Earth in the Balance: Ecology and the Human Spirit.* New York: Houghton Mifflin.

Goulet, Dennis. 1971. *The Cruel Choice: Value Conflicts in Technology Transfer.* New York: Atheneum.

Gradwohl, J. and R. Greenberg. 1978. *Saving the Tropical Forests.* Washington, D.C.: Smithsonian Institute.

Gray, Elizabeth Green. 1988. *Paradise Lost.* Wellesley, Mass.: Roundtable Press.

Griffin, Susan. 1978. *Women and Nature: The Roaring Inside Her.* New York: Harper & Row.

Grof, Stanislav. 1976. *Realms of the Human Unconscious.* New York: Dutton.

Hammond, M., Howarth, J. and R. Kent, eds. 1991. *Understanding Phenomenology.* Oxford: Blackwell.

Hammond, H. 1992. *Seeing the Forest Among the Trees: A Guide to Wholistic Forestry.* Vancouver: Polestar Books.

Harding, Jim, ed., et al. 1982. *Tools for the Soft Paths.* San Francisco: Friends of the Earth.

Hargrove, Eugene. 1989. *Foundations of Environmental Ethics.* New York: Prentice Hall.

Harker, D. and K. Evans. S. and M. eds. 1992. *Landscape Restoration Handbook.* Boca Raton, Fla.: Lewis Park.

Harner, M. 1986. *The Way of the Shaman.* New York: Bantam.

Harris, Larry D. 1984. *The Fragmented Forest: Island Biogeography Theory and the Preservation of Biotic Diversity.* Chicago: University of Chicago Press.

Harrison, H. P. 1992. *Forests: Shadow of Civilization.* Chicago: University of Chicago Press.

Hawken, Paul. 1993. *The Ecology of Commerce: A declaration of sustainability.* New York: Harper Collins.

Hawking, Stephen W. 1988. *A Brief History of Time.* New York: Bantam.

Head, S. and R. Heinzman, eds. 1990. *Lessons of the Rain Forest.* San Francisco: Sierra Club Books.

Heidegger, Martin. 1977. *The Question Concerning Technology and Other Essays.* New York: Norton.

Henderson, Hazel. 1978. *Creating Alternative Futures: The End to Economics.* New York: Harper & Row.

———. 1991. *Paradigms in Progress: Life Beyond Economics.* Indianapolis: Knowledge Systems.

Herrigel, E. 1953. *Zen and the Art of Archery.* New York: Vintage.

Hess, Karl, Jr. 1992. *Visions Upon the Land.* Covelo, Calif.: Island Press.

Hick, John. 1983. *Introduction to Philosophy of Religion.* Englewood Cliffs, N.J.: Prentice Hall.

Hickman, Larry. 1990. *John Dewey's Pragmatic Technology.* Bloomington: Indiana University Press.

———, ed., 1990. *Technology as a Human Affair.* New York: McGraw Hill.

Highwater, Jamake. 1981. *The Primal Mind: Vision and Reality in Indian America.* New York: Harper & Row.

Howard, Sir Albert. 1956. *The Soil and Health*. London: Oxford.

Hughes, D. 1983. *American Indian Ecology*. El Paso, Texas: Texas Press.

Huxley, Aldous. 1946. *Brave New World*. New York: Bantam.

————. 1962. *Island*. New York: Harper & Row.

Hyams, E. 1976. *Soil & Civilization*. New York: Harper & Row.

Hyland, Drew. 1984. *The Question of Play*. New York: University Presses of America.

Hynes, Patricia H. ed. 1991. *Reconstructing Babylon: Essays on Women & Technology*. Bloomington: Indiana University Press.

Ihde, Don. 1983. *Existential Technics*. Albany: SUNY.

————. 1990. *Technology & the Lifeworld: From Garden to Earth*. Bloomington: Indiana University Press.

Illich, Ivan. 1970. *Deschooling Society*. New York: Harper & Row.

————. 1973. *Tools for Conviviality*. New York: Harper & Row.

————. 1977. *Medical Nemesis: The Expropriation of Health*. New York: Bantam.

Jackson, Wes. 1985. *New Roots for Agriculture*. Lincoln: University of Nebraska.

Jackson, W., W. Berry, & B. Colman. 1984. *Meeting the Expectations of the Land: Essays in Sustainable Agriculture*. San Francisco: North Point Press.

Jacobs, Jane. 1985. *Cities & The Wealth of Nations*. New York: Vintage.

————. 1992. *Systems of Survival: A Dialogue on the Moral Foundations of Commerce & Politics*. New York: Random House.

James, William. 1902. *Varieties of Religious Experience*. New York: Modern Library.

Jantsch, Erich. 1980. *The Self-Organizing Universe: Scientific & Human Implications of the Emerging Paradigm of Evolution*. New York: Pergamon Press.

Johnston, Mark. 1993. *Moral Imagination*. Chicago: University of Chicago Press.

Jordan, W. R., M. E. Gilpin and J. D. Abers, eds. 1987. *Restoration Ecology: A Synthetic Approach to Ecological Research*. London & New York: Cambridge.

Kant, I. 1963. *The Critique of Pure Reason.* New York: MacMillan.

Kapleau, Phillip. 1966. *Three Pillars of Zen.* New York: Harper & Row.

Kaza, S. 1993. *The Attentive Heart: Conversations with Trees.* Ballantine, New York: Fawcett Columbine.

Keller, Evelyn Fox. 1985. *Reflections on Gender & Science.* New Haven: Yale University Press.

Kerby, A. P. 1991. *Narrative & the Self.* Bloomington: Indiana University Press.

Krishnamurti, J. 1953. *Education & the Significance of Life.* New York: Harper & Row.

Kuhn, Thomas. 1970. *The Structure of Scientific Revolutions.* Chicago: University of Chicago Press.

Kusler, J. and M. Kentulla, eds. 1990. *Wetlands Creation & Restoration.* Covelo, Calif.: Island Press.

LaChapelle, Dolores. 1978. *Earth Wisdom.* Silverton, Colo.: Way of the Mountain Center.

————. 1988. *Sacred Land, Sacred Sex: The Rapture of the Deep.* Silverton, Colo.: Finn Hill Arts.

Lappé, Francis M. and Joseph Collins. 1979. *Food First: Beyond the Myths of Scarcity.* New York: Ballantine.

Lao Tzu. 1963. *Tao Te Ching.* Trans. D. C. Lau. New York: Penguin.

Leiss, William. 1976. *The Limits to Satisfaction: An Essay on the Problem of Needs & Commodities.* Toronto: University of Toronto.

Leopold, A. 1949. *Sand County Almanac.* New York and London: Oxford.

Livingston, John. 1981. *The Fallacy of Wildlife Conservation.* Toronto: McClelland & Stewart.

Logsdon, Gene. 1977. *Small-Scale Grain Raising.* Emmaus, Penn.: Rodale.

Lovins, Amory B. 1979. *Soft-Energy Paths: Toward a Durable Peace.* New York: Harper Colophon.

Lovins, Amory & L. Hunter Lovins. 1986. *Power Unbound.* San Francisco: Sierra Club Books.

Macy, J. 1991. *World As Lover, World as Self.* Berkeley: Parallax Press.

Mander, Jerry. 1978. *Four Arguments for the Elimination of Television.* New York: Quill.

———. 1991. *In the Absence of the Sacred: The Failure of Technology & The Survival of the Indian Nations*. San Francisco: Sierra Books.

Maser, C. 1988. *The Redesigned Forest*. San Diego: R & E Miles.

———. 1990. *The Forest Primeval*. San Francisco: Sierra Books.

Matthews, F. 1991. *The Ecological Self*. Savage, Maryland: Barnes & Noble.

Maturana, H. and F. Varela. 1980. *Autopoiesis & Cognition: The Realization of the Living*. Dordrecht, Holland: Reidel.

Maxwell, Nicolas. 1967. *What's Wrong With Science: Toward a People's Rational Science of Delight & Compassion*. London: Bran's Head Books.

———. 1984. *From Knowledge to Wisdom: A Revolution in the Aims & Methods of Modern Science*. Oxford: Basil Blackwell.

McHarg, Ian. 1971. *Design With Nature*. New York: Natural History.

McIntyre, A. 1984. *After Virtue*. Notre Dame, Ind.: Notre Dame Press.

McKibben, Bill. 1989. *The End of Nature*. New York: Random House.

McTarney, William. 1987. *The Freshwater Aquaculture Book*. Point Roberts, Wash.: Hartley & Marks.

McLaughlin, A. 1993. *Regarding Nature: Industrialism & Deep Ecology*. Albany: SUNY.

McLuhan, Marshall. 1964. *Understanding Media: The Extension of Man*. New York: Mentor.

McRobbie, G. 1981. *Small Is Possible*. London: Abacas.

Meadows, D. and D. Meadows. 1972. *The Limits to Growth*. New York: Universe (Club of Rome Study).

Meadows, D. H., Meadows, D. ., and J. Randers. 1992. *Beyond the Limits: Confronting Global Collapse and Envisioning a Sustainable Future (Sequel to The Limits of Growth)*. Post Mill, Vermont: Chelsea Green Pub.

Meeker-Lowry, Susan. 1992. *Economics as if the Earth Mattered*. Philadelphia: New Society Publishers.

Merchant, Carolyn. 1980. *The Death of Nature: Women, Ecology & the Scientific Revolution*. New York: Harper & Row.

Merton, Thomas. 1960. *Wisdom of the Desert*. New York: New Directions.

———. 1978. *The Monastic Journey*. New York: Image Books.

Messner, M. A. 1992. *Power at Play: Sports & The Problem of Masculinity*. Boston: Beacon Press.

Milbrath, Lester. 1989. *Envisioning a Sustainable Society: Learning Our Way Out.* Albany: SUNY.

Miller, A. 1990. *Banished Knowledge: Facing Childhood Injuries.* New York: Doubleday.

Miller, W. M. 1959. *A Canticle for Leibowitz.* New York: Bantam.

Mitchell, C. T. 1993. *Redefining Designing.* New York: Van Nostrand Reinhold.

de Moll, Jane, ed., et al. 1977. *Rainbook: Resources for Appropriate Technology.* New York: Schocken.

de Moll, Jane and Gigi Coe, eds. 1978. *Stepping Stones: Appropriate Technology & Beyond.* New York: Schocken.

Mollison, Bill. 1990. *Permaculture: A Practical Guide for a Sustainable Future.* Covelo, Ca.: Island Press.

Morgan, Arthur, 1984. *The Small Community.* Ohio: Yellow Spring: Community Service.

Moustakis, Clark. 1961. *Loneliness.* Englewood Cliffs, N.J.: Prentice Hall.

Muir, John. 1954. *The Wilderness World of John Muir.* Edwin Way Teale, ed. New York: Houghton-Mifflin.

Mumford, Lewis. 1961. *The City of History: Its Origins, Its Transformations, and Its Prospects.* New York: Harcourt Brace.

————. 1967. *The Myths of the Machine: Vol. I. Technics & Human Development.* New York: Harcourt Brace.

————. 1970. *The Myths of the Machine: Vol. II. The Pentagon of Power.* New York: Harcourt Brace.

Myers, Norman & Gaia Ltd. Staff. 1984. *An Atlas of Planet Management.* Garden City, New York: Anchor/Doubleday.

Naess, A. 1991. *Ecology, Community & Lifestyle.* London: Cambridge University Press.

————. 1974. *Ghandi and Group Conflict. An Exploration of Satyragraha, Theoretical Background.* Oslo: Universitets-Forlaget.

Nash, Roderick. 1973. *Wilderness & the American Mind.* New Haven: Yale University Press.

Nearing, Helen & Scott. 1970. *Leading the Good Life.* New York: Schocken.

Needleman, Carla. 1979. *The Work of Craft: An Inquiry Into the Nature of Crafts and Craftsmanship.* New York: Knopf.

Needleman, Jacob. 1980. *Lost Christianity.* New York: Doubleday.

Neihardt, John. 1975. *Black Elk Speaks.* New York: Pocket Books.

Noble, David F. 1977. *America By Design: Science, Technology and The Rise of Corporate Capitalism.* New York: Oxford University Press.

Noble, D. D. 1991. *The Classroom Arsenal: Military Research, Information Technology and Public Education.* London: Falmer Press.

Norberg-Hodge, Helena. 1991. *Ancient Futures: Learning From Ladakh.* San Francisco: Sierra Club Books.

Ong, Walter. 1982. *Orality & Literacy: Technologizing of the Word.* New York and London: Methuen.

Orr, D. 1992. *Ecological Literacy: Education & the Transition to a Post Modern World.* Albany: SUNY.

Orwell, George. 1966. *1984.* New York: Harcourt Brace.

O'Toole, R. 1988. *Reforming the Forest Service.* Covelo, Calif.: Island Press.

Pacey, Arnold. 1983. *The Culture of Technology.* Oxford: Blackwell.

Papanek, Victor. 1973. *Designs For The Real World.* New York: Bantam.

Parker, Tom. 1983. *Rules of Thumb.* Boston: Houghton-Mifflin.

Perlin, J. 1989. *A Forest Journey: The Role of Wood in The Development of Civilization.* New York: Norton.

Pianka, E. 1978. *Evolutionary Ecology.* New York: Harper & Row.

Plato. 1977. *Plato's Republic.* Trans. G. Grube. Indianapolis: Hackett.

Quinn, Daniel. 1993. *Ishmael.* New York: Bantam Books.

Rader, Melvin. 1981. *The Right to Hope: Crisis & Community.* Seattle: University of Washington Press.

Raphael, R. 1981. *Tree Talk: The People & Politics of Timber.* Covelo, Calif.: Island Press.

Rapp, Frederick. 1981. *Analytical Philosophy of Technology.* Dordrecht, Holland: Reidel.

Register, Richard. 1987. *Ecocity Berkeley: Building Cities for a Healthy Future.* Berkeley: North Atlantic Books.

Rifkin, Jeremy. 1983. *Algeny*. New York: Viking.

Rifkin, Jeremy. 1987. *Time Wars: The Primary Conflict in Human History*. New York: Henry Holt.

Robinson, G. 1988. *The Forest and The Trees: Guide to Excellent Forestry*. Covelo, Calif.: Island Press.

Rodale, Robert. 1981. *Our Next Frontier: A Personal Guide for Tomorrow's Lifestyle*. Emmaus, Penn.: Rodale Press.

Rodale, R. and M. Gabel, et al. 1985. *Regenerating America: Meeting the Challenges of Building Local Economies*. Emmaus, Penn.: Rodale.

Rolston, Holmes. 1986. *Philosophy Gone Wild: Essays in Environmental Ethics*. Buffalo, New York: Prometheus Books.

Romanyshyn, Robert. 1989. *Technology as Symptom & Dream*. London: Routledge.

Rorabaugh, W. J. 1986. *The Craft Apprentice: From Franklin to the Machine Age in America*. London & New York: Oxford University Press.

Roszak, Theodore. 1978. *Person/Planet*. New York: Anchor.

————. 1986. *The Cult of Information*. New York: Pantheon.

Rothenberg, David. 1993. *Hand's End: Technology & The Limits of Nature*. Berkeley, C.A.: University of California Press.

Rowe, Stan. 1990. *Home Place: Essays on Ecology*. Edmonton, A.B.: NeWest.

St. John, A. 1992. *Sourcebook for Sustainable Design*. Boston: Boston Soc. of Architects.

Sahlins, Marshall. 1972. *Stone Age Economics*. New York: Aldine.

Sale, Kirkpatrick. 1980. *Human Scale*. New York: Coward McCann & Geohegan.

————. 1985. *Dwellers on the Land: The Bioregional Vision*. San Francisco: Sierra Club Books.

Savory, Allan. 1988. *Holistic Resource Management*. Covelo, Calif.: Island Press.

Schumacher, E. F. 1973. *Small Is Beautiful*. New York: Harper & Row.

————. 1979. *Good Work*. New York: Harper & Row.

Seabrook, J. 1990. *The Myth of the Market*. Bideford, U.K.: Green Books.

————. 1993. *Pioneers of Change: Experiments in Creating a Humane Society*. Philadelphia: New Society Publishers.

Seamon, David, ed. 1993. *Dwelling, Seeing & Designing: Toward a Phenomenological Ecology.* Albany: SUNY.

Seed, J., J. Macy, P. Fleming, and A. Naess. 1988. *Thinking Like a Mountain: Towards a Council of All Beings.* Philadelphia: New Society Pub.

Seidenberg, Roderick. 1950. *Posthistoric Man.* New York: Harper & Row.

Senge, P. 1990. *The Fifth Discipline: The Art and Practice of the Learning Organization.* New York: Doubleday.

Shephard, Paul. 1973. *The Tender Carnivore & The Sacred Game.* New York: Scribners.

Shephard, P. and D. McKinley. 1967. *The Subversive Science: Essays Toward An Ecology of Man.* New York: Houghton-Mifflin.

Shiva, Vandana. 1993. *Monocultures of the Mind: Biodiversity, Biotechnology and the Third World.* Penong: Third World Network.

Shulgin, Alexander T. 1991. *Pihkal.* Berkeley: Transform Press.

Skinner, B. F. 1962. *Walden Two.* New York: MacMillan.

———. 1975. *Beyond Freedom & Dignity.* New York: Bantam.

Skolimowski, Henryk. 1983. *Technology & Human Destiny.* Madras, India: University of Madras.

Smith, Houston. 1982. *Beyond the Post Modern Mind.* New York: Crossroad.

Smith, J. R. 1950. *Tree Crops: A Permanent Agriculture.* Covelo, Calif.: Island Press.

Smuts, Jan. 1967. *Holism and Evolution.* New York: Viking.

Snyder, Gary. 1977. *The Old Ways.* San Francisco: City Light Books.

———. 1990. *The Practice of the Wild.* San Francisco: North Point.

Sontag, Susan. 1990. *Illness as Metaphor and AIDS and Its Metaphors.* New York: Doubleday.

Soulé, M. and M. Wilcox. 1980, 1986. *Conservation Biology,* vols. 1 & 2. New York: Sinauer.

Stevens, John. 1988. *The Marathon Monks of Mount Hiei.* Boston: Shambhala.

Stone, Merlin. 1976. *When God Was a Woman.* New York: Harcourt Brace.

Streng, Frederick. 1985. *Religious Life.* Belmont, Calif.: Wadsworth.

Szazs, Thomas. 1975. *Ceremonial Chemistry.* New York: Anchor.

Tarthang, Tulka. 1978. *Skillful Means.* Emeryville, Calif.: Dharma.

Tawney, R. H. 1960. *Religion & The Rise of Capitalism.* New York: Mentor.

Teich, A. H. ed. 1977. *Technology & Man's Future.* New York: St. Martins Press.

Thurgood, J. V. 1981. *Man & the Mediterranean Forest: A History of Resource Depletion.* New York: Academic Press.

Thomas, Keith. 1983. *Man & The Natural World: A History of Modern Sensibility.* New York: Pantheon.

Thoreau, Henry David. 1980. *The Natural History Essays.* Layton, Utah: Gibbs M. Smith.

Todd, John and Nancy Josh Todd. 1980. *The Village as Solar Ecology.* Falmouth, Mass.: New Alchemy Institute.

Todd, Nancy and Jack. 1984. *Bioshelters, Ocean Arks, City Farming: Ecology and the Basis for Design.* San Francisco: Sierra Club Books.

Toulmin, Stephen. 1990. *Cosmopolis: The Hidden Agenda of Modernity.* New York: Free Press.

Trebach, Arnold S. 1987. *The Great Drug War.* New York: Macmillan.

Tresemer, David. 1982. *The Scythe Book.* Brattleboro, Vermont: Hand & Foot.

Trungpa, Chogyam. 1984. *Shambhala: The Sacred Path of the Warrior.* Boston: Shambhala Books.

Turnbull, Colin. 1962. *The Forest People.* New York: Simon & Schuster.

Turner, Frederick. 1980. *Beyond Geography: The Western Spirit Against the Wilderness.* New York: Viking Press.

Ueshiba, K. 1985. *The Spirit of Aikido.* Tokyo and New York: Kodansha.

Ueshiba, Morihei. 1991. *Budo: Teachings of the Founder of Aikido.* Tokyo: Kodansha.

Vanderburg, Willem H. 1985. *The Growth of Minds and Cultures: A Unified Theory of the Structure of Human Experience.* Toronto: University of Toronto Press.

Vasey, Daniel E. 1989. *An Ecological History of Agriculture.* Ames: Iowa State University Press.

Weizenbaum, Joseph. 1976. *Computer Power & Human Reason.* San Francisco, C.A.: Freeman.

Wenk, E. 1979. *Margins for Survival: Overcoming Political Limits in Steering Technology.* Oxford, U.K.: Pergamon Press.

Wilber, Ken. 1981. *Up From Eden: A Transpersonal View of Human Evolution.* New York: Anchor.

————. 1984. *A Sociable God.* Boulder, Colo.: Shambhala.

Wilkinson, M. and R. Loomis. 1991. *Wildwood: A Forest for the Future.* Gabriola, B.C.: Reflections.

Wilson, E. O. 1992. *The Diversity of Life.* Cambridge: Harvard Press.

Winner, Langdon. 1977. *Autonomous Technology.* Cambridge: M.I.T. Press.

————. 1986. *The Whale and the Reactor: A Search for Limits in an Age of High Technology.* Chicago: University of Chicago.

Wittgenstein, L. 1953. *Philosophical Investigations.* London: Macmillan.

Worster, Donald. 1985. *Nature's Economy: A History of Ecological Ideas.* Cambridge, U.K.: Cambridge University Press.

Zaleznik, Abraham. 1989. *The Managerial Mystique: Restoring Leadership in Business.* New York: Harper & Row.

Zamyatin, Y. 1972. *We.* New York: Bantam.

Zimmerman, Michael E. 1990. *Heidegger's Confrontation With Modernity: Technology, Politics & Art.* Bloomington: Indiana University Press.

Index